1

iPray

A Simple Prayer Book for Ministry,
Mercy and Multiplication

By James D. Buckman

Special thanks to Peter Meier and Mike Ruhl for their leadership and partnership in ministry.

Published by Church Beyond The Walls
Bridgewater – New Jersey

*"Equipping the Priesthood of the Baptized to assist their Pastors
in planting new worshipping communities."*

For additional copies and other resources, visit our web site:
www.HouseChurchPlanter.com

ISBN: 9780988973206
5th Edition (2013.10.15)

All Scriptural quotations are from the NIV unless otherwise indicated, are taken from the Holy Bible, New International Version®, NIV®. Copyright © 1973, 1978, 1984, 2011 by Biblica, Inc. ™ Used by permission of Zondervan. All rights reserved worldwide. www.zondervan.com The "NIV" and "New International Version" are trademarks registered in the United States Patent and Trademark Office by Biblica, Inc.™

All citations from the works of Martin Luther are from *Luther's Works*. American Edition. 55 vols. Edited by Jaroslav Pelikan and Helmut T. Lehman. Philadelphia: Muehlenberg and Fortress, and St. Louis: Concordia, 1955-86.

Unless otherwise noted, all references to the Lutheran Confessions are from Theodore G. Tappert, ed., *The Book of Concord: The Confessions of the Evangelical Lutheran Church.* (Philadelphia: Fortress, 2000, 1959).

Abbreviations are as follows:

AC The Augsburg Confession
Apol Apology of the Augsburg Confession
SA The Smalcald Articles
SC The Small Catechism
LC The Large Catechism
LW Luther's Works
FC Formula of Concord

Where there are underlinings, boldface, and / or italics within a quoted source, those emphases have been added by the author.

Edited by Martha Streufert Jander.

The Center for United States Missions

Mission Statement

The Center for United States Missions provides research, training, coaching, consultation and resources for accelerating church multiplication in the United States of America.

Core Values

The Center for United States Missions deeply values being a ministry which is:

- Christ centered
- Scripture based
- Mission driven
- Service oriented

Purpose

Responding to Jesus' Great Commission to "make disciples of all nations" (Mt 28:18), and convinced of Jesus' promise, "I will build My church and the gates of hell will not prevail against it" (Mt 16:18), the Center for United States Missions focuses on the church multiplication facet of the Great Commission.

As a grass-roots advocate for multiplying mission, the Center identifies, equips, coaches and encourages local congregations and church planters to prepare and launch Gospel-centered faith communities. Our prayer and goal is that each of the faith communities we seed intentionally invites others to know Jesus Christ, feeding those it encounters through Word and Sacrament ministry.

Partners

The Center for US Missions is a partnership between Concordia University in Irvine, California, the districts of the Lutheran Church – Missouri Synod, and Concordia Seminary in St. Louis, Missouri.

For a list of seminars, training, resources, newsletters and other services visit our website at **www.c4usm.org**, or contact us directly:

- Rev. Dr. Peter Meier, Executive Director |952-657-2182 | peter.meier@cui.edu
- Rev. Michael Ruhl, Director of Training | 743-648-0185 | michael.ruhl@cui.edu

Equipping God's People to Multiply the Harvest

"I pray" (Jacob, Genesis 32:11)
"I pray" (David, Psalm 5:2)
"I pray" (Jesus, Mark 14:32)
"I pray" (Paul, Acts 26:29)
"I pray" (John, 3 John 2)

"Ons Vader wat in die hemel is…" (Afrikaans)
"Abbun Dbashmayo Abbun dbashmayo, netquadash shmokh titeh malkutock…" (Aramaic)
"Onze Vader, die in de hemel zijt…" (Belgium/Flemish)
"Pare nostre que esteu en el cel…" (Catalan)
"Dawe wa twese uri mw'ijuru…" (Burundi)
"Wo men zai tian shang de fu…" (Chinese)
"Oce nas, koji jesi na nebesima, sveti se ime tvoje…" (Croatia)
"Otce nas, jenz jsi na nebesich…" (Czech)
"Vor Fader, du som er i Himlene!..." (Danish)
"Onze vader die in de hemel zijt…" (Dutch)
"Our Father, who art in Heaven…" (English)
"Patro nia, kiu estas en la cielo…" (Esperanto)
"Isa meidan, joka olet taivaissa!..." (Finnish)
"Notre Pere qui es aux cieux…" (French)
"Vater unser im Himmel…" (German)
"Tata nostru, se jesci pa nour!..." (Gipsy)
"Pater (h)emon 9h)o en tois ouranois…" (Greek)
"Bapa kami yang ada di surga…" (Indonesian)
"Padre nostro, che sei nei cieli…" (Italian)
"Ten ni orareru watashitachi no Chichi yo…" (Japanese)
"Mi Atyank, aki a mennyekben vagy…" (Magyarul)
"Amay nmon,nga yara ks sa langit…" (Ilongo, Philippines)
"Padre nuestor, que estas en el cielo…" (Spanish)
"Baba yetu uliye mbiguni, jina lako lisifiwe…" (Swahili)
"Goklerdeki Babamyz, adyn kutsal kylynsyn…" (Turkish)

(For a more complete list, go to http://www.marypages.com/TheLordPrayer.htm)

"Before we explain the Lord's Prayer part by part, it is very necessary to exhort and draw people to prayer, as Christ and the apostles also did.

"The first thing to know is this: It is our duty to pray because God has commanded it. We were told in the Second Commandment, 'You shall not take God's name in vain.' Thereby we are required to praise the holy name and pray or call upon it in every need. For to call upon it is nothing else than to pray. Prayer, therefore, is as strictly and solemnly commanded as all the other commandments, such as having no other God, not killing, not stealing, etc.

"Let no one think that it makes no difference whether *I pray* or not, as vulgar people do who say in their delusion: 'Why should I pray? Who knows whether God heeds my prayer or cares to hear it? If I do not pray, someone else will.'"[1]

---

[1] LC III, 4-6 in Tappert,. ed., ,.

"iPray"

"My house will be called a house of Prayer, for all nations."
(Isaiah 56:7; Matthew 21:13; Mark 11:17; Luke 19:46)

A Simple Prayer Book for Ministry, Mercy and Multiplication

I have tried to keep acronyms to a minimum; but sometimes space required it
HC = House Church
PT = Prayer Team
LCMS = The Lutheran Church Missouri Synod (my church body--www.lcms.org)
LW = Luther's Works (the bound collection containing much of his writings)
PW = Prayer Walking

Thank You

First of all, I want to thank my Lord and Savior Jesus Christ, who died on a cross to pay for my sins. I confess with my mouth, "Jesus is Lord" and believe in my heart that God raised Him from the dead. I am a sinner saved by grace; every day is a good day for me; thank you Holy Spirit for this gift of faith to me.

Secondly, I want to thank my wife Cathy- you raised our children when I was away on orders or working late nights trying to help plant churches (or write books). You have put the ministry before personal preferences and you put God's word first in our relationship and family. Love you always. I also want to thank my children- Jacob, Jim, Sarah, John and Grace; you have been a bigger blessing to me than you can ever imagine. I pray that God watches over both your coming in and your going out, this day and even forevermore. You have grown up so fast; but then again, time flies when you are having fun.

Third, I want to thank my parents- the Rev. Dr. Al & Carol Buckman. I was born into a great family. From a young age, you taught me two things- the meaning of life is to share the Good News found in Jesus with others and to always Pray. I am so proud of your volunteer ministry now for immigrants and refugees.

Jane Basuino--your passion for Prayer Walking in the Westfield Business District is a model for all.
Rev. Bill Beckham--it was truly a blessing to have you as a guest in our home; blessings on your ministry.
Rabbi Yaakov Bindell--I count you as a true friend; you have been a blessing to me and are in my Prayers.
Shirley Carpenter--it has been such a blessing to train House Church Planters through Leaders and Learners
Caitlin Dinger--for all you do to communicate the Mission Vision in the Garden State!
Rev. Andrew Dinger--for all you do with the Mission teams; House Church planting and your perspective.
Lt. Col. Chuck French—the biggest Yellow Ribbon event in AFRC couldn't have happened without you.
Maj. Rob Fritz--first true friend in the Air Force; Rob runs a bank now; God's blessings, buddy.
Rev. Lawrence Gboeah--you and Martha have made such sacrifices for the Gospel; may God refresh you
Rev. Steve Gewecke--there are some people you trust with the store; you are one of those kind of people.
Matthew Hass--your intensity for the Gospel is an inspiration to us all; run the race!
Rev. Bob Herring--fellow St. Louis Cardinals fan and Barnabas in the ministry; God bless you always!
Rev. Paul Huneke--your partnership and planting of our first military House Church is a blessing.
Rev. Andy Keltner--first Pastor to sign up to raise funds for my mission work in New Jersey; go AFSOC!
Chaplain (LTC) Herman Kemp--best boss I ever had in the Chaplaincy, hands down; keep it real Sir.
Rev. Dr. Robert Kolb--you are an inspirational Professor and a heritage to the Church.
Rev. Garrett Knudson--thank you for helping us to keep the main thing the main thing.
Rev. Paul Kritsch--your love for Jesus; His flock and the lost is inspiringly evident in your life and work.
Rev. Bob Kuppler--you planted two Hispanic House Churches; I praise God for His work through you.
Rev. Craig Lutz--thank you for your mission heart; both here and overseas; you are a blessing.
Edna McClure--you stepped up when Jane had to move out of state and you kept on stepping up.
Rev. Bob Mueller--for all you do to help with the New Jersey Jam and sharing the Gospel beyond Texas.
Rev. Dr. Herb Mueller--thank you for your time and commitment to the Gospel; you are an encouragement.
Pr. Haron Orutwa--you have done so much, with so little; thank you for your faithfulness to the fight.
Rick Porter--your heart for the lost and vision for ministry through LCEF is so refreshing to us all.
SMSgt Cindy Roller--the very best Air Force Wing Chapel NCOIC ever.
Elaine Schleifer--you are a blessing to work with in the New Jersey District Office!
Rev. Chris Schonberg--thank you for your support of our mission teams and our mission in general.
Rev. Scott Seidler--I hope you are pleased. Thank you for everything.
Rev. Mark Stillman--your desire to share the Gospel is a delight; looking forward to Prayer Walking.
Rev. Rick Vossler--your use of Congregational Prayer Ministry in education inspired several key ideas.
Rev. Deric Taylor--your community and church are so blessed; looking forward to medical missions.
Rev. Dr. Tom Zehnder--thank you for your emails of encouragement along the way.

Being a network supported church worker is a journey which requires your help. Thank you too.

With Cathy and our children- Jacob, Jim, Sarah, John and Grace; I just received the Meritorious Service Medal from Col Steve Arthur (now General)- at Whiteman AFB, MO. Home of the 442nd Fighter Wing.

Introduction

When I was a little boy growing up in Africa, my dad asked me one day, "What is the meaning of life?" I thought about it for a while and I don't believe I had an answer to his question. What I absolutely do remember were his next words, "The meaning of life is to share Jesus with others."

I personally believe my Dad's words to be true; I have come to find great joy in personally sharing Jesus with others, and an equal joy in helping others grow in their ability and desire to do the same--and watching their joy in this. My hope is that this simple book will be used by the Holy Spirit to help you share Jesus as well.

By God's grace, as I have grown in my faith, I have personally experienced the power of Prayer in my life. In 1998 just before my family moved to Springfield, Missouri, to help plant a new church, my wife, Cathy, had a miscarriage. To make matters worse, when we arrived in Springfield, our furniture was delayed; this meant the first night we all slept on the floor in a strange house. My wife and I cried ourselves to sleep that night.

God blessed us with our daughter Sarah, born in 1999 and our son John in 2001. In 2003 we were expecting our next child. I will never forget the doctor's visit. After the normal tests, our doctor came into the room unexpectedly and said, "I have bad news." We asked what it was. He said, "It has a growth on the side of its head; its placenta is falling apart; its chromosomes aren't right and it has an irregular heartbeat. You have options." I don't know what made me angrier: him calling our baby "it" or saying "you have options."

As he talked, I was rejecting everything he said and immediately began praying in my spirit. When Cathy and I left, we went home and cried some more. We prayed, read God's Word and talked about it. I absolutely believed that, unlike the last time with the miscarriage, this time we could do something--this time we could pray. As part of the Pastoral Leadership Institute (class of 2000), I asked if they would share our prayer request with the other Pastors and churches, which they did. Cathy and I shared our Prayer request with our little mission start, which met in the basement of a strip mall. We asked everyone we knew to join us in praying.

God blessed Cathy and me with peace. Our prayer was two-fold: heal our baby or make us to be the kind of parents He would want us to be for a special needs child. God gave us peace. Before we went back to see that doctor, we had peace. This peace did not come from any human being; it did not come from a medical test; this peace passed all human understanding; this peace came from God. Back for another visit, the same doctor was there. After more tests he came into our room and the first words out of his mouth were, "It is a miracle." Cathy and I smiled and looked at him, waiting to hear more. He continued, "It is all gone. It is a miracle." I asked what he meant. He said, "The growth on the head is gone; the chromosomes are fine; the placenta is fine; the heartbeat is fine. It is a miracle." We all smiled at each other; Cathy and I praised God and shared that we and our friends were had been praying for the baby.

I was there by his side when this doctor brought Grace into the world.. I am sure he had seen hundreds of babies born by this point in his career, but the look of amazement on his face as he examined her was priceless. Doctors like him are in a hard position when faced with sharing difficult news. Our prayer is that this experience toned down his rush to judgment in the future.

My wife and I experienced a miscarriage and we experienced this miracle. We know what both situations feel like. Prayer is not some magical act by which you get whatever you want. Prayer is what the Holy Spirit produces in true believers. Our daughter Grace is a beautiful, healthy child who understands just enough about her story to know God's grace for us all.

Through my experiences as a church planter (twice) and now as a mission strategist working with hundreds of churches, I have come to believe very strongly in the power of Prayer for Ministry, Mercy and Multiplication. The concepts in this book are not theory. I have been using them personally for over 10 years and I am blessed to have partners in ministry with solid experience as well. In this book are real examples from actual Lutheran Church–Missouri Synod (LCMS) congregations who have put them into practice. As a mission strategist, I have been blessed to help congregations apply these principles in urban, suburban and rural settings; among the affluent and the indigent; with recent immigrants as well as with members whose families have been in this country for many generations. So let us put to rest the question, "Will it work in our area?"

In my study of prayer, I have been blessed to read much of Luther's thoughts on this topic. I was delighted to read of Luther's love for prayer and the importance of prayer in the Reformation and early Lutheran church. I enjoyed reading the following commentary on Luther and Prayer and share it with you:

"In the *Personal Prayer Book* (1522) he (Luther) provided a positive and practical substitute for laymen to use instead of the traditional, medieval prayer books in which they had sought a model of Christian faith and life."[2]

"Luther's immensely popular *Personal Prayer Book* of 1522 summed up the basics of a Christian's faith and conduct in a way the ordinary person could understand. Along with Luther's German Bible and the new evangelical hymnal, the *Personal Prayer Book* offered laymen clear guidance as they flocked to the Reformation and looked for practical alternatives to the old forms of medieval piety with which they had grown up."[3]

"The immediate occasion for compiling and writing the *Personal Prayer Book* of 1522 was the rapid and confused advance of the Reformation while Luther was absent from Wittenberg and in hiding at the Wartburg. Returning to Wittenberg in this crisis Luther realized that evangelical piety had to be communicated in terms that any layman would readily accept and understand. For this reason he did not publish something new in appearance, but simply adopted the outward form of the highly regarded personal prayer books of the Roman church while changing the content. He reduced their complex catalogues of sins for use in preparation for confession to the Ten Commandments alone, with a pithy listing of ways to break and ways to observe each commandment. He interpreted the Ten Commandments as requiring a person's complete self-giving love to God and neighbor and, as such, a fully adequate code of conduct and aid to self-examination. As a substitute for the elaborate steps to gain salvation listed in the old prayer books, Luther gave a personal testimony of what a living, existential faith means by expounding the Apostles' Creed. For the traditional miscellaneous collection of prayers with their fantastic promises of protection and reward, Luther elucidated the Lord's Prayer as an instruction in how to pray and as the only prayer a Christian needs to know. Unlike the former prayer books, Luther limited his edition of 1522 to biblically related content."[4]

"To this he added the traditional Hail Mary, which every Roman Catholic prayer book contained, but gave to it a thoroughly evangelical interpretation. Adding a dedication and a preface, Luther rushed the manuscript to the printer Johann Grünenberg of Wittenberg, in the spring of 1522 and it was published on June 2. So great was the demand for it that the printer did not hold his press for the two revisions Luther had finished before the original was published; he simply issued both revisions later in the year."[5]

"Nine editions of the *Personal Prayer Book* appeared in 1522, four in 1523, four in 1524, two in1525, and one each year through 1530. As the number of editions indicates, the *Personal Prayer Book* enjoyed a quick and wide sale."[6]

---

[2]Martin Luther, AE 43. *43*. Fortress.
Ibid.
[4]Ibid., p. 6-7.
[5]Ibid., p. 7.
[6]Ibid.

Luther's book was meant as a tool to help individual Christians in their personal prayer life. Another of Luther's books on prayer titled, "A Simple Way to Pray," was written for Peter, his friend and barber (this title provided the inspiration for the subtitle of this book).

This Prayer book is meant to help the Church (individual Christians) in her prayer life so that Ministry, Mercy and the Multiplication of believers might increase; all to the glory of God! May we in the Lutheran church be zealous once again for Prayer.

My great-great Grandfather John Buckman immigrated to this country from Germany in 1872. John came through New York, his goal being North Dakota, where he wanted to get a homestead and start farming. John worked in Chicago for about 10 years as a day laborer, doing construction, saving his money. John and his best friend married two sisters. Then they got on a train for North Dakota and got off in Belfield, North Dakota. John and Christine got a Quarter of land (160 acres) just north of town (which is still in our family), and began homesteading. John, like most immigrants, worked two jobs; in addition to being a farmer, he also worked full time for the railroad on the section that ran through Belfield.

When John and Christine Buckman got to Belfield, there was no Lutheran church. So, the first year they built their home, then went to the other farmers, inviting them to their home for worship. There was no Pastor to help; there was no denominational church planting expert; there were just John and Christine and the Holy Spirit.

By God's grace, a worshipping community was formed, and in time, they called their first Pastor. It is worth noting that this prairie House Church had their congregational church building completely erected before their first called Pastor arrived. The church God began in their home is now called "St Peter Evangelical Lutheran Church of the Unaltered Augsburg Confession."

My grandmother Eleanor played the organ for over 60 years, finally retiring on her 90th birthday. When Rev. Dr. Al Barry was president of our church body, he personally wrote Grandma a letter, thanking her for her service. Grandma was always proud of this letter. John Buckman would have been too. When my grandmother was called Home, my dad and his father were in the hospital room. Grandpa said to Dad, "Let's pray the Lord's Prayer." They did and then left the room. Prayer is what we do as Christians--in all seasons. The best inheritance you can pass on is a strong family faith.

A lot of good books have been written on Prayer: books to help you with your personal Prayer life; books to give you ideas for how to use Prayer in worship; books that provide great devotions on Prayer from Scripture; even books that document the history of Prayer over the centuries within Christianity.

This book is not meant to be a book like that. It is my hope, that by God's grace and the work of the Holy Spirit, this book can serve as a practical manual on how to use Prayer for Ministry to members, visitors, and your community. My hope is that this book will help you develop a robust Mercy ministry in your congregation that is largely focused on meeting the needs people share with us in their Prayer requests, and that this Mercy Ministry in your Congregation will grow so everyone in your Church can participate in this ministry of Prayer and Care.

Ultimately, I hope this book will help you and your church use Prayer to reach out into your community (just as John and Christine Buckman did, this time with the oversight and support of your called and ordained Pastor); initiating relationships through intentional Prayer outreach; increasing the faith of others through Mercy ministry, which is intentionally focused on these new friends found through Prayer; and ultimately, planting House Churches through your local congregation. If these House Churches develop into constituted congregations (like St. Peter in Belfield, North Dakota), remain satellite outposts" or become something else is between the Holy Spirit and your congregation. ☺

I pray that you are reasonable and patient with the brothers and sisters in your congregation. As you read this book, you may be inspired to see great things happening in your area. Please remember, God works through His body--the local Church and this local Church is part of a larger gathering of Christians; there is accountability and good order. Please, don't try to do "the right thing" with the wrong methods. This is neither profitable nor pleasing to the Holy Spirit. Trust me; this is not where you want to be.

May God richly bless you and yours.

In the 1920 census below- my grandfather, Franklin Buckman was 8 years old. His dad, William is listed as the head of the home; because Williams's dad, John had passed away. William was married to Lillie at the time of this census. I met Lillie when we came back from Africa for a short visit, when I was a little boy. William's mother, Christine was 67 at the time of this census and she is listed above William's wife.

May God bless our efforts on His behalf to do His good works so that names would be added to His book of life (Revelation 21:27).

I. Prayer in Scripture

What Does God Tell Us About Prayer?

Before we talk about any aspect of Prayer, let's first look at what God says about Prayer. For us, Scripture is the foundation and the measurement of anything we say about ministry. This chapter has almost 100 passages revealing God's thoughts on Prayer. There are many books about Prayer and it is common to hear preachers talk about Prayer; opinions regarding Prayer are endless; but it is critical that we dig down to the bedrock of Scripture and begin with Christ as our cornerstone.

In the following chapters we will look at our teaching regarding Prayer; Prayer in worship; the connection between Prayer and Mercy Ministry--serving our neighbor; and then the practical examples of Prayer for: Ministry, Mercy and Multiplication. Let us now give God our full attention.

What Is Prayer?

1. Prayer is the belief that we are talking with God, that He listens and responds. A person with a strong faith may even attempt to get God to change His mind about something.

> *"Moses sought the favor of the LORD his God. "O LORD," he said, "why should your anger burn against your people, whom you brought out of Egypt with great power and a mighty hand?"* (Exodus 32:11) *"Does he who implanted the ear not hear? Does he who formed the eye not see?* (Psalm 94:9) *"We know that in all things God works for the good of those who love Him.* (Romans 8:28)

2. Prayer is the expression of the desire to commune with God:

> *"My soul thirsts for God, for the living God."* (Psalm 42:2)

3. Prayer is a public statement of a personal sentiment:

> *"Isaac built an altar there and called on the name of the LORD."* (Genesis 26:25)

4. Prayer is properly presented by the Holy Spirit Himself on our behalf:

> *"We do not know what we ought to pray for, but the Spirit intercedes for us."* (Romans 8:26)

5. Believers pray God's Word to Him:

> *"When they heard this, they raised their voices together in prayer to God. "Sovereign Lord," they said, "you made the heaven and the earth and the sea, and everything in them.* (Acts 4:24)
> *"You are my portion, O LORD; I have promised to obey your words. I have sought your face with all my heart; be gracious to me according to your promise."* (Psalm 119:57-58)

Discipleship Question:
  *Describe your parents' prayer life and its impact on you: _____

  _____

What Happens When We Pray?

1. God may choose to answer our prayers with a miracle:

   > *"Because [Samson] was very thirsty, he cried out to the LORD, "You have given your servant this great victory. Must I now die of thirst and fall into the hands of the uncircumcised?" Then God opened up the hollow place in Lehi, and water came out of it."* (Judges 15:18-19)

2. Believers are happy with the answer God gives to their prayer, regardless:

   > *"Three times I pleaded with the Lord to take it away from me. But he said to me, "My grace is sufficient for you, for my power is made perfect in weakness." Therefore I will boast all the more gladly about my weaknesses, so that Christ's power may rest on me."* (2 Corinthians 12:8-9)

3. Believers hope for their will to be conformed to the will of God; as God grants grace, true believers aspire to have the mind of Christ. In this way we are able to ask, "Not our will, but Your will be done. To believers with this mindset, Christ says the following amazing words:

   > *"Ask and it will be given to you; seek and you will find; knock and the door will be opened to you."* (Matthew 7:7)

   > *"If you remain in me and my words remain in you, ask whatever you wish, and it will be given you. This is to my Father's glory, that you bear much fruit, showing yourselves to be my disciples."* (John 15:7-8)

   > *"This is the confidence we have in approaching God: that if we ask anything according to his will, he hears us."* (1 John 5:14)

4. Sometimes, our prayers will shake the very building we are in:

   > *"After they prayed, the place where they were meeting was shaken"* (Acts 4:31)

Discipleship Question:
   *Do you "make deals" with God when you pray? How? _____

How Do We Pray?

1. Prayer must come from a believer's heart; otherwise, it is a waste of time:

   > *"Anyone who comes to him must believe that he exists and that he rewards those who earnestly seek him."* (Hebrews 11:6)

2. Prayers should also include "Praise Reports," not just an endless list of requests, worries and sorrow:

   > *"Then Hannah prayed and said: "My heart rejoices in the LORD; in the LORD my horn is lifted high."* (1 Samuel 2:1)

3. A believer speaks plainly, without pretense to God in prayer:

   > *"But Abram said, "O Sovereign LORD, what can you give me since I remain childless and the one who will inherit my estate is Eliezer of Damascus?"* (Genesis 15:2-3)

4. The Lord's Prayer is plural, not singular; this speaks to the communal, not individual nature of the Christian faith:

   > *"This, then, is how you should pray: 'Our Father…'"* (Matthew 6:9)

5. Prayer is pouring out your deepest held emotions to God:

> *"Hannah replied, "I am a woman who is deeply troubled. I have not been drinking wine or beer; I was pouring out my soul to the LORD... I have been praying here out of my great anguish and grief."* (1 Samuel 1:15-16)

6. Incense is the symbol of Prayer:

> *"May my prayer be set before you like incense."* (Psalm 141:2)

7. Believers have the freedom to observe patterns for prayer they feel may be helpful for their practice of prayer / witnessing to those who have not yet confessed Christ:

> *"One day Peter and John were going up to the temple at the time of prayer -- at three in the afternoon."* (Acts 3:1)

8. Our physical posture when we pray is not limited; we can pray kneeling, standing, bowing or prostrate on our faces:

> *"When Solomon had finished all these prayers and supplications to the LORD, he rose from before the altar of the LORD, where he had been <u>kneeling</u> with his hands spread out toward heaven."* (1 Kings 8:54)

> *"Going a little farther, he <u>fell with his face to the ground</u> and prayed.* (Matthew 26:39)

> *"Then <u>Solomon stood</u> before the altar of the LORD in front of the whole assembly of Israel, <u>spread out his hands</u> toward heaven... ."* (1 Kings 8:22)   *Then the man <u>bowed down</u> and worshiped the LORD."* (Genesis 24:26)

What Did Jesus' Prayer Life Look Like?

1. <u>Jesus prayed for miracles:</u>

> *"We have here only five loaves of bread and two fish," they answered. "Bring them here to me," he said. And he directed the people to sit down on the grass. Taking the five loaves and the two fish and looking up to heaven, he gave thanks and broke the loaves. Then he gave them to the disciples, and the disciples gave them to the people. They all ate and were satisfied, and the disciples picked up twelve basketfuls of broken pieces that were left over. The number of those who ate was about five thousand men, besides women and children.* (Matthew 14:17-21)

> *"How many loaves do you have?" Jesus asked. "Seven," they replied, "and a few small fish." He told the crowd to sit down on the ground. Then he took the seven loaves and the fish, and when he had given thanks, he broke them and gave them to the disciples, and they in turn to the people. They all ate and were satisfied. Afterward the disciples picked up seven basketfuls of broken pieces that were left over. The number of those who ate was four thousand, besides women and children."* (Matthew 15:34-38)

> *"Then Jesus said, "Did I not tell you that if you believed, you would see the glory of God?" So they took away the stone. Then Jesus looked up and said, "Father, I thank you that you have heard me. I knew that you always hear me, but I said this for the benefit of the people standing here, that they may believe that you sent me." When he had said this, Jesus called in a loud voice, "Lazarus, come out!" The dead man came out, his hands and feet wrapped with strips of linen, and a cloth around his face. Jesus said to them, "Take off the grave clothes and let him go."* (John 11:40-44)

2. <u>Jesus took time to be in Prayer with the Father, by Himself:</u>

> *"Immediately Jesus made the disciples get into the boat and go on ahead of him to the other side, while he dismissed the crowd. After he had dismissed them, he went up on a mountainside by himself to pray."* (Matthew 14:22-23)

3. <u>Parents wanted Jesus to Pray over their children:</u>
>   *"Then little children were brought to Jesus for him to place his hands on them and pray for them."* (Matthew 19:13)

4. <u>Jesus took the idea of a House of Prayer seriously:</u>
>   *"Jesus entered the temple area and drove out all who were buying and selling there. He overturned the tables of the money changers and the benches of those selling doves. "It is written," he said to them, "'My house will be called a house of prayer,' but you are making it a 'den of robbers.'"* (Matthew 21:12-13)

5. <u>Even though Jesus was God in human form, He did not consider equality with the Father something to be grasped, but humbled Himself and became obedient, even to death on a cross:</u>
>   *"Then Jesus went with his disciples to a place called Gethsemane, and he said to them, "Sit here while I go over there and pray." He took Peter and the two sons of Zebedee along with him, and he began to be sorrowful and troubled. Then he said to them, "My soul is overwhelmed with sorrow to the point of death. Stay here and keep watch with me." Going a little farther, he fell with his face to the ground and prayed, "My Father, if it is possible, may this cup be taken from me. Yet not as I will, but as you will." Then he returned to his disciples and found them sleeping. "Could you men not keep watch with me for one hour?" he asked Peter. "Watch and pray so that you will not fall into temptation. The spirit is willing, but the body is weak." He went away a second time and prayed, "My Father, if it is not possible for this cup to be taken away unless I drink it, may your will be done." When he came back, he again found them sleeping, because their eyes were heavy. So he left them and went away once more and prayed the third time, saying the same thing. Then he returned to the disciples and said to them, "Are you still sleeping and resting? Look, the hour is near, and the Son of Man is betrayed into the hands of sinners. Rise, let us go! Here comes my betrayer!"* (Matthew 26:36-46)

6. <u>Jesus expressed frustration, doubt and abandonment in His prayers also:</u>
>   *"About the ninth hour Jesus cried out in a loud voice, "Eloi, Eloi, lama sabachthani?"-which means, "My God, my God, why have you forsaken me?"* (Matthew 27:46)

7. <u>When Jesus commanded something, He was talking with His Father (praying) and at the same time focusing on the object of His command:</u>
>   *"When Jesus saw that a crowd was running to the scene, he rebuked the evil spirit. "You deaf and mute spirit," he said, "I <u>command</u> you, come out of him and never enter him again." The spirit shrieked, convulsed him violently and came out. The boy looked so much like a corpse that many said, "He's dead." But Jesus took him by the hand and lifted him to his feet, and he stood up. After Jesus had gone indoors, his disciples asked him privately, "Why couldn't we drive it out?" He replied, "This kind can come out only by <u>prayer</u>."* (Mark 9:25-29)

8. <u>Prayer, not the Transfiguration, was the primary purpose of the climb up the mountain:</u>
>   *"About eight days after Jesus said this, he took Peter, John and James with him and went up onto a mountain <u>to pray</u>. As he was praying, the appearance of his face changed, and his clothes became as bright as a flash of lightning. Two men, Moses and Elijah, appeared in glorious splendor, talking with Jesus."* (Luke 9:28-31)

9. <u>God talked out loud to Jesus when He prayed:</u>
>   *"Now my heart is troubled, and what shall I say? "Father, save me from this hour"? No, it was for this very reason I came to this hour. Father, glorify your name!" Then a voice came from heaven, "I have glorified it, and will glorify it again." The crowd that was there and heard it said it had thundered; others said an angel had spoken to him."* (John 12:27-29)

10. <u>Here is the longest Prayer of Jesus recorded in Scripture:</u>

"*After Jesus said this, he looked toward heaven <u>and prayed</u>: "Father, the time has come. Glorify your Son, that your Son may glorify you. For you granted him authority over all people that he might give eternal life to all those you have given him. Now this is eternal life: that they may know you, the only true God, and Jesus Christ, whom you have sent. I have brought you glory on earth by completing the work you gave me to do. And now, Father, glorify me in your presence with the glory I had with you before the world began.*

"I have revealed you to those whom you gave me out of the world. They were yours; you gave them to me and they have obeyed your word. Now they know that everything you have given me comes from you. For I gave them the words you gave me and they accepted them. They knew with certainty that I came from you, and they believed that you sent me. I pray for them. I am not praying for the world, but for those you have given me, for they are yours. All I have is yours, and all you have is mine. And glory has come to me through them. I will remain in the world no longer, but they are still in the world, and I am coming to you. Holy Father, protect them by the power of your name--the name you gave me--so that they may be one as we are one. While I was with them, I protected them and kept them safe by that name you gave me. None has been lost except the one doomed to destruction so that Scripture would be fulfilled.

"I am coming to you now, but I say these things while I am still in the world, so that they may have the full measure of my joy within them. I have given them your word and the world has hated them, for they are not of the world any more than I am of the world. My prayer is not that you take them out of the world but that you protect them from the evil one. They are not of the world, even as I am not of it. Sanctify them by the truth; your word is truth. As you sent me into the world, I have sent them into the world. For them I sanctify myself, that they too may be truly sanctified.

"My prayer is not for them alone. I pray also for those who will believe in me through their message, that all of them may be one, Father, just as you are in me and I am in you. May they also be in us so that the world may believe that you have sent me. I have given them the glory that you gave me, that they may be one as we are one:I in them and you in me. May they be brought to complete unity to let the world know that you sent me and have loved them even as you have loved me.

"Father, I want those you have given me to be with me where I am, and to see my glory, the glory you have given me because you loved me before the creation of the world.
"Righteous Father, though the world does not know you, I know you, and they know that you have sent me. I have made you known to them, and will continue to make you known in order that the love you have for me may be in them and that I myself may be in them." <u>When he had finished praying</u>, Jesus left with his disciples and crossed the Kidron Valley. (John 17:1--18:1)

11. <u>Jesus prays for our faith to be strengthened:</u>

"*But I have prayed for you, Simon, that your faith may not fail. And when you have turned back, strengthen your brothers.*" (Luke 22:32)

12. <u>Jesus modeled prayer before eating:</u>

"*Then he took the seven loaves and the fish, and when he had given thanks, he broke them and gave them to the disciples*". (Matthew 15:36)

Jesus quoting Isaiah said that God's house was to be "…*a house of Prayer, for all the nations.*" In Acts 6:4 we read a Scriptural job description for Pastors- it has two priorities- Prayer and the ministry of the Word. If my Church is a "*house of Prayer*":
 -How does that impact my Pastor's schedule? _____
 -Who will feed widows etc (Acts 6:1-3) so Pastor can focus on Prayer and the Word?_____
 -How do we know if we are actually helping believers grow in their Prayer life? _____
 -How should Pastor, staff and leadership model a strong Prayer life? _____

How and What Did Jesus Teach His Disciples to Pray?

"And when you pray, do not be like the hypocrites, for they love to pray standing in the synagogues and on the street corners to be seen by men. I tell you the truth, they have received their reward in full. But when you pray, go into your room, close the door and pray to your Father, who is unseen. Then your Father, who sees what is done in secret, will reward you. And when you pray, do not keep on babbling like pagans, for they think they will be heard because of their many words. Do not be like them, for your Father knows what you need before you ask him.

"This, then, is how you should pray:

'Our Father in heaven, hallowed be your name, your kingdom come, your will be done on earth as it is in heaven. Give us today our daily bread. Forgive us our debts, as we also have forgiven our debtors. And lead us not into temptation, but deliver us from the evil one.'

For if you forgive men when they sin against you, your heavenly Father will also forgive you. But if you do not forgive men their sins, your Father will not forgive your sins." (Matthew 6:5-15)

The context of the Lord's Prayer is clearly one where Jesus is teaching His disciples <u>how</u> they should pray. He does not want us making Prayer into a public show, but to be done privately. And Jesus is very specific regarding how we should pray in a way that is pleasing to God; this is why He gives us this specific Prayer and introduces it by saying, *"This then is how you should pray..."*

<u>Can a believer pray a prayer other than the Lord's Prayer? Of course! What Scripture does not command or forbid, neither do we command or forbid.</u>

But, to dismiss offhandedly the Prayer Jesus taught His disciples when they asked Him how to pray by saying, "This is just an example, it is not something we are actually supposed to pray," is undercutting the teaching of Jesus and setting up a human teacher on a higher pedestal regarding Prayer. In Matthew 7:24 Jesus says to us, *"Everyone who hears my words and puts them into practice is like a wise man."* (See also Luke 6:46)

Discipleship Question:
  *Why is it wise to pray the Lord's Prayer? _____

---

1. <u>Jesus taught His disciples to Pray boldly</u>:
   "Again, I tell you that if two of you on earth agree about anything you ask for, it will be done for you by my Father in heaven. For where two or three come together in my name, there am I with them." (Matthew 18:19-20)
   "If you believe, you will receive whatever you ask for in prayer." (Matthew 21:22)
   "So I say to you: Ask and it will be given to you; seek and you will find; knock and the door will be opened to you. For everyone who asks receives; he who seeks finds; and to him who knocks, the door will be opened. "Which of you fathers, if your son asks for a fish, will give him a snake instead? Or if he asks for an egg, will give him a scorpion? If you then, though you are evil, know how to give good gifts to your children, how much more will your Father in heaven give the Holy Spirit to those who ask him!" (Luke 11:9-13)

2. <u>Jesus taught His disciples how to Pray during the Tribulation</u>:
   "Pray that your flight will not take place in winter or on the Sabbath. For then there will be great distress, unequaled from the beginning of the world until now—and never to be equaled again. If those days had not been cut short, no one would survive, but for the sake of the elect those days will be shortened." (Matthew 24:20-22)

3. Jesus taught His disciples to Pray without ceasing, and the New Testament Church did that:

"*Then Jesus told his disciples a parable to show them that they should <u>always pray</u> and <u>not give up</u>. He said: "In a certain town there was a judge who neither feared God nor cared about men. And there was a widow in that town who kept coming to him with the plea, 'Grant me justice against my adversary.' "For some time he refused. But finally he said to himself, 'Even though I don't fear God or care about men, yet because this widow keeps bothering me, I will see that she gets justice, so that she won't eventually wear me out with her coming!'" And the Lord said, "Listen to what the unjust judge says. And <u>will not God bring about justice for his chosen ones, who cry out to him day and night</u>? Will he keep putting them off? I tell you, he will see that they get justice, and quickly.*" (Luke 18:1-8a)

"*<u>Always keep on praying</u> for all the saints.*" (Ephesians 6:18)

4. Jesus taught His disciples to Pray humbly:

"*To some who were confident of their own righteousness and looked down on everybody else, Jesus told this parable: "Two men went up to the temple to pray, one a Pharisee and the other a tax collector. The Pharisee stood up and prayed about himself: 'God, I thank you that I am not like other men—robbers, evildoers, adulterers—or even like this tax collector. I fast twice a week and give a tenth of all I get.' But the tax collector stood at a distance. He would not even look up to heaven, but beat his breast and said, 'God, have mercy on me, a sinner.' I tell you that this man, rather than the other, went home justified before God. For everyone who exalts himself will be humbled, and he who humbles himself will be exalted.*" (Luke 18:9-14)

5. Jesus taught us to pray for the gift of the Holy Spirit:

"*If you then, though you are evil, know how to give good gifts to your children, how much more will your Father in heaven give the Holy Spirit to those who ask him!*" (Luke 11:13)

How Is Christian Prayer Different from the Prayers of Other Religions?

1. Our prayers are Trinitarian:

"*May the grace of the Lord Jesus Christ, and the love of God, and the fellowship of the Holy Spirit be with you all.*" (2 Corinthians 13:14)

2. Jesus taught us to pray in agreement and to pray in His Name:

"*Again, I tell you that if two of you on earth agree about anything you ask for, it will be done for you by my Father in heaven. For where two or three come together in my name, there am I with them.*" (Matthew 18:19-20)

23

What Should We NOT Do When We Pray?

1. Prayer is not for show; it is a sincere communication between the believer and the Father:
>"And when you pray, do not be like the hypocrites, for they love to pray standing in the synagogues and on the street corners to be seen by men. *But when you pray, go into your room, close the door and pray to your Father, who is unseen. Then your Father, who sees what is done in secret, will reward you.*" (Matthew 6:5-6)

2. Be in disagreement when we pray:
>"*I want men everywhere to lift up holy hands in prayer, without anger or disputing.*" (1 Timothy 2:8)

Discipleship Question:
*What causes separation between me and others?

_____

What Things Can STOP My Prayers?

1. How a husband treats his wife:
>"*Husbands, in the same way be considerate as you live with your wives, and treat them with respect as the weaker partner and as heirs with you of the gracious gift of life, so that nothing will hinder your prayers.*" (1 Peter 3:7)

2. Cherishing a sin:
>"*If I had cherished sin in my heart, the Lord would not have listened.*" (Psalm 66:18)

3. Ignoring God's direction for our life:
>"*If anyone turns a deaf ear to the law, even his prayers are detestable.*" (Proverbs 28:9)

4. God may command us not to pray for someone:
>"*Then the LORD said to me, "Do not pray for the well-being of this people. Although they fast, I will not listen to their cry.*" (Jeremiah 14:11-12a; see also Jeremiah 7:16; 11:14)

Why Should We Pray?

1. We should look to God for His blessing upon every aspect of our daily life:
>"*Then he prayed, "O LORD, God of my master Abraham, give me success today.*" (Genesis 24:12)

2. Believers look, expectantly, for God to answer their prayer:
>"*To the LORD I cry aloud, and he answers me from his holy hill.*" (Psalm 3:4)

3. Prayer is not some sort of church growth program; Prayer is part of our identity and it is something our Heavenly Father looks for in us:
>"*If my people, who are called by my name, will humble themselves and pray and seek my face and turn from their wicked ways, then will I hear from heaven and will forgive their sin and will heal their land.* (2 Chronicles 7:14)

4. We should pray for God's intervention over enemies of the Gospel:
> "*Now David had been told, "Ahithophel is among the conspirators with Absalom." So David prayed, "O LORD, turn Ahithophel's counsel into foolishness.*" (2 Samuel 15:31)

5. Believers pray for God to scatter the enemies of the Gospel:
> "*Whenever the ark set out, Moses said, "Rise up, O LORD! May your enemies be scattered; may your foes flee before you.*" (Numbers 10:35)

> "*Yet my prayer is ever against the deeds of evildoers; their rulers will be thrown down from the cliffs, and the wicked will learn that my words were well spoken.*" (Psalm 141:5b-6)

For Whom Do We Pray Besides Ourselves?

1. Believers pray for those in authority:
> "*I urge, then, first of all, that requests, prayers, intercession and thanksgiving be made for everyone--for kings and all those in authority, that we may live peaceful and quiet lives in all godliness and holiness. This is good, and pleases God our Savior, who wants all men to be saved and to come to a knowledge of the truth.*" (1 Timothy 2:1-4)

2. Believers pray for the persecuted:
> "*So Peter was kept in prison, but the church was earnestly praying to God for him.*" (Acts 12:5)

3. Believers pray for those who are persecuting them, even when the believer knows that God is punishing the evil:
> "*After Moses and Aaron left Pharaoh, Moses cried out to the LORD about the frogs he had brought on Pharaoh.*" (Exodus 8:12)

4. Prayer is something the entire family engages in together:
> "*[Cornelius] and all his family were devout and God-fearing; he gave generously to those in need and prayed to God regularly.*" (Acts 10:2)

5. We should pray for our community:
> "*I have posted watchmen on your walls, O Jerusalem; they will never be silent day or night. You who call on the LORD, give yourselves no rest.*" (Isaiah 62:6)

6. We pray for Pastors, Teachers, and Others Proclaiming God's Word:
> "*Brothers, pray for us.*" (1 Thessalonians 5:25)

7. We pray for those in need:
> "*[Cornelius] and all his family were devout and God-fearing; he gave generously to those in need and prayed to God regularly.*" (Acts 10:2)

Discipleship Question:
  *What percentage of my prayers are for others?
  _____

How Should We Pray for Others to Be Changed?

1. We should pray for love to increase in others:
>   "*And this is my prayer: that your love may abound more and more in knowledge and depth of insight.*" (Philippians 1:9)

2. We should pray for others to be strengthened:
>   "*I pray that out of his glorious riches he may strengthen you with power through his Spirit in your inner being, so that Christ may dwell in your hearts through faith.*" (Ephesians 3:16-17)

3. Believers thank other believers who pray for them:
>   "*You help us by your prayers.*" (2 Corinthians 1:11a)

How Should We Pray for God's Kingdom to Grow on Earth?

1. Jesus taught us to pray for workers to be sent out into the Harvest fields:
>   "*Ask the Lord of the harvest, therefore, to send out workers into his harvest field.*" (Mt 9:38)

2. Jesus taught us to pray for God's Kingdom to come on earth as it is in Heaven:
>   "*This, then, is how you should pray: "'Our Father in heaven, hallowed be your name, your kingdom come…*" (Matthew 6:9-10)

3. Believers pray for others to be active in sharing their faith:
>   "*I pray that you may be active in sharing your faith.*" (Philemon 6)

4. Believers pray for others to be equipped:
>   "*May the God of peace, who through the blood of the eternal covenant brought back from the dead our Lord Jesus, that great Shepherd of the sheep, equip you with everything good for doing his will.*" (Hebrews 13:20-21)

Should We Only Pray Or Should We Also Act?

Prayer and work are complementary to each other:
>   "*But we prayed to our God and posted a guard day and night to meet this threat.*" (Neh 4:9)

Action Question:
  *Does God inspire you to action? In what way?
  _____

How Can Believers Grow in Their Prayer Life?

1. Prayer grows in times of persecution:
   "*Now when Daniel learned that the decree had been published, he went home to his upstairs room where the windows opened toward Jerusalem. Three times a day he got down on his knees and prayed, giving thanks to his God, just as he had done before.*" (Daniel 6:10)

2. The Holy Spirit works in believers to produce new and fruitful life:
   "*And we, who with unveiled faces all reflect the Lord's glory, are being transformed into His likeness with ever-increasing glory, which comes from the Lord, who is the Spirit.*" (2 Corinthians 3:18)

3. Jesus' disciples have always desired to grow in their prayer life:
   "*One of his disciples said to him, "Lord, teach us to pray.*" (Luke 11:1)

How Did the New Testament Church Pray?

1. The New Testament Church devoted itself to Prayer:
   "*They devoted themselves to the apostles' teaching and to the fellowship, to the breaking of bread and to prayer.*" (Acts 2:42)

2. The Apostle Paul highly valued prayer, as was evidenced in his life:
   "*We continually remember before our God and Father…*" (1 Thessalonians 1:3)

3. The Apostle Paul exhorted the New Testament Church to be strong in prayer:
   "*And pray in the Spirit on all occasions with all kinds of prayers and requests. With this in mind, be alert and always keep on praying for all the saints.*" (Ephesians 6:18)
   "*Pray continually.*" (1 Thessalonians 5:17)

4. The New Testament Church was birthed in an atmosphere of Prayer:
   "*They all joined together constantly in prayer, along with the women and Mary the mother of Jesus, and with his brothers.*" (Acts 1:14)

5. The New Testament Church used incense as part of their Prayers:
   "*And when the time for the burning of incense came, all the assembled worshipers were praying outside.*" (Luke 1:10)

Action Question:
   *How does Jesus want us to imitate His prayer life? _____

   *What changes do I need to make? _____

   *How does not caring for the needs of others affect ministry? _____

   *When we Pray for others, in what ways can we then serve them? _____

   *Would it be healthy for our members to look for ways to serve those we pray for? _____

<u>The following story comes from the Rev. Dr. Scott Rische; the Director, City Transformation Ministries:</u>

"When Jesus sent out the disciples in Luke 10:1ff, Jesus told them not to take any money along with them. What they were going to need was going to come from the people they were going to meet, reach, and serve. When Jesus fed the 5,000, the food that fed the people didn't come from the disciples, (though it could have if they had been willing to give it). Rather, the food came from a little boy, one of those who were being reached and served by Jesus.

Church planter, Rev. Justin Laughridge, who is planting in San Diego and a part of the City Transformation Ministries network, believes that God provides for the harvest from the harvest. For that reason, early in his church planting work, Justin prayed that God would provide for the work he was doing through the work he was doing; that he too would meet "persons of peace" who would invest in the work he was doing, even though they were the ones that he was reaching and serving himself.

This happened one day. Justin was teaching a group of young boys in the home of one of the people he was reaching out to. One of the fathers was listening to and watching Justin. After Justin had finished and the boys were leaving, the father came up to Justin and said, "Though I do not yet believe everything you are teaching them, I believe in what you are doing for them." With that, the father reached out his hand to Justin and gave him a one hundred dollar bill.

Justin put ninety-nine dollars and forty-eight cents into his ministry account, and put fifty-two cents (for the five loaves and two fish) into his pocket and has carried it with him since to remind himself and others of the amazing ways that God will provide.

"He who did not spare his own Son, but gave him up for us all—how will he not also, along with him, graciously give us all things?" *Romans 8:32*"

+   +   +

<u>Some reflection and discipleship questions:</u>

1. If Jesus knew in advance that there was going to be a shortage of food (in Luke 10); why did He still let this problem happen?

_____

2. What causes believers to be hesitant about asking for help from those they are reaching out to with the Gospel?

_____

3. Pr. Laughridge carries fifty-two cents with him as a visible reminder of God's word coming true in his life. Do you have something like this?

_____

Short term mission team members from Concordia Lutheran Church in Kirkwood, MO
(with the Rev. Dr. Scott Seidler) are Prayer Walking in East Orange, New Jersey

+ + +

"I want to point out to you a correct way of studying theology, for I have had practice in that. If you keep to it, you will become so learned that you yourself could (if it were necessary) write books just as good as those of the fathers and councils…

"This is the way taught by holy King David (and doubtlessly used also by all the patriarchs and prophets) in the one hundred nineteenth Psalm.

"There you will find three rules, amply presented throughout the whole Psalm. They are:

Prayer (*Oratio*),
Meditation (*Meditatio*), and
Testing (*Tentatio*)."[7]

Interestingly, this inscription appears in the gate of the Lutheran Seminary located near Seoul, Korea.

+ + +

Community Youth Fellowship in Eat Orange- youth from Concordia Lutheran Church Prayer Walked with our Liberian House Church in East Orange in order to build relationships with over 100 youth.

---

[7]Martin Luther, AE 43:285. "Fortress.

II. Prayer in Our Doctrine

We began first with Scripture, because <u>God's Word is the source and norm for all Christian teaching and preaching</u>. The Word of God as contained in the 66 canonical books of the Old and New Testaments is in fact the inerrant and inspired Word of God; His Word is a lamp for our feet and a light unto our path. (Psalm 119:105). Now, we will look briefly at our doctrine regarding Prayer.

The U.S. Army has an entire major command known as TRADOC; this stands for "Training and Doctrine". The <u>reality</u> of war has taught our military the necessity of a clearly defined doctrine; while at the same time allowing the commander on the ground certain flexibility in how this doctrine is applied. The idea that those who follow in Christ's steps would do so without Spiritual doctrine is silliness at best (see 1 Corinthians 14:8). Some people tried to discourage me from talking about doctrine; they said it would sell more books; but if you don't write what you believe, what would the point be? Acting like we have agreement in everything just for appearances means we really have agreement in nothing.

I would like to take a minute to share what we confess as Christians of the Lutheran tribe, regarding Prayer. Perhaps this will encourage you to dig deeper into your doctrines as well.

The following quotes are from the Book of Concord and Christian Dogmatics, Volume #3. These are some of the writings of the Lutheran Church, which all Pastors of my church body--The Lutheran Church Missouri Synod give their promise to uphold and teach faithfully when they are ordained; we also agree to have our lives and ministry evaluated according to them. We hold these writings to be the correct understanding and explanation of Scripture. Having said all that, we also hold that The Lutheran Church Missouri Synod is <u>not</u> the visible church on earth. <u>We freely and joyfully confess that the true Church is invisible regarding human organization and that many believers from an almost endless list of churches will join us in heaven</u>. Salvation by grace is a gift of God and faith comes by hearing the Word of God.

My prayer is that this book is helpful to my tribe of Christians and any others who read it.

Theology itself, which measures all preaching and teaching ultimately, falls to the local Pastor who is called and ordained for this purpose. However, as we look at the following doctrinal statements, prepare your heart and mind to contemplate ways in which the Holy Spirit could also use Deaconesses, Parish Nurses, Directors of Christian Education, Directors of Christian Outreach and others from the Priesthood of the Baptized who would truly enjoy the opportunity to provide Mercy to those identified through your Congregational Prayer Ministry efforts as needing care.

God Only Listens to Christian Prayer:

I have been blessed to know Pr. Jacob Preuss; he was my academic advisor as a Seminary student and I have always known him to be someone that I could have robust and enjoyable conversations with on almost any topic, but especially Lutheran doctrine. At a conference in 2013 we ran into each other and he asked about my ministry; this led to a good conversation about Prayer and the Lutheran perspective on it.

In the course of our conversation, Pr. Preuss said two things that really struck me. The first was his observation that the Book of Concord is not an exhaustive catalog of our doctrine. Pr. Preuss pointed out that the Book of Concord was written largely in response to allegations and accusations during the Reformation. We are grateful for the Book of Concord but the need for a more comprehensive and organized gathering of our doctrinal positions was needed, this led Rev. Dr. Franz Pieper to write his three volume "Christian Dogmatics". The second thing that Pr. Preuss said to me was by way of encouragement- his suggestion was that I look again at Pieper's writings and see what he said about Prayer.

Shortly after the conference, I got my three volumes of Pieper's Dogmatics down. There are two sections of Volume 3 devoted to Prayer. The second section addresses the question, "Is prayer a means of grace?" Some Christians have taught this; we do not. The first section regarding Prayer is found in the chapter on Sanctification (the holy things that the Holy Spirit does in the life of a Christian). It was interesting to me that the section on Prayer, "The Christian Life and Prayer" immediately follows, "The Christian Life and the Cross". The life of the Christian is found at the foot of the cross, from which comes our Prayer life. <u>Here are some quotes from Pieper on Prayer</u>:

"… all prayer which does not flow from faith in the reconciliation effected by Christ is the result of natural emotions. The (cause) of such praying is not the Holy Ghost… but the devil." (pg. 78)
*This fact creates a moral obligation for Christians to know the needs of their unsaved neighbors and to pray for them and their salvation.

"Luther, 'Without communion with Christ, no on can pray even one word which would count before God or be pleasing to Him." (pg. 78)
"Scripture expressly declares that the things which the Gentiles sacrifice- and that includes their prayers- 'they sacrifice to devils and not to God' (1 Cor. 10:20)" (pg. 78)

"The prayer of Christians has its effect on all occurrences in the Church and in the world… It is owing to their (the Christians) prayer that the State is preserved and prosper." (pg. 80)
*We must pray for those in authority, <u>especially</u> if their decisions are contrary to Scripture.

"A Christian prays… even when by reason of great sorrow and grief he imagines that he <u>cannot</u> pray." (pg. 77)
*Faith is not the lack of doubt, but trust and hope in God, through His Son, by His Spirit.

"The prayers of all saints have ever been based on Christ's righteousness, on God's grace and mercy in Christ, <u>never</u> on their own worthiness." (pg. 80)

"Prayer has been fittingly compared to the heartbeat of physical life: it never ceases. Luther says, 'Where there is a Christian, there is the Holy Ghost, who is <u>always</u> engaged in prayer.'" (pg. 77)

What Is Prayer?

1. *Prayer is a confident conversation between a sister or brother of Christ and their Father*:
Jesus teaches us to pray, *"Our Father who art in heaven."* What does this mean?
Answer: Here God would encourage us to believe that he is truly our Father and we are truly his children in order that we may approach him boldly and confidently in prayer, even as beloved children approach their dear father."[8]

---

[8] SC III. 1-2.

2. *Prayer is commanded of believers, just as firmly as any of the 10 Commandments*:
"Prayer, therefore, is as strictly and <u>solemnly commanded as all the other commandments</u>, such as having no other God, not killing, not stealing, etc." [9]

3. *Prayer is our fortress from the devil*:
"Since the devil is not only a liar but also a murderer,[3] he incessantly seeks our life and vents his anger by causing accidents and injury to our bodies. He breaks many a man's neck and drives others to insanity; some he drowns, and many he hounds to suicide or other dreadful catastrophes. [116] Therefore <u>there is nothing for us to do on earth but to **pray constantly** against this arch-enemy</u>. For if God did not support us, we would not be safe from him for a single hour."[10]

4. *Prayer is a Eucharistic Sacrifice that we offer to God*:
"<u>There are two, and only two, basic types of sacrifice</u>. One is the <u>propitiatory sacrifice</u>; this is a work of satisfaction for guilt and punishment that reconciles God or placates his wrath or merits the forgiveness of sins for others. <u>The other type is the eucharistic sacrifice</u>; this does not merit the forgiveness of sins or reconciliation, but by it those who have been reconciled <u>give thanks</u> or show their gratitude for the forgiveness of sins and other blessings received.[11]"...
"<u>There has really been only one propitiatory sacrifice in the world, the death of Christ</u>."[12]...
"The rest are eucharistic sacrifices, called '<u>sacrifices of praise</u>': the proclamation of the Gospel, faith, <u>prayer</u>, thanksgiving, confession, the afflictions of the saints, yes, all the good works of the saints. These sacrifices are <u>not</u> satisfactions on behalf of those who bring them, nor can they be transferred to merit the forgiveness of sins or reconciliation for others.... Those who bring them are <u>already</u> reconciled. [26] The sacrifices of the New Testament are of this type, as Peter teaches in 1 Peter 2:5, 'A holy priesthood, to offer spiritual sacrifices.'[13]

What Does God Do with Our Prayers?

1. *God responds to the prayer of every good Christian*:
"For whenever a good Christian prays, 'Dear Father, thy will be done,' God replies from on high, 'Yes, dear child, it shall indeed be done in spite of the devil and all the world.'[14]

2. *We believe in specific prayer*:
"Let this be said as an admonition in order that men may <u>learn above all to value prayer as a great and precious thing</u> and may clearly <u>distinguish between vain babbling and praying for something definite</u>."[15]

3. *God answers every one of our prayers*:
"In the second place, we should be all the more urged and encouraged to pray because <u>God has promised that our prayer will surely be answered</u>, as he says in Psalm 50:15: 'Call upon me in the day of trouble, and I will deliver you,' and Christ says in Matthew 7:7-8, 'Ask and it will be given you,' etc. "For everyone who asks receives." [20] <u>Such promises certainly ought to awaken and kindle in our hearts a desire</u> and love to pray. For by his Word <u>God testifies that our prayer is heartily pleasing to him</u> and will assuredly be heard and granted, so that we may not despise or disdain it or pray uncertainly."[16]

---

[9]LC III. 6.
[10]Ibid., 115.
[11]Apol 1, XII. 19. .
[12]Ibid., 22.
[13]Ibid., 25-26.
[14]LC III. 32.
[15]Ibid., 33.
[16]Ibid., 19-20.

In June 1540, a very good friend of Martin Luther was sick; in fact, he was nearly dead. Luther prayed fervently for his friend and God did restore him. On September 20, 1542, Luther's daughter Magdalene died in his arms; in spite of his prayers throughout her illness, she was taken Home. For us, we always pray that "the Lord's will be done." (Rev. Dr. Al Collver, *"Fides Heroica? Luther's Prayer for Melanchthon's Recovery from Illness in 1540"*; Volume 76, January/April of the *Concordia Theological Quarterly*)

4. *Every believer's prayer is equally precious in God's eyes*:
"We allow ourselves to be hindered and deterred by such thoughts as these: 'I am not holy enough or worthy enough; if I were as godly and holy as St. Peter or St. Paul, then I would pray.' Away with such thoughts! He can boast of no better or holier commandment than I.
[16] "Therefore you should say: "The prayer I offer is just as precious, holy, and pleasing to God as those of St. Paul and the holiest of saints."[17]

If God Knows Everything, Why Should We Pray?

1. *God has forgiven us before we even ask Him; but we pray as a sign that we accept His forgiveness*:
"Here again there is great need to call upon God and pray, 'Dear Father, forgive us our debts.' Not that he does not forgive sin even without and before our prayer; and he gave us the Gospel, in which there is nothing but forgiveness, before we prayed or even thought of it. But the point here is for us to recognize and accept this forgiveness."[18]

2. *Prayer trusts in God's mercy*:
"Therefore prayer relies upon the mercy of God when we believe that we are heard because of Christ the high priest, as he himself says (John 16:23): 'If you ask anything of the Father, he will give it to you in my name.' 'In my name,' he says, because without the high priest we cannot draw near to the Father."[19]

3. *God's punishments of us are lightened by our prayers*:
"Afterwards, as we readily admit, the punishments that chasten us are lightened by our prayers and good works, indeed by our complete penitence, according to the words, 'If we judged ourselves, we would not be judged by the Lord'" (1 Corinthians 11:31); 'If you are converted, I will convert you' (Jeremiah 15:19); 'Return to me and I will return to you'" (Zechariah 1:3); 'Call upon me in the day of trouble' (Psalm 50:15)"[20]

4. *A mark of a true Christian is that he or she prays*:
"To pray, as the Second Commandment teaches, is to call upon God in every need. This God requires of us; he has not left it to our choice. It is our duty and obligation to pray if we want to be Christians."[21]
"For this is the essence of a genuinely Christian life, to acknowledge that we are sinners and to pray for grace."[22]

5. *Penitence (confession of sin) should produce the fruit of increased Prayer in a believer*:
"We have testified often enough that penitence ought to produce good fruits. (tr-307) What these fruit are, we learn from the commandments — prayer, thanksgiving, the confession of the Gospel, the teaching of the Gospel."[23]

---

[17]Ibid., 15-26.
[18]Ibid., 88.
[19]Apol 1, III. 212.
[20]Ibid., 147.
[21]LC III. 8.
[22]LC VI. 9.

6. *Prayer should be esteemed as much as a Sacrament*:
"Ultimately, if we should list as sacraments all the things that have God's command and a promise added to them, then <u>why not prayer, which can most truly be called a sacrament</u>? It has both the command of God and many promises. If it were placed among the sacraments and thus given, so to speak, a more exalted position, this would (tr-313) move men to pray." [24] (Earlier in the text, we include Confession and Absolution as a Sacrament; Prayer is a similar New Testament, non-extra-material means of Grace; but just to clarify--we are not advocating that Prayer be considered a Sacrament.☺)

Lutheran Kenyan men's basketball team in Jersey City, NJ

What Do Believers Think Will Happen with Their Prayers?

1. *We pray, believing that God will provide for our earthly needs*:
"The fault lies wholly in that shameful unbelief which does not look to God even for enough to satisfy the belly, let alone expect, without doubting, eternal blessings from God. Therefore <u>we must strengthen ourselves against unbelief</u> and let the kingdom of God be the first thing for which we pray. Then, surely, we shall have all the other things in abundance, as Christ teaches, 'Seek first the kingdom of God, and all these things shall be yours as well.'[4] <u>For how could God allow us to suffer want in temporal things when he promises that which is eternal and imperishable?</u>"[25]

2. *Reason cannot believe that God hears prayer*:
"It is false, too, that by its own strength, reason can love God above all things and keep his law, truly fear him, truly believe that he hears prayer, willingly obey him in death and in his other visitations, and not covet.[26]

Discipleship Questions:
   *How can you keep track of God's answers to your Prayers?
   _____

   *How can you give God the glory and tell others what He has done for you?
   _____

---

[23]Apol 1, VI. 77.
[24]Ibid. 1, VII. 16.
[25]LC III. 58.
[26]Apol 1. II. 27.

How Do We Know the Right Words to Say in a Prayer?

God gives us the desire and the words to pray:

"Furthermore, we should be encouraged and drawn to pray because, in addition to this commandment and promise, <u>God takes the initiative and puts into our mouths the very words we are to use</u>." [27]

What Is the Right Way to Pray?

1. *We should pray without ceasing*:

"It has been prescribed for this reason, also, that we should reflect on our needs, which ought to drive and impel us to ^(tr-705) pray <u>without ceasing</u>." [28]

2. *Emotions are expected and a sign of Godly prayer*:

"If you pray the petition <u>whole-heartedly</u>, you can be sure that God is pleased." [29]

3. *The Lord's Prayer is not just a model for prayer, but an actual prayer we should pray*:

"That we may know what and how to pray, our Lord Christ himself has taught us both the way and the words, as we shall see." [30]

4. *The best prayer for us to actually pray is the Lord's Prayer*:

"So this prayer is far superior to all others that we might ourselves devise. For in the latter our conscience would always be in doubt, saying, 'I have prayed, but who knows whether it pleased him, or whether I have hit upon the right form and mode?' Thus there is no nobler prayer to be found on earth,[9] for <u>it has the excellent testimony that God loves to hear it</u>. This we should not trade for all the riches in the world." [31]

5. *We should be taught from the time of our youth to pray for others*:

"Each of us should form the habit from his youth up to pray daily for all his needs, whenever he is aware of anything that affects him or other <u>people around him</u>, such as preachers, magistrates, neighbors, servants." [32]

6. *True prayer requires no teaching, but comes from an earnest heart*:

"But where there is true prayer <u>there must be earnestness</u>. We must <u>feel</u> our need, <u>the distress</u> that impels <u>and drives us to cry out</u>. Then prayer will come spontaneously, as it should, <u>and we shall not need to be taught how to prepare for it or how to generate devotion</u>." [33]

What Is Required for an Acceptable Prayer?

We can offer acceptable prayers to God only <u>after</u> we have been justified:

"After we have been justified and regenerated by faith, therefore, we begin to fear and love God, to pray and expect help from him, to thank and praise him…" [34]

---

[27] LC III. 22.
[28] Ibid., 24.
[29] Ibid., 48.
[30] Ibid., 3.
[31] Ibid., 23.
[32] Ibid., 28.
[33] Ibid. 26.

What If Believers Don't Feel Like Praying?

1. *We are commanded by God to pray*:

"The first thing to know is this: It is our duty to pray because God has commanded it. We were told in the Second Commandment, 'You shall not take God's name in vain.' <u>Thereby we are required to praise the holy name and pray or call upon it in every need</u>. For to call upon it is nothing else than to pray."[6] "Prayer, therefore, is as strictly and solemnly commanded as all the other commandments, such as having no other God, not killing, not stealing, etc. <u>Let no one think that it makes no difference whether I pray or not</u>, as vulgar people do who say in their delusion: 'Why should I pray? Who knows whether God heeds my prayer or cares to hear it? If I do not pray, someone else will.' Thus they fall into the habit of never praying, alleging that since we reject false and hypocritical prayers we teach that there is no duty or need to pray."[35]

2. *The devil does not want us to pray*:

"I would like to see the people brought again to pray rightly and not act so crudely and coldly that they become daily more inept at praying. This is just what the devil wants and works for with all his might, for <u>he is well aware what damage and harm he suffers when prayer is in proper use</u>."[36]

3. *Failure to pray is a fruit of the Fall into Sin*:

"Here we must confess what St. Paul says in Romans 5:12, namely, that sin had its origin in one man, Adam, through whose disobedience all men were made sinners and became subject to death and the devil. This is called original sin, or the root sin.
[2] <u>The fruits of this sin are all the subsequent evil deeds</u> which are forbidden in the Ten Commandments, such as unbelief, false belief, idolatry, being without the fear of God, presumption, despair, blindness-- in short, ignorance or disregard of God-- and then also lying, swearing by God's name, <u>failure to pray and call upon God</u>, neglect of God's Word, disobedience to parents, murder, unchastity, theft, deceit, etc."[37]

4. *Prayer is done in obedience, but not as a good work; we pray in order to <u>receive from God</u>*:

"Therefore we have rightly rejected the prayers of monks and priests, who howl and growl frightfully day and night; not one of them thinks of asking for the least thing. If we gathered all the churches together, with all their clergy, they would have to confess that <u>they never prayed whole-heartedly for so much as a drop of wine</u>. None of them has ever undertaken to pray out of obedience to God and faith in his promise, or out of consideration for his own needs. They only thought, at best, of doing a good work as a payment to God, <u>not willing to receive anything from him, but only to give him something</u>."[38]

5. *Pastors should model a strong Prayer life for their church members*:

"Now that they are free from the useless, bothersome babbling of the Seven Hours,[4] it would be fine if every morning, noon, and evening they would read, instead, at least a page or two from the Catechism, the Prayer Book,[5] the New Testament, or something else from the Bible and would pray the Lord's Prayer for themselves and their parishioners."[39]

6. *It is necessary for us to exhort people to pray*:

"Before we explain the Lord's Prayer part by part, <u>it is very necessary to exhort and draw people to prayer</u>, as Christ and the apostles also did."[40]

---

[34]Apol 1. III. 4.
[35]LC III. 5-6.
[36]Ibid., 29.
[37]SA 3. I. 1-2.
[38]LC III. 25.
[39]LC III.
[40]Ibid., III. IV.

7. *Choosing not to pray is an act of disobedience to God*:
"What we shall pray, and for what, we should regard as demanded by God and done in obedience to him. We should think, 'On my account this prayer would amount to nothing; but it is important because God has commanded it.' So, no matter what he has to pray for, <u>everybody should always approach God in obedience to this commandment</u>."[41]

8. *God's foreknowledge and election does NOT remove from us the need to witness or pray*:
"God's eternal election, however, not only foresees and foreknows the salvation of the elect, but by God's gracious will and pleasure in Christ Jesus it is also a cause which creates, effects, helps, and furthers our salvation and whatever pertains to it… Such a view, however, leads many to (unfortunately) draw and formulate <u>strange, dangerous, and pernicious opinions and causes and fortifies in people's minds either false security and impenitence or anxiety and</u> [(tr-1067)] <u>despair</u>.

"As a result <u>they trouble themselves with burdensome doubts and say: Since God has foreordained his elect to salvation</u> 'before the foundations of the world were laid' (Ephesians 1:4) and since God's foreknowledge can never fail and no one can ever change or hinder it (Isaiah 14:27; Romans 9:19, 11), therefore if I have been foreknown to salvation, <u>it will do me no harm if I live in all kinds of sin and vice without repentance, despise Word and sacraments, and do not concern myself with repentance, faith, prayer, and godliness</u>. On the contrary, I shall and must be saved since God's foreknowledge must be carried out. But if I am not foreknown, then everything is in vain, even though I were to hold to the Word, repent, believe, etc., since I cannot hinder or alter God's foreknowledge."[42]

For What Things Should We Pray?

1. *We pray for God's kingdom to come among us*:
"Just as God's name is holy in itself and yet we pray that it may be holy among us, so also his kingdom comes of itself without our prayer and yet we pray that it may come to us."[43]

2. *We pray for ourselves to live Holy lives*:
"We pray here at the outset that all this may be realized in us and that God's name may be praised through his holy Word <u>and our Christian lives</u>." [44]

3. *The saved must pray for God to keep them from falling into sin*:
"Therefore, even though at present we are upright and stand before God with a good conscience, <u>we must pray again that he will not allow us to fall and yield to trials and temptations</u>. Temptation (or, as the ancient Saxons called it, *Bekörunge*)[9] is of three kinds: of the flesh, the world, and the devil."[45]

4. *We pray for the unsaved to be saved and for the saved to be sanctified*:
"Now, [(tr-713)] we pray for both of these, that it may come to those who are not yet in it, and that it may come by daily growth here and in eternal life hereafter to us who have attained it."[46]

5. *We pray for God's Name to be treated in a Holy way*:
"… we pray for exactly the same thing that God demands in the Second Commandment: that his name should not be taken in vain by swearing, cursing, deceiving, etc., but used rightly to the praise and glory of God." [47]

---

[41]Ibid., III. 13.
[42]FC II. XI. 10.
[43]LC PFP III. 50.
[44]LC III. 52.
[45]Ibid., 100-101.
[46]Ibid., 53.
[47]Ibid., 45.

For Whom Should We Pray Besides Ourselves?

1. *Christians in general, should pray for their neighbors*:
"I urge that supplications, prayers, intercessions, and thanksgivings be made for all men."[48]

2. *We pray for the Holy Spirit to save many from eternal damnation*:
"So we pray that, led by the Holy Spirit, many may come into the kingdom of grace and become partakers of salvation, so that we may all remain together eternally in this kingdom which has now made its appearance among us."[49]

3. *We pray for our military to be successful against the Muslims and all who attack us*:
Again, to ask God to endow the emperor, kings, and all estates of men, and especially our princes, counselors, magistrates, and officials, with wisdom, strength, and prosperity to govern well and to be victorious over the Turks and all our enemies; to grant their subjects and the people at large to live together in obedience, peace, and concord.[50]

4. *We pray without ceasing for the failure of all enemies of the Gospel*:
"Therefore, there is just as much need in this case as in every other case to pray without ceasing: 'Thy will be done, dear Father, and not the will of the devil or of our enemies, nor of those who would persecute and suppress thy holy Word or prevent thy kingdom from coming; and grant that whatever we must suffer on its account, we may patiently bear and overcome, so that our poor flesh may not yield or fall away through weakness or indolence.'"[51]

5. *We pray for God's blessing over every aspect of our life on this earth*:
"When you pray for 'daily bread'" you pray for everything that is necessary in order to have and enjoy daily bread and, on the contrary, against everything that interferes with enjoying it. You must therefore enlarge and extend your thoughts to include not only the oven or the flour bin, but also the broad fields and the whole land which produce and provide for us our daily bread and all kinds of sustenance. For if God did not cause grain to grow and did not bless and preserve it in the field, we could never take a loaf of bread from the oven to set on the table.
[73] To put it briefly, *this petition includes everything that belongs to our entire life in this world*; only for its sake do we need daily bread. Now, our life requires not only food and clothing and other necessities for our body, but also peace and concord in our daily business and in associations of every description with the people among whom we live and move-- in short, everything that pertains to the regulation of our domestic and our civil or political affairs. For where these two relations are interfered with and prevented from functioning properly, there the necessities of life are also interfered with, and life itself cannot be maintained for any length of time. [74] Indeed, the greatest need of all is to pray for our civil authorities and the government, for chiefly through them does God provide us our daily bread and all the comforts of this life."[52]

---

[48]SC PFP VIII.
[49]LC PFP III. 52.
[50]Ibid., 77.
[51]Ibid., 67.
[52]Ibid., 72-24.

What Things Can Make My Prayer Ineffective?

1. *A prayer said with doubt is no prayer at all*:
"… they receive nothing, as St. James says, 'If anyone prays, let him ask in faith, with no doubting, for he who doubts is like a wave of the sea that is driven and tossed by the wind. For that person must not suppose that he will receive anything from God.'[4] [124] Behold, <u>such is the importance that God attaches to our being certain that we do not pray in vain</u>"[53]

2. *Prayer should not be used as an excuse for lack of marital relations*:
"Good men know, too, that Paul commands each one to possess his vessel in holiness. (1 Thessalonians 4:4) They know that <u>sometimes</u> they must withdraw to have opportunity for prayer, but Paul does not want this to be perpetual. (1 Corinthians 7:5)"[54]

3. *We do not pray to Saints; it is ineffective and idolatrous to pray to anyone other than God*:
"… the Scriptures do not teach us to pray to the saints or seek their help, for the only mediator, propitiation, high priest, and intercessor whom the Scriptures set before us is Christ." [55]
"However, <u>it cannot be proved from the Scriptures that we are to invoke saints or seek help from them</u>. 'For there is one mediator between God and men, Christ Jesus' (1 Timothy 2:5)… He alone has promised to hear our prayers. [3] Moreover, according to the Scriptures, the highest form of divine service [(tr-59)] is sincerely to seek and call upon this same Jesus Christ in every time of need. [4] 'If anyone sins, we have an advocate with the Father, Jesus Christ the righteous. (1 John 2:1)"[56]
"Even if the saints do pray fervently for the church, it does not follow that they should be invoked."[57]

How Does Prayer Help Me?

1. *Prayer is a tool to help us resist temptation*:
"… we cannot be harmed by the mere feeling of temptation as long as it is contrary to our will and we would prefer to be rid of it. If we did not feel it, it could not be called a temptation. But to consent to it is to give it free rein and neither resist it nor pray for help against it."[58]

2. *The power of "Amen"*:
"…the efficacy of prayer consists in our learning also to say 'Amen' to it-- that is, not to doubt that our prayer is surely heard and will be granted. [120] <u>This word is nothing else than an unquestioning affirmation of faith</u> on the part of one who does not pray as a matter of chance but knows that God does not lie since he has promised to grant his requests." [59]

3. *"Protect us from evil" is last in the Lord's Prayer, because everything else must come first*:
"… this petition he has put last, for if we are to be protected and delivered from all evil, his name must first be hallowed in us, his kingdom come among us, and his will be done. Then he will preserve us from sin and shame and from everything else that harms or injures us."[60]

4. *Children pray prayers that are pleasing to God*:
"So children pray, 'I believe in one holy Christian church.'"[61]

---

[53]Ibid., 123-124.
[54]Apol 1. XI. 43.
[55]AC "The Confession of Faith." 2. XXI. 2.
[56]Ibid., 2.
[57]Apol 1. IX. 10.
[58]LC III. 108.
[59]Ibid., 119-120.
[60]Ibid., 118.
[61]SA III. XII. 3.

What Did Luther Personally Say About Prayer?

As I mentioned at the beginning of this chapter; all the quotes are from the Book of Concord and explained why this is important for us as Lutherans. The following quotes are of Luther, regarding prayer and they are taken from throughout his writings.

I am always surprised by Lutherans who dismiss what Luther has to say outside of the Book of Concord. Just my opinion, but if you want to know what Luther meant by what he said in the Book of Concord, the best place to turn is to Luther and look at his other writings. I am always a little cautious when I hear a Lutheran today who puts forward his or her opinion regarding Luther as being more authoritative than what Luther himself had to say.

I am blessed to have Luther's Works on my laptop. With the search engine you can grind through all his writings and quickly research what you are looking for; truly a blessing for us today. Here are a couple of statistics regarding Luther and Prayer that I found interesting and that quantify the strength of his emphasis on Prayer:

The words "prayer" and "neighbor" occur together:
-105 times in 16 articles in the Book of Concord
-625 times in all of Luther's Works

The words "God" and "pray" occur 15,427 times in Luther's writings.

Luther's Five Parts to Prayer:

"But elsewhere I have often taken up and discussed the component parts and the characteristics which every real prayer has to possess,[3] and therefore I shall only summarize them briefly here. They are as follows:

first, the urging of God's commandment, who has strictly required us to pray;

second, His promise, in which He declares that He will hear us;

third, an examination of our own need and misery, which burden lies so heavily on our shoulders that we have to carry it to God immediately and pour it out before Him, in accordance with His order and commandment;

fourth, true faith, based on this word and promise of God, praying with the certainty and confidence that He will hear and help us—

and (fifth) all these things in the name of Christ, through whom our prayer is acceptable to the Father and for whose sake He gives us every grace and every good."[62]

Luther's Six Types of Prayer

(1) "For to pray [*beten*] is really to repeat the words of a prayer such as the Psalms or the Lord's Prayer.

(2) But to petition [*bitten*] is to accompany such a spoken prayer with one's own special need and indicate it by name, just as the Lord's Prayer contains seven such petitions, and so forth.

(3) To plead [*flehen*] is to go beyond the petition in one's prayer and to admonish God through something that He prizes very highly, such as his mercy, name, honor, truth, or through Christ, and so forth.

(4-6) In addition there is also intercession for others, and praise and thanksgiving."[63]

---

[62]Martin Luther, 21: Matthew 6:7. Concordia.
[63]Ibid., 36:292..Fortress.

Luther Believed Prayer Is a Ministry All Believers Practice

"The sixth function is to *pray for others*… For Christ gave the Lord's Prayer to all his Christians. By this alone we are sufficiently able to prove and confirm that the priesthood is one and the same to all, whereas the papal priesthood is a falsehood devised outside the church of God and through mere effrontery brought into the church. To pray for others is to go between and make intercession of God, which is befitting Christ only and all his brethren…"[64]

"This is the great honor which belongs to Christians: He has anointed us and made us worthy, so that we may appear before God in prayer. Those who are not Christians can neither teach nor pray nor sacrifice rightly, no matter how presumptuous and boastful they may be about trying to teach all the world to sacrifice, chatter, sing, and groan in the churches day and night. They do not have this Mediator and High Priest. Everything must have its source in Him. Only through Him does anything avail in the sight of God. But if, for example, a young child who is baptized prays the Ten Commandments, the Creed, and the Lord's Prayer each morning or evening at the table, it is a true prayer; and God hears him. Such a child prays as a Christian and a priest, born in Baptism and ordained by Christ. Every Christian has and practices such priestly works." [65]

"… after we have become Christians through this Priest and His priestly office, incorporated in Him by Baptism through faith, then each one, according to his calling and position, obtains the right and the power of teaching and confessing before others this Word which we have obtained from Him. Even though not everybody has the public office and calling, every Christian has the right and the duty to teach, instruct, admonish, comfort, and rebuke his neighbor with the Word of God at every opportunity and whenever necessary. For example, father and mother should do this for their children and household; a brother, neighbor, citizen, or peasant for the other. Certainly one Christian may instruct and admonish another ignorant or weak Christian concerning the Ten Commandments, the Creed, or the Lord's Prayer. And he who receives such instruction is also under obligation to accept it as God's Word and publicly to confess it."[66]

"Meanwhile they pray for others and celebrate masses for them, as if prayer and the mass were their possession and not entrusted to the whole congregation." [67]

"Not only are we the freest of kings, we are also priests forever, which is far more excellent than being kings, for as priests we are worthy to appear before God to pray for others and to teach one another divine things. These are the functions of priests, and they cannot be granted to any unbeliever. Thus Christ has made it possible for us, provided we believe in him, to be not only his brethren, co-heirs, and fellow-kings, but also his fellow-priests. Therefore we may boldly come into the presence of God in the spirit of faith [Heb. 10:19, 22] and cry 'Abba, Father!' pray for one another, and do all things which we see done and foreshadowed in the outer and visible works of priests."[68]

"We must often reflect how horribly demented and infatuated the whole world was through the papists, canonists, and sophists, who limited the invocation and worship of God to the monasteries only, as though God could not be worshiped and invoked in common life."[69]

"Therefore we must not put aside our concern for our descendants, but we must diligently pray for them."[70]

---

[64]Ibid., 40:29-30.
Ibid., 13: Psalm 110:5. Concordia.
[66]Ibid., 13: Psalm 110:5. Concordia.
[67]Ibid.,52.
[68]Ibid., 31:355. Fortress.
[69]Ibid., 6: Genesis 37:15. Concordia. enesis 37:15
[70]Ibid., "Chapters 6-14," 6:Genesis 7:2

"But it is impossible for the ungodly to pray. Let no one, therefore, hope for any prayer from our adversaries, the papists. We are praying for them and setting ourselves up like a wall against the wrath of God; and if by any chance they were to come to repentance, they would, without a doubt, be saved through our tears and groanings." [71]

"With these and the following words Christ also demonstrates what constitutes a Christian's true office and function, and how necessary the exercise of this is in Christendom. The prophet Zechariah refers to this when he says (12:10) that Christ will pour out and grant the spirit which is called 'a spirit of compassion and supplication.' For in all Christians He will effect and produce these two things: First, He will convince and assure their hearts that they have a compassionate God; secondly, He will enable them to help others by their supplication. The result of the first is that they are reconciled to God and have all they need for themselves. Then, when they have this, they will become gods and will be **saviors of the world by their supplication.** Through the spirit of compassion they themselves will become children of God; and then, as children of God, they will mediate between God and their neighbor, and will serve others and help them attain this estate too.

"For once a Christian begins to know Christ as his Lord and Savior, through whom he is redeemed from death and brought into His dominion and inheritance, God completely permeates his heart.[51] Now he is eager to help everyone acquire the same benefits. For his greatest delight is in this treasure, the knowledge of Christ. Therefore he steps forth boldly, teaches and admonishes others, praises and confesses his treasure before everybody, prays and yearns that they, too, may obtain such mercy. There is a spirit of restlessness amid the greatest calm, that is, in God's grace and peace. A Christian cannot be still or idle. He constantly strives and struggles with all his might, as one who has no other object in life than to disseminate God's honor and glory among the people, that others may also receive such a spirit of grace and through this spirit also help him pray. For wherever the spirit of grace resides, there we can and dare, yes, must begin to pray.

"Therefore Christ wants to say here: 'When you believe in Me and have received the spirit by which the heart is assured of the grace of God'" (Christ had said above: 'He who has seen Me has seen the Father'), 'then you will certainly be constrained to pray.' For prayer is the true work characteristic only of Christians. Before we become Christians and believe, we do not know how or what to pray. And even if a man prays most fervently, the spirit of grace is not yet present. Then the heart is still disposed to say: 'Dear Lord, I ask you to regard my life, my intense suffering, or the merit of this or of that saint, the intercession and the good works of pious people.' This is not faith in divine grace and mercy through Christ." [72]

"**For My house shall be called a house of prayer for all peoples**, as if to say, "I have not built My temple for Jews only, because this temple at Jerusalem must be glorious for all peoples. It must be a place of prayer for all, and therefore the temple was also built for eunuchs and foreigners.

"This is a passage of supreme consolation, and it has converted many Gentiles to God, since they came with confidence to the worship of God. They have appropriated it to themselves like children. This is what Isaiah saw, that Abraham would be the father of many nations."[73]

Action Question:
   *How can we give members more opportunities to Pray?

_____

---

[71] Ibid., Genesis 6:8
[72] Ibid., 24: John 14:15. 24:John 14:15
[73] Ibid., 17: Isaiah 56:8. Concordia.

Luther's Thoughts on What Makes Prayer Effective or Ineffective

"If you have someone whom you do not forgive, you pray in vain. Therefore let each one look to his neighbor, if he has been offended by him, and forgive him from the heart; then he will be certain that his sin too has been forgiven. Not that you are forgiven on account of your forgiveness, but freely, without your forgiveness, your sins are forgiven. He, however, enjoins it upon you as a sign, that you may be assured that, if you forgive, you too will be forgiven."[74]

"When we plan to come before God in prayer for what we are to obtain, we must not be disunited or divided into schisms, factions, and sects, but we must be tolerant toward one another in love and remain of one mind. When this is the case, the Christian man is perfect; he believes correctly, and he loves correctly. Whatever other faults he may have, these are to be consumed in his prayer, and it is all forgiven and remitted." [75]

"The devil who besets us is not lazy or careless, and our flesh is too ready and eager to sin and is disinclined to the spirit of prayer."[76]

"...whatever we need will surely be granted and given to us if we only pray in faith and in the name of Christ."[77]

"To summarize, God will hear and acknowledge only what is presented in the name of Christ." [78]

"It would be one of the worst blasphemies--a blasphemy which calls God a liar--for you to pray because of God's command and promise, also in the name of Christ, and yet to waver by saying: "Who knows whether I am praying properly, whether my prayer is heard?"[79]

"But Scripture testifies that "whatever does not proceed from faith is sin" (Romans 14:23) and, on the other hand, that what proceeds from faith is righteousness. Therefore in taking possession of a house, in an administrative office in the state, and in the whole course of material life we should pray in faith in the Mediator and **be convinced that that prayer is pleasing to God and is heard by Him**.
In our times we have gained a wonderful victory against the pope by means of prayer and faith. Although arms and swords are not lacking, the church conquers the pope by means of prayer alone, slays him, and strips him of his arms and that thunderbolt of excommunication even among his subjects and confederates. And we shall do still greater things if we persevere in faith and prayer." [80]

"He refuses to hear and accept anyone's prayer but his who comes in the name of Christ, and throws himself on pure mercy and grace, and who says with the publican: 'God, be merciful to me a sinner!'"[81]

"God bestows on those who call upon Him more and greater things than the human heart can comprehend or request; for we worship Him whose power and beneficence are boundless. Indeed, He also determines all the particulars, the place, the time, and the person far better and more successfully than we would prescribe with our thinking. Therefore let us habituate and stir up our hearts to prayer, in order that many may pray together; for the greater the number of those who will pray, the more quickly and more

---

[74]Ibid., 51:178-179. Fortress.
[75]Ibid., 21: Matthew 6:16. Concordia.
[76]Ibid., 43:194. Fortress.
[77]Ibid., 24: John 15:17. Concordia.
[78]Ibid., John 16:25.
[79]Ibid., John 16:24.
[80]Ibid.,8: Genesis 49:14.
[81]Ibid., 24:John 14:15.

abundantly they will get what they ask for. But one must pray in the name of Christ, not of Mary, Peter, or other saints, as the papists are in the habit of doing. But of this we have often spoken elsewhere."[82]

"… and this is **the true incense** of Christians—**to pray earnestly**…"[83]

"And here the advantage is that when Christians thus come together their prayers are twice as strong as otherwise. One can and one really should pray in every place and every hour; but prayer is nowhere so mighty and strong[5] as when the whole multitude prays together. Thus the dear patriarchs gathered with their families, and anybody else who happened to be with them, under a tree, or put up a tent, and erected an altar, and this was their temple and house of God, where they talked about Christ, the coming seed who was promised to them, sacrificed together, called upon God, and gave thanks to him. And thus they were always glad to be with the multitude whenever they could, even though they also meditated upon God's Word and promise and prayed by themselves in private."[84]

Luther on Abraham's Prayer Life

"When Moses states here that at this place Abram called *in* the name of the Lord, it is the same as if he said that he erected a public chapel or an altar, at which he preached and taught about the true religion-- mainly, of course, to his household but then also to the neighboring Canaanites who came together at this place."[85]

"Abraham teaches us by his example that everything indeed should be done for the sake of one's neighbor,"[86]

"Now go ask our popes and bishops: 'Who anointed Abraham to fill this priestly office among his people?'"[87]

Discipleship Question:
*How would your family describe your Prayer life? _____

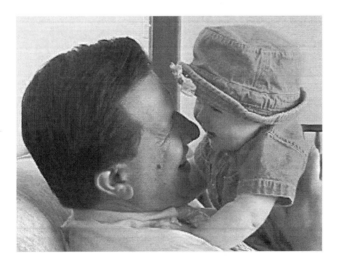

With Grace soon after she was born.

---

[82]Ibid. 4: Genesis 24:16.
[83]Ibid., 51:353-355. Fortress.
[84]Ibid., 337-338.
[85]Ibid., 2: Genesis 13:4. Concordia.
[86]Ibid., 4: Genesis 21:17.
[87]Ibid., 2: Genesis 12:9.

III. Prayer in Worship

We looked at Scripture first regarding Prayer because Scripture is the objective basis of the Christian faith. Next we looked at our explanation of Scripture regarding Prayer and encouraged others to look at their own church body's explanation of Scripture regarding Prayer. Now, on the foundation of Scripture and its explanation, we will look at Worship and specifically, Prayer in our Worship life.

What Role Does Prayer Have in Our Worship?

"It has been said that how we worship is how we live our faith." (Prof. Ron Feuerhahn, Emeritus)

"Where now are those who desire to know and to do good works? Let them undertake just prayer alone and rightly exercise themselves in faith, and they will find that it is true, as the holy fathers have said, that there is no work like prayer. Mumbling with the mouth is easy, or at least considered easy. But to follow the words in deep devotion and sincerity of heart, that is, with desire and in faith, so that one earnestly desires what the words say and does not doubt that they will be heard, that is a great deed in God's sight."[88]

Prayer is found throughout our worship. So, Prayer should be reflected throughout the daily life of a Christian. As we pause to reflect on how heavily we emphasize Prayer in our Worship, we will see the Spiritual unfolding of Prayer for: Ministry, Mercy and Multiplication; by God's gracious enlightenment from the Holy Spirit, we will be directed in how to use Prayer to serve our fellow members better, as well as the visitors to our churches and those around us in our communities.

As Scripture teaches, *This is how we know what love is: Jesus Christ laid down his life for us. And we ought to lay down our lives for our brothers. If anyone has material possessions and sees his brother in need but has no pity on him, how can the love of God be in him?* ***Dear children, let us not love with words or tongue but with actions and in truth****.* (1 John 3:16-18)

Prayer is not some "program"; it is not a human invention in which we trust. For us as Lutherans, Prayer ministry is the 6th function of the Priesthood of the Baptized (see Luther's Works, volume 40; pgs.29-30 for the full list). Prayer is like breathing; it comes naturally for a Christian. Any suggestions regarding Prayer had better be based on Scripture, backed up with accepted Christian teaching, and bear the blessings of fruitfulness that comes only from the Holy Spirit.

Discipleship Question:

  *What parts of my Sunday worship experience do I repeat during the week?

_____

---

[88] Ibid., 44:61-62. Fortress.

A. The Role of Prayer in the House Church Worship Era (32 A.D. – 313 A.D.)

In preparing this part of the book, I reached out to Pastor Will Weedon who serves as the Director of Worship for T0he Lutheran Church--Missouri Synod (my tribe). Pastor Weedon was very collegial and took time from his busy schedule to respond and share thoughts and resources. Thank you, Pastor Weedon.

A book Pastor Weedon recommended to me regarding Prayer and Worship was Dom Dix's: *The Shape of Liturgy*. This book, while not inexpensive, does make for a <u>very good</u> research resource regarding the historic Christian liturgy. Not every part of this 777 page book relates to Prayer in Worship, but much of it applies to my focus. The following quotes are taken from Dix's book; they are meant as a fair sample of his thoughts. The purpose of Dix's book intrigued me--"The subject of the paper--the structure of actions <u>and prayers</u> which forms the eucharist…" (pg. xi). <u>Prayer has always been a vital part of our Christian worship.</u>

My contention is that what we say and sing in worship should be seen in our walk, which is why I appreciated these thoughts from Dix: "It is sometimes forgotten by the advocates of the vernacular liturgy that our Lord… never attended a strictly vernacular service in His life…. The Jewish services… were in the liturgical Hebrew, which was not understood by the people without special instruction…. According to Saint Mark it was the <u>liturgical</u> Hebrew, not the vernacular Aramaic, which rose to His lips in prayer at the supreme moment of His passion." (pg. 616) <u>Jesus' prayer in public reflected His prayer in worship.</u> The old covenant with its rules and regulations regarding worship was seconds within being replaced as Jesus hung on the tree for us; He was about to usher in a new reality.

Dix goes on: "Real efforts were made in the fourteenth and fifteenth centuries to provide vernacular devotions for the layfolk to use during mass. Most unfortunately these do not seem anywhere to have taken the form of translations of the prayers actually used at the altar, <u>which would have enabled the laity to participate more intelligently in the rite itself</u>." (pg. 618)

I had to smile when I read--"… we may note in passing that the arguments by which the retention of Latin for the liturgy is now defended are the precise opposite of those which originally brought about the introduction of a Latin rite at Rome." (pg. 619)

My focus on Prayer in the historic Lutheran / Christian liturgy is <u>not</u> in order to make a statement regarding worship "style"; in fact Dix states at the outset of his book, "… the primitive outline of the liturgy, was from the first prescribed, not by an authoritative code, but by the tradition of custom alone." (pg. 3) This is a nice balance with an earlier and equally true observation regarding "spontaneous prayer," where Dix says this prayer is "… still largely drawn from what he (the person praying) has learned from others--his teachers... mother… from the tradition of prayer evolved in the worshipping church." (pg. xii)

My hope is that if we can see from <u>the historic worship style of Christianity</u> how important Prayer has been and how richly Prayer was used, <u>that Christians of today, especially those who do not do much praying outside of Church or out loud in public, might come to see that Prayer is definitely something we do as Christians</u>--always have, always will; all the time; in all sorts of places.

"We regard Christian worship… as essentially a *public* activity… The apostolic and primitive church, on the contrary, regarded all Christian worship, and especially the eucharist, as a highly *private* activity… Christian worship was intensely corporate, but it was not 'public'… They met in one another's houses for the Breaking of Bread…. It was not that the church did not desire converts; she was ardently missionary to all… But propaganda meetings were rigidly separate from 'worship,' <u>so that they were not even accompanied by prayer</u>." (pg. 16-17)

"<u>Christianity</u>… <u>concentrated itself instead in those 'house churches'</u> which meet us everywhere in the N.T. and the 2nd century…. <u>Worship was entirely at home, and their atmosphere</u> also informed the spirit and the arrangements of the liturgical worship… It was this originally domestic spirit of Christian worship… that preserved the clear understanding of its corporate nature. <u>The understanding of this began to</u>

fade at once when it was transformed into a 'public' worship in the great basilicas of the fourth century. " (pg. 17-18)

"Until the third century the word 'church' (*ecclesia*) means invariably *not* the building for Christian worship but the solemn assembly for the liturgy… There were of course plenty of other meetings of groups of Christians in one another's houses for prayer and edification… But these gatherings were never called 'ecclesia', 'the general assembly…' but *syneleuseis* or 'meetings'… what distinguished the liturgical *ecclesia* from even the largest private meeting was the official present of the *liturgical* ministry, the bishop, presbyters and deacons, and their exercise there of those special 'liturgical' functions in which they were irreplaceable. Without these it is not called an *ecclesia.*" (pg. 19-20)

This differentiation is maintained in the Lutheran understanding that Church has seven outward characteristics: the Word, Baptism, Communion, Confession and Absolution, a called Pastor, Prayer and Praise, and a cross. (For a more complete description, see Volume 41 of *Luther's Works*.)

I know that Latin and Greek words can cause people to roll their eyes and accuse clergy of educational pride; but on n pg. 20 Dix retells a very touching story (recorded in Roman legal records) about an early Christian by the name of Justin who was martyred for his faith. Justin was caught, with seven other Christians, worshipping in a home. The judge tried to learn the whereabouts of any larger group of Christians of which Justin might be a part. Sensing this, Justin always answered the judge with the word *syneleuseis* and only described the small meeting group; Justin never answered the judge with the word *ecclesia* because to do so would have revealed the rest of the Christians in Justin's House Church. Pretty touching stuff! The early Christians were very matter-of-fact; when pressed to sell out other Christians, a frequent response was, "We are not informants. I have told you about my faith."

In the early Christian Church, the greatest personal expression of faith, the liturgy of the individual believer, was participation in the Eucharist, the reception of Christ's body and blood. In so doing, they proclaimed Christ's death, until He came again. Taking Communion in those times was not some passé event. It was a public statement of a personal faith. This was the liturgical role for the individual believer in the Early Church's worship.

"Thus Saint Ignatius writes… 'as the Lord did nothing without the Father… so neither do anything without the bishop' This (single Eucharistic assembly) remained the ideal, until it was finally lost to sight in the later middle ages… Ignatius already recognizes that the bishop may have to delegate his 'special liturgy' to others at minor Eucharistic assemblies: 'Let that be counted a valid eucharist which is either under the bishop or under one to whom the bishop has assigned this.' The last church to abandon this was… Rome…. right down to the fourteenth century, and did not wholly die out until 1870." (pg. 21)

Dix stresses that for the Early Church, worship was something believers did, not said. Rev. Dr. Bob Scudieri in his book, *The Apostolic Church: One, Holy, Catholic and Missionary*, makes much the same point, stressing that "Apostolic" in the Early Church always referred to what the Apostles did (the Apostles were one who were sent out), not what they said; the point being the Early Church focused on doing.

"For centuries it was the custom at Rome to dispatch to each of these by an acolyte the *fermentum*, a fragment from the Breads consecrated by the Pope at 'the' eucharist of the whole church, to be placed in the Chalice at every parish eucharist, in token that each of these was still, in Ignatius' phrase, 'under the bishop,' as the 'liturgy' of the presbyter whom 'the bishop had assigned it.'" (pg. 21)

"In the idea of Ignatius, and of the primitive writers generally, it is *the church as a whole,* and not any one order in it, which not so much 'represents' as 'is' Christ on earth… The primitive church took this concept with its fullest force… the ***whole church* prayed in the Person of Christ**; the *whole church* was charged with the office of 'proclaiming' the revelation of Christ…" (pg. 29)

"It is in the fourth century, when the peace of the church and the immense growth of numbers had made it impossible for bishops in most place still to act as the only ministers of all sacraments to their churches, that we find the real change taking place in the function of the presbyter. He becomes the permanent liturgical minister of a separate congregation, to whom he… supplies most of those 'liturgies' of sacraments and teaching for which the pre-Nicene church had habitually looked to the bishop." (pg. 34)

"The bishop absorbs more and more of its administrative authority, but in return parts with his liturgical monopoly. The only sacramental function he retains in his own hands is the bestowal of 'order' in the church—confirmation, which admits to the order of the laity, and ordination, which admits to the orders of deacon, presbyter or bishop." (pg. 34)

"But by immemorial tradition they (the deacons) never directly address God on behalf of the church; that is the 'liturgy' of the bishop. The deacon, even in 'bidding' the prayers of the church, speaks *to the church,* not to God." (pg. 34)

Hippolytus who wrote the earliest recorded Prayer for worship, said regarding widows in the Church, "the widow is appointed for prayer, and this is (a function) of all." (pg. 35) Prayer has always been a function of all believers.

To summarize some thoughts from Dix (pgs. 36-47): the earliest Christian worship service had two basic parts: the service of the Word and the service of Communion.

The service of the Word was taken largely from the Jewish order of service with one significant exception--Prayer. Whereas the Jewish service had Prayer at the beginning, the Christian service had Prayer at the end.

Only believers were admitted into the second half of the worship service for Communion; when the sermon was completed in the first half of the worship service, all who had not entered the order of the laity were dismissed before the Prayers were offered up by the Church. This is because "the church is the body of Christ and prays 'in the name' of Jesus, *i.e.,….* 'in His *Person.'*… those who had not yet put on Christ by Baptism (Galatians 3:27) and thus as 'sons' received His Spirit by confirmation *cannot* join in offering that prevailing Prayer.

All who had not entered the order of the laity were therefore without exception turned out of the assembly after the sermon. The catechumens who had accepted the faith, but had not yet been added to the church by the sacraments, first received a special blessing from the bishop." (pgs. 41-42)

The idea is not that Christians refused to pray for non-Christians, but rather that early Christians did not do things "just for appearance's sake." The early Church prayed "in Jesus' Name"; they could not honestly pray in this way with a non-believer. They could and did pray for those in authority and all others, but they prayed as a Christian community.

When people talk about the Early Church dismissing all who were not yet Disciples before Communion was offered, they should remember that this happened when worship was done in people's homes. Once the Constantinian church model came into effect, people were no longer dismissed. You will look long and hard to find any Lutheran congregation today that literally dismisses people from their Sanctuary before offering Prayers and Communion. My point is not that we should do this, but just to say that the House Church approach to worship demonstrated a tighter control than the Constantinian model.

This ancient understanding of worship, a worship established by Christ and the Early Church in people's homes, was something Martin Luther wanted to see reestablished. And when you look closely at Luther's understanding of worship and the benefits the Christian community experienced through more personal worship in people's homes, you see that Luther longed for the worship experience of the early Christian church:

"The third kind of service should be a truly evangelical order and should not be held in a public place for all sorts of people. But those who want to be Christians in earnest and who profess the gospel with hand and mouth should sign their names and meet alone in a house somewhere to pray, to read, to baptize, to receive the sacrament, and to do other Christian works. According to this order, those who do not lead Christian lives could be known, reproved, corrected, cast out, or excommunicated, according to the rule of Christ, Matthew 18 [:15–17]." (Volume 53, *Luther's Works*)

Dix is very passionate about liturgical worship, but he is also very transparent:

"It (the Eucharistic Prayer) was subject to constant development and revision, so that it varied considerably from church to church and from period to period, and even (probably within narrower limits) from celebrant to celebrant." (pg. 156) I was impressed with Dix's integrity. This is hardly the analysis of someone who is trying to force liturgy through legalism.

"The traditions we shall chiefly consider now are three--those of Rome, Egypt and Syria, for Rome, Alexandria and Antioch were the three most important churches in pre-Nicene times. But there were other traditions of the Prayer elsewhere, some of them equally ancient, in North Africa, Spain and Gaul in the West, and in the apostolic churches of the Balkans and Asia Minor in the East. Unfortunately, by the accidents of history it happens that no texts of the Eucharistic prayers of these churches have survived from Pre-Nicene times, or indeed from any period at which their evidence can usefully serve for even a tentative comparison with the really ancient material." (pg. 156)

Regarding Congregational Prayer, for the entire Pre-Nicene period, for all locations of Christianity, it appears that we have only Hippolytus' Eucharistic Prayer.

Martin Luther observed, "… as for the example of the fathers, [their liturgical orders] are partly unknown, partly so much at variance with each other that nothing definite can be established about them, evidently because they themselves used their liberty. And even if they would be perfectly definite and clear, yet they could not impose on us a law or the obligation to follow them."

The following is a statement of faith for confessional Lutherans, "We believe, teach, and confess that no church should condemn another because it has fewer or more external ceremonies not commanded by God, as long as there is mutual agreement in doctrine and in all its articles as well as in the right use of the holy sacraments, according to the familiar axiom, "Disagreement in fasting does not destroy agreement in faith." (The Formula of Concord: 1, X, 7)

For Dix, this incredible loss of early Christian worship records would not produce significant change if they were found. He believes that these other documents would basically agree with Hippolytus' Eucharistic Prayer (pg. 157). .

In my humble opinion, the strength of the historic Christian liturgy is that it has stood the test of time; endured false doctrines; been a steady hand in seasons of persecution as well as prominence. When we use the historic Christian liturgy, we are confident that what we are saying and doing, proclaims Christ and Him crucified, that we are announcing the truth that God was reconciling all nations to Himself, through His Son, by the power of the Holy Spirit.

We have freedom in worship; but with the exercise of freedom come the responsibility to be held accountable and measured according to Scripture and doctrine. If a Pastor is too proud for the Bereans of today to examine Scripture and judge his actions, then he is no true Pastor.

Two themes that run throughout Dix's book ("*The Shape of the Liturgy*") are these:

1. Worship in the early Church was something done by the community (vs. a focus on the individual's experience); the community was the "Body of Christ."
2. Worship was something thought of in terms of action, not words. The early Church always spoke of "doing the Eucharist"; Communion was an action and every person had a role.

This focus on the whole body, acting out her faith, is the picture of Prayer in the Church of today, which this book hopes to communicate.

It is my belief that Prayer is much more than just words; Prayer is the Church in action, living out her faith in loving service to others, for the purposes of Ministry, Mercy and Multiplication.

Have You Ever Read the Oldest Prayer Written by the Early Church?

I am just a history geek at heart, but I think this is pretty cool stuff. Here is Hippolytus' Eucharistic Prayer, taken from Dix's book (I did delete one sentence from the Prayer, which Dix believed was added in the 4th century):

"We render thanks unto Thee, O God, through Thy Beloved Servant Jesus Christ, Whom in the last times Thou didst send (to be) a Savior and Redeemer and the Angel of Thy counsel; Who is Thy Word inseparable (from Thee)

Through Whom Thou made all things and in Whom Thou was well-pleased;

Whom Thou didst send from heaven into the Virgin's womb, and Who conceived within her was made flesh, and demonstrated to be Thy Son, being born of Holy Spirit and a Virgin;

Who fulfilling Thy will and procuring for Thee an holy people, stretched forth His hands for suffering (or for the passion) that He might release from sufferings them who have believed in Thee;

Who when He was betrayed to voluntary suffering (*or* the passion) in order that He might abolish death and rend the bonds of the devil and tread down hell and enlighten the righteous and establish the ordinance and demonstrate the resurrection,
Taking bread (and) making eucharist to Thee, said: 'Take, eat; this is My Body, which is (*or* will be) broken for you.

Likewise also the cup, saying: 'This is my Blood which is shed for you. When ye do this ye do (*or* make My 'anamnesis' [remembrance]) now, therefore, doing the 'anamnesis' of His death and resurrection we offer to Thee the bread and cup making eucharist to Thee because Thou hast made us worthy to stand before Thee and minister as priests to Thee

And we pray Thee that Thou would grant to all who partake to be made one, that they may be fulfilled with (the) Holy Spirit for the confirmation of (their) faith in truth;

That we may praise and glorify Thee through Thy Servant Jesus Christ through Whom honor and glory (be) unto Thee with (the) Holy Spirit in Thy holy church, now and forever and world without end. Amen."

That is pretty cool. When is the last time you prayed a prayer that was used by the Christian church in the 2nd century? (Just to be clear, there are other Prayers that claim to go back as far as Hippolytus' Prayer, but these other Prayers all had additions and deletions / were built on entirely different Prayers).

B. The Role of Prayer in the Constantinian Church Worship Era (313 A.D. – Today)

It is argued that we are today in the Post-Constantinian era of the Church- the Church in America does not enjoy the centrality in culture or assumed favor in legal decisions it once did; the 10 Commandments are not posted in public schools and Nativity scenes are not welcome at municipal buildings

Constantine was a European emperor and in Europe, the state Church is still financed with public tax funds; this is true also of the state Church in Canada; the largest landholder in the world is still the Church and the most popular series on cable T.V. was the recent "Bible" production on the History channel. Before Constantine, the government often rounded up Christians and fed them to lions; this is not the case in any Western country today. Muslim persecution of Christians has always been here; so that is not new.

I do not dispute that circumstances for Christianity in America today are not what they were 50 years ago, but in the broad picture of things it is a little dramatic to say we are "Post Constantinian" just yet. Drama is fine, it wakens people up; just make sure you have a map forward to share at that point.

The very first page of the *Lutheran Service Book* is titled, "Prayers for Worship," and has seven prayers offered to help the worshipper. The very last page of the *Lutheran Service Book* has the Lord's Prayer printed on it… The first and last pages of our hymnal focus on Prayer. For a Lutheran, there is no mistaking the role of Prayer in worship.

We have a whole section of hymns on the theme of Prayer--hymns 766 through 780 are specifically focused on Prayer. Verse 9 of Martin Luther's, "Our Father, Who from Heaven Above" (one of his catechism hymns), resonates with me; maybe it's because Luther uses "amen" somewhere other than at the end of the hymn, or maybe it's because you can hear the confidence of his conviction:

> "Amen, that is, so shall it be. Make strong our faith in You, that we
> May doubt not but with trust believe that what we ask we shall receive.
> Thus in Your Name and at Your Word, We say, "Amen, O hear us, Lord!"

Words Traditionally Used in Worship with Prayer

"**Amen**"--simply means, "it is true." It is a statement of agreement spoken individually or congregationally.

"**Collect**"-- usually a brief prayer, yet having five parts: (1) calling upon God; (2) basis for the prayer; (3) our need/concern/praise, etc.; (4) the result we would like; (5) a Trinitarian conclusion.

"**Compline**"--a service of Prayer; at the close of the day

"**Litany**"--a printed series of prayers; usually done responsively.

"**Matins**"--Morning service of psalms, readings and prayers

"**Ordinary Prayers**" and "**Proper Prayers**"--Ordinary Prayers are those that do not change in the worship service, —e.g., the Lord's Prayer. Proper Prayers are those that change each week, e.g., the Collect. Hopefully, all prayers are "proper," yet none too "ordinary."

"**Suffrages**"--A worship service focused on Prayer, with special emphases for morning, afternoon or evening.

I am indebted to the *Lutheran Service Book*, from which I adapted the above definitions; it has a very fine glossary of worship terms (pgs. xxiv-xxv).

Which Historic Liturgical Worship Services Focus on Prayer?

In the *Lutheran Service Book*, we have the following worship services, which are either built around Prayer / emphasize Prayer:

-Morning Prayer
-Evening Prayer
-Compline (Prayer at the Close of the Day)
-The Service of Prayer and Preaching

Additionally, we also have these prepared Worship resources to help with our focus on Prayer:
-Responsive Prayer 1 (Suffrages)
-Responsive Prayer 2
-The Litany
-Daily Prayer for Individuals / Families
-Table of Psalms for Daily Prayer
-Prayers, Intercessions and Thanksgivings
-The Small Catechism

What Is the Role of Prayer in the Official Acts of the Congregation?

In the historic Lutheran liturgy, we have prepared Prayers for the following aspects of ministry (some prefer to Pray *ex corde*, that is "from the heart," and forego the use of prepared Prayers; even if this is your preference, you may find following historic Prayers of benefit in your preparation and reflection):
those we Baptize;
the youth we Confirm;
the Members we receive;
if we have to excommunicate someone, we still pray for them;
in our weddings (and anniversary celebrations), we pray for the couple;
in our visitation / Communion ministry to the sick and infirm, we pray for their needs;
when someone is near death, we minister to them in Prayer;
when someone has died, we pray for their loved ones;
if a child is stillborn, we pray for the grieving family;
when we ordain and install Pastors, we pray for them and their congregations;
when we commission and install Teachers, Directors of Christian Education, Ministers of Music, Deaconesses, and other church workers, , we pray for them;
when we install congregational officers and / or other servants, we pray for them and their ministry;
in the dedication of our buildings, property, cemeteries, etc., we pray to God;
when we pay off a bank loan, we praise God and we pray;
in the gatherings of our Districts or our Synod, we definitely pray.

For all these (and more) situations, we have prepared Prayers that may be used. Prayer is thoroughly a part of our life together. Anyone who has been to a Congregational Meeting will appreciate the following suggested opening prayer:

".... Let your Holy Spirit rule and direct our hearts that, in the spirit of Christian   love, we may peaceably present and discuss matters and be kindly disposed to one
another..."

Luther on the Need, Definition and Desire of "True Prayer":

"Be constant in prayer."

This is spoken in opposition to those who only read the Psalms without any heart. And we must be on our guard that the prayers in church in our day do not become more of a hindrance than a help.

First, because we offend God more by reading them when our heart is not in it, as He says: "This people honors Me with their lips, etc." (Matthew 15:8; Mark 7:6; Isaiah 29:13)

Second, because we are deceived and made secure by the appearance of these things, as if we had truly prayed properly. And thus we never become really attached to the desire for **true prayer**, but when we pray these things, we think that we have prayed and are in need of nothing more. This is a terrible danger. And in return for these things we then at our leisure and in security consume the income and the pensions and subsidies of the people!

This is the reason why he inserted the word "constant," a great watchword that must be noted and respected by all, and especially by clerics. For this word signifies that we must put real work into our praying. And it is not in vain. For as the ancient fathers have said: "There is no work like praying to God."[36] Therefore when a man wants to enter the priesthood, he must first consider that he is entering a work which is harder than any other, namely, the work of prayer. For this requires a subdued and broken mind and an elevated and victorious spirit. But at this point the lawyers introduce a nice explanation, that to pray the hours is not commanded, but rather to "read" them or to "say" them is. For in this manner they encumber the canon law with words and snore on in peace. But even if we omit the canonical hours, we need to say something about prayer.

Prayer is of two kinds. There is the vocal prayer,[37] of which it is presently the custom to say that a virtual intention is sufficient--a nice little cover for laziness and negligence! For on the basis of this, in the first place, they must by force tear from themselves the good intention, and then being satisfied with this they immediately give up every other attempt.

And in this type of prayer there is a threefold attentiveness: the material, or sensual, attentiveness, whereby one pays attention only to the words, as monks and others, such as simple lay people do, who do not understand even the Lord's Prayer. And this is real prayer no more than material is the real thing, that is, according to its own nature it is not prayer in the proper sense of the word, but only in an extrinsic sense, by which every other good work can be called prayer. To pray in this way is merely to perform an act of obedience which makes it pleasing to God. Such prayer is not to be despised, because in addition to this, that it is a work of obedience, it is good in many other ways.

First, because it drives away the devil, even if the prayer is only recited in the simplicity of the heart, that is, if "it is sung in the spirit" (1 Corinthians 14:15) and thus brings the Holy Spirit to us. This is symbolized in David's playing the harp before Saul. For the devil cannot endure even having the Word of God read, as we know from many examples. 1 Corinthians 14:2: "For one who speaks in a tongue speaks to God."

Second, because the divine Word by nature affects the soul, even if it is not understood. For it is a Word of grace, as we read in Psalm 45:2: "Grace is poured upon your lips." Likewise: "Your lips distil nectar" (Song of Solomon 4:11)

Third, it gives to the intellect and the emotions an occasion which they would not have otherwise, as we see it symbolized in the minstrel of Elisha.[38]

Fourth, although many people who pray this way do not have the full emotional effect of these words, yet they often have a common and elevated spirit toward God.

There is also the intellectual attentiveness, whereby one gives attention to the sense and meaning of the words. The better educated and intelligent must pay attention to this, for each must pay his talent to God.

Then there is the spiritual or emotional attentiveness, whereby one is <u>attentive to the emotional</u> or spiritual effect of the words, as when one <u>laments</u> with those who lament, <u>rejoices</u> with those who rejoice, <u>shouts for joy</u> with those who are shouting for joy, <u>and accommodates himself to every movement of the words</u>. **This is true prayer**. Of these two points the apostle says, 1 Corinthians 14:15: "I will sing with the spirit, and I will sing with the mind also." By using the expression to "sing with the spirit" <u>he is calling attention to the sensual attentiveness, apart from the intellectual attentiveness</u>, and yet intimately connected with the emotional attentiveness, as in the case of devout nuns and uneducated people. By using the expression "to sing with the mind" he is describing the intellectual attentiveness, which can be aroused both without the spirit as well as with the spirit. <u>The mental prayer is the ascent of the mind, as well as the spirit, to God</u>. This is the prayer of which he is speaking when he says: "Be constant in prayer." In this passage he is emphasizing that Christians ought to engage in frequent as well as diligent prayer. <u>For "to be constant" means not only to take a great deal of time, but also to urge, to incite, to demand</u>. For just as there is no work which for Christians ought to be more frequent, so **no other work that requires more labor and effort and therefore is more efficacious and fruitful**. For here "the kingdom of heaven has suffered violence, and men of violence take it by force." (Matthew 11:12) For prayer in my opinion is a constant violent action of the spirit as it is lifted up to God, as a ship is driven upward against the power of the storm. This is why it is said of blessed Martin to his credit that **he had an inconquerable spirit because he never released it from prayer**.[39]

This violence decreases and disappears, to be sure, whenever the Spirit draws and carries our heart upward by grace, or surely, when a present and major anxiety compels us to take refuge in prayer. And without these two factors, prayer becomes a most difficult and tedious thing. <u>But its effect is tremendous. For **true prayer is omnipotent**</u>, as our Lord says: "For everyone who asks receives, etc." (Matthew 7:8) <u>Thus we must all practice violence and remember that he who prays is fighting against the devil and the flesh</u>."[89]

Personal Reflection:
    *What would constant Prayer look like in my life? _____

    *Do you agree that Prayer drives the devil away? _____

    *How did Jesus express emotions when He prayed? _____

    *What sort of emotions do you experience in your Prayers? _____

God has ordained the praises of infants and the prayers of all believers who draw near with a sincere and contrite heart. His house is to be a House of Prayer, for all nations. May our Prayers rise up when we lift our hands, as the incense arises with the evening sacrifice; may this sweet aroma fill the Heavens and the earth. Even as Zechariah came into Your house to burn incense and the faithful gathered outside for Prayer, so may we also come before You.

Prayer Is Part of Our Personal / Family Worship

Worship happens throughout a believer's week. Luther wanted believers to be in worship as much as possible. He developed simple "orders of service" to help parents in their family devotions. *"Reading the Psalms with Luther--The Psalter for Individual and Family Devotions"* (published by CPH) is a book I bought in large quantity as a Pastor, to give to people on all sorts of occasions.

What I appreciate about this resource is that Luther writes a short commentary for each Psalm and then after the Psalm, he has prepared a Prayer to read and reflect on or to offer to God. In the back of the book are two very practical reading charts you can use. Get a copy if you don't have one.

---

[89]Martin Luther, 25. Concordia.

IV. Prayer and Mercy Ministry

Are we willing to take detours in our schedule for the needs in someone else's life?   Christ gave no indication that it was His plan to stay in Sychar for two days; but because of the woman at the well, He did.

What Is the Connection Between Prayer and Mercy?

None of us are mind readers. This forces us to talk with other people (or at least text). We try to avoid doing this by sending out mass mailers or printing announcements in bulletins; then we tell ourselves, "I have done my job." No, we haven't.

One time a blind man cried out to Jesus for help. Jesus, being God in human form--unlike us--knew everything. Yet, Jesus asked him, "What do you want Me to do for you?"
Jesus didn't have to ask this question; He already knew the answer. Part of the reason Jesus asked is because He genuinely cared and He wanted this man to know His care.

When we ask members, **"How can I pray for you?"** we are showing them that we care. More importantly, we are reminding them that Jesus cares. *It is important to follow up Prayer with Action.*

The blind man was no fool; he told Jesus what he wanted! He wanted to see!!

We see people all the time who are blind spiritually; even believers can have specks or logs in their eyes. It is understandable to despair when we see an older person who has had their blindness for decades and doubt that they could ever change. When the person is a fellow Church member and you have known them for many years, it is easy to become more focused on their problems than on the power of our Savior.

But then we should ask ourselves a question: do people see Jesus when they see me? Are we as Luther said, "the mask (the face) of God" to unbelievers"?

Jesus wanted that blind man to know He was going to care precisely for what this man cared about (his blindness). When we ask people, "How can I pray for you?" we are doing the same; we are telling them, person to person, that we care precisely for what they care about.

One day Luther was riding his horse back to law school and got caught in a terrible storm; he feared for his life and cried out for God to spare him. As I was told the story, Luther made a deal with God; if his life was spared, he would enter the ministry. God did and Luther did.

Here is an interesting aspect to that story--Luther prayed to a dead saint. He didn't know any better; that was the best he could pray. We should be more charitable towards those today who don't know any better when it comes to praying. Even we who are believers don't know how to pray, but the Holy Spirit intercedes for us. (Romans 8:26)

Jesus could have done many different things for that blind man. Jesus could have fed him or washed his feet, maybe painted his house. But Jesus wanted to provide care, specifically for what mattered to that man.

When we ask a member, "How can I pray for you?" we will learn how we can specifically provide care that matters. Yes, we will pray and we will care for their physical needs to the best of our abilities.

And here is the great part--our churches are filled with people who want to help others. Dietrich Bonhoeffer said, "The church is the church only when it exists for others."

When we ask fellow members how we can pray for them, we will be able to direct the care we provide into efforts that are of the most importance to those receiving them. There is perhaps nothing more frustrating than to work very hard, thinking you are helping others only to learn later that they did not want what you were doing. Jesus could have done many good things for that blind man; but He wanted the blind man to know that He was going to focus on what was most important to him.

People looking for a new church (especially younger people) are looking for a one that is making a difference, a church that cares about others and values finding ways for members to serve others. When a church makes it clear that Mercy matters, it is speaking to the hearts of many.

Action Question:

It is good for a church to communicate clearly its process of:
1. gathering prayers (Sunday a.m.; Bible Class; Pastoral visits; Prayer Walking, etc.)
2. praying
3. translating these prayers into care and finally
4. closing the loop by following up to check on the condition of the things being prayed for

What do we need to do in our church regarding this? _____

This should be done in writing as well as electronically; it should be reinforced regularly through the social media communication channels, lifted up in worship and highlighted in congregational leadership meetings. When Congregational Prayer Ministry has line items in the official budget, this will be a significant indicator of its priority and place in ministry.

For Luther, Prayer for Our Neighbor Was the Best Way to Love Our Neighbor:

"Then proceed to the Second Table of the commandments (commandments regarding other people). See how disobedient you have been and still are toward father and mother and all in authority; how you sin against your neighbor with anger, hatred, and evil words; how you are tempted to unchastity, covetousness, and injustice in word and deed against your neighbor. In this way you will without a doubt find that you are full of all need and misery, and that you have reason enough to weep even drops of blood, if you could." [90]

"How could God have endowed us more richly with His grace than by hanging such a common baptism around our necks and attaching it to the Lord's Prayer, a baptism that everyone discovers in himself when he prays and forgives his neighbor?" [91]

"… a godly mistress of the household is not proud; for she is vexed and humbled in various ways when countless annoyances are put in her way by the domestics, by her husband, by the children, by the neighbors, etc. Thus opportunities are nowhere lacking for the practice both of faith and of prayer." [92]

---

[90]Martin Luther, 44.
[91]Ibid., 21: Matthew 6:16. Concordia.
[92]Ibid., 3: Genesis 18:10.

"Give us this day our daily bread." [13] What does this mean?

"Answer: To be sure, God provides daily bread, even to the wicked, without our prayer, but we pray in this petition that God may make us aware of his gifts and enable us to receive our daily bread with thanksgiving.

[14] **What is meant by daily bread?**

"Answer: Everything required to satisfy our bodily needs, such as food and clothing, house and home, fields and flocks, money and property; a pious spouse and good children, [tr-549]trustworthy servants, godly and faithful rulers, good government; seasonable weather, peace and health, order and honor; true friends, **faithful neighbors**, and the like."[93]

Luther Saw that Prayer for Your Neighbor Leads to Care for Them Also:

"… you pray in love when, prompted by a kindly attitude toward your brother, you pray for him," [94]

"… do deeds of mercy, prayers, and things of benefit to your neighbor. In this way you depart from evil and do good." [95]

"But the true Sabbath works consist in doing the works of God, hearing the Word, praying, doing good in every way to the neighbor." [96]

"The commandments are summed up in this sentence: 'You shall love your neighbor as yourself.'" (Romans 13:9) "I urge that supplications, prayers, intercessions, and thanksgivings be made for all men." (1 Timothy 2:1) Let each his lesson learn with care And all the household well will fare."[9]

What Are Some Basic Principles of Prayer Based Care?

-Prayer based care is given in almost an endless variety of settings and situations.

-Through Prayer, we can better focus our service to members, visitors and those in our community.

-Prayer based care is about building relationships through Prayer; for the purpose of ministry, mercy and multiplication

-Prayer based care begins by asking simply, "How can I pray for you?"

-Prayer itself is the first step in Prayer based care.

-It is easy and natural to build relations with new people when this happens in the context of delivering Prayer based care to them.

-Never stop discussing in your Church how your Mercy Ministry can work even more effectively in serving those we are connected with through Prayer requests.

---

[93]SC III, 11-14.
[94]Martin Luther, 27: Galatians 5:15. Concordia.
[95]Ibid., 10: Psalm 34:14.
[96]Ibid., 17: Isaiah 58:13.

Progression from Prayer to Care to Planting— An Overview

F O C U S		Prayer Ministry	Mercy Ministry	Plant House Churches
	Community	5.	6.	9.
	Visitors	3.	4.	8.
	Members	1.	2.	7.

FUNCTION

   ** *Boxes one through four are the most important*. If by God's grace you just do these four well; you should be ok. You will be taking care of those God gave you and those He brings. Remember," the best advertising is word of mouth". If you are taking care of members and visitors; they will tell others.

   It is <u>critical</u> to identify who coordinates Prayer request follow up and for all Prayer requests received to be gathered into one database. When you can give yourself a "B" in box 1, move on to box 2 and so on.

   The diagram above is for <u>existing</u> congregation, showing the steps through planting House Churches. If you are planting a new Church, through the planting of House Churches, just begin with box 5 (also, look at a sample development plan for this, on pg. 153)

   Existing churches- please resist the temptation to jump straight to planting H.C.'s in the community (box #9) also, resist the temptation to jump straight to Prayer Walking in the Community (box #5). Start instead by evaluating the Prayer and Mercy Ministry you <u>currently</u> provide your members. Members will support an outreach they have experienced as a blessing. Interview community leaders and partner where possible.

   Scripture tells us not to be hasty in placing people into leadership- it is vital to have a properly trained House Church Planter (or more) who works under your Pastor's supervision. Jesus spent a night in Prayer before choosing the disciples; Prayer is key to this process.

House Church Planter training available at www.HouseChurchPlanter.com

---

   Some people have asked, "Does this process have to result in House Churches; can you use it to plant Bible studies or missional communities?" Yes, you can use this process to start a wide variety of groups. But in the end, <u>we want the Sacraments</u> in our Christian community; ultimately we desire to <u>be</u> Church. The truth of the matter is that most House Churches do not start offering Communion from the very beginning; most Pastors find that their new House Church members are not yet ready and need instruction. We are not in a rush to try and get people to take communion with us. But the Sacraments are a goal and are part of the clearly stated "DNA" of the House Church from the infancy of it. Remember- we need to be the Church (see the 7 marks of the Church in LW, volume 41) <u>beyond the walls of our current churches</u>.

God has already provided everything you need for your ministry. Do not put your trust anywhere other than in Him! What are the strengths of your church in the following areas?

-Worship: _____

-Hospitality: _____

-Mercy: _____

-Mentoring: _____

-Corporate Connections: _____

-Children's Ministry: _____

-Social Media: _____

-High Visibility People: _____

-Physical Plant and Church Property: _____

-Community Events: _____

-Education / Discipleship _____

-Other Areas: _____

What contacts do I have outside the Church? How will I recruit them? How will we organize?

_____

You must see your community in terms of the Stakeholders already there. Take a moment to list the Stakeholders you know in your community:

-Civic / Corporate Leaders: _____

-Politicians: _____

-Clergy: _____

-Chamber of Commerce: _____

-First Responders: _____

-Sports / Entertainment / Media: _____

-Others _____

What do they value? What do they think your priorities should be? How can they help you to help them? How will they hold you accountable? _____

Our Congregational Prayer Ministry Coordinator
-An Initial Worksheet-

1. How do we gather member's Prayers? _____

2. Why should we do more than Pray? _____

3. How are we blessed by helping others? _____

4. How can members help each other? _____

5. What ministries could offer care in response to Prayer requests received? _____

Progression from Prayer to Care to Planting— An Overview

FOCUS		Prayer Ministry	Mercy Ministry	Plant House Churches
	Community	5.	6.	9.
	Visitors	3.	4.	8.
	Members	1.	2.	7.

FUNCTION

6. How will the Coordinator be chosen? _____

7. How will we measure effectiveness? _____

8. How will we encourage them? _____

9. How will we communicate this ministry to the members? _____

10. How will the Coordinator train those who want to help? _____

11. How will the Coordinator interact with Pastor / Church leadership? _____

12. How much Prayer ministry will we have in church "business" meetings? _____

13. What areas of Prayer in the lives of the members need attention first? _____

14. How can members contribute specifically for the Prayer Ministry of the Church? _____

15. What written guidance does the Church have regarding Prayer Ministry? _____

On line Congregational Prayer Ministry is available at www.HouseChurchPlanter.com

The 12 Universal Cultural Domains and the Connection to Mercy Ministry

The 2009 UNESCO Framework for Cultural Studies (the result of a four-year effort by the Institute for Statistics and Culture Sector of their organization) said the following about "culture":

> "Culture plays a key role in all societies around the world, influencing various facets of peoples' lives, from leisure to professional activities. The role of culture in development has also recently emerged as an important policy issue. However, preserving and respecting the specificity of each individual culture as well as the distinctive qualities of other cultures is the challenge that must be met globally."

The RAND Corporation does a lot of research for the United States government and its various entities. Later, I share the story of how I came across this information during my training to be a Wing Chaplain.

UNESCO identifies seven Cultural Domains; the RAND Corporation has a more comprehensive understanding of Cultural Domains and it identifies 12 Cultural Domains. My list below has 12 Cultural Domains; it draws heavily from the RAND list, but also reflects the influence of UNESCO's list as well as my input as a mission strategist:

-Language
-Religion
-Gender
-Politics
-Economics
-Kinship / Blood
-Knowledge / Learning
-Recreation / Sports
-Health / Sustenance
-Technology
-Time / Space
-History / Myths

> Understanding the local culture is critical to any successful mission.

Here is the important point to understand--these 12 cultural domains are present in your community.

Start looking at your community in terms of these 12 categories. Focus on a different one each month, developing different leadership teams within your congregation that focus on each area.

Now for the great Lutheran follow up question, "So, what does this mean?" There are no cookie cutter answers worth a hoot,; but here are some possible ideas that might work. You are going to have to do the research and investigation for your local context.

Language--
What issues regarding language are present in your community? Perhaps there are immigrants who could benefit from ESL (English as a Second Language) classes. When it comes to worship do you have the language resources necessary to communicate your Word and Sacrament ministry to people who speak languages other than English? Many people in your community who come to mind when you think of "language" could possibly also use help with citizenship classes. Would it be a good thing if your church was known as a community of Christians that helped answer questions for your new neighbors?
        *My ideas: _____

Religion-

What are the world religions evident in your community? Have you met with leaders from other religions / denominations? What are the significant differences between their faith and ours? What are their fears / concerns? What divisions exist within these religions? What aspects of their faith seem to provide a respectful way to present the Good News found in Christ? Are there efforts in which you could work together?

One of the best outreaches I was blessed by God to do as a Pastor involved the movie, *The Passion,* by Mel Gibson. The buildup to the release of this movie drew a firestorm from the anti-Christian elements of the media and society. Every night saw ads for the movie for which we did not have to pay, followed up by news stories and interviews on all the popular news outlets about the movie. By the time the movie opened, there couldn't have been very many people in America who did not know about it.

God blessed me with the idea to approach a donor (who, by the way, was not even a member of the church) to provide the funds so our church could reserve the first showings of *The Passion* in our area. By God's grace, the donor gladly gave all the money needed; I arranged with the national office of the movie theatre chain for us to have all the tickets to the first night of the movie's release in our area. I next worked with the local Christian radio station to promote the event and do a live feed.

I worked with the local movie theatre so before every showing, I could address the audience--something they happily agreed to. I can tell you that as a direct result of that outreach God directed us to and provided all our needs for, we had many families come to worship with us.

The local media covered our opening of the movie very favorably. We got movie banners to put up at church so visitors who came through the movie had the connection reinforced. Our members loved the community visibility; many took the opportunity to tell their friends about their church's ministry. For a very small amount of money, we were able to leverage something huge, for the purpose of communicating the Gospel in our community.

*In any of these 12 cultural domains, the basic principle is still the same--identify the changes that are occurring; and then, gain understanding about how you can leverage this change to help you communicate the Gospel. That's it; it ain't rocket science! Git r done! Make it happen!

*My ideas: _____

Gender-

What are the roles, expectations and cultural taboos regarding men and women in your community? For example, with recent immigrants, what struggles are they having with American culture regarding women?

*My ideas: _____

Politics-

Who are your elected officials? How often do you meet? What are their expectations of your ministry? Is there a way you can serve them with Prayer and the Ministry of the Word? What items are they advocating for in your community?

*My ideas: _____

Economics-

Who are the largest employers? What employers are hiring? What needs do the Human Resources people in these successful companies identify? When speaking with new people, ask them what their economic expectations, frustrations and hopes are. Are there financial planners / real estate agents your church can partner with to offer workshops?

*My ideas: _____

Kinship / Blood-

Immigrants especially are under great stress because of their extended family and loved ones back in their country of origin. Many immigrants work two and three jobs; partly because their loved ones back home see America as a place "made of gold" and their loved one here as the pipeline to that gold. In a down economy, long term citizens of this country are dealing with the stress of loved ones moving in with them. Great questions regarding "Kinship / Blood" include: "What are the demands on your time, money, allegiance, travel, etc.?" Also, it is valuable to learn the unique cultural traditions of the different groups within your community; these will often provide portals to enter with the Gospel.

The Honorable Martha Karua is a Presidential candidate in Kenya; I met her in New Jersey, through Pastor Haron Orutwa, who serves our Kenyan immigrant congregation, Tumaini Kristo in Jersey City, New Jersey. Like many Kenyan politicians, Martha raises most of her money in the United States. I was blessed to be asked to share the Invocation for the Kenyan immigrant association for northern New Jersey, a group that counts 10,000 Kenyan immigrants just in its area.

What are the immigrant networks and associations in your community? Could a short term mission team from your congregation visit their country and provide assistance on the ground?
        *My ideas: _____

Knowledge / Learning-

Immigrants place a tremendous value on education. The Lutheran Church--Missouri Synod has a rich educational history that should be leveraged by the congregation serious on outreach. We have the second largest Christian education system in this country (quite a feat considering we equal only 1% of the population). Church members will find a ready connection with a vision for connecting immigrants to Jesus through our educational model. This is one of the institutional approaches to missions that still works (for Catholics, another would be their extensive hospital system).
        *My ideas: _____

Recreation / Sports-

Outreach can be fun too. Relaxing is an important part of any culture. What are their annual festivals and can you be a part? What are traditional ways in which a family in their culture relaxes (daily, weekly, seasonally, annually)? What changes regarding recreation / sports have happened in recent years? Who are the national / cultural sports stars? Which American athletes are popular? Why?
        *My ideas: _____

Health / Sustenance-

Questions you can ask your community, to connect in this cultural domain might include, "What medical challenges are you facing?" Or, "Would a partnership with a hospital or perhaps a medical supply company be a way for our church members to offer free medical screenings?" Some churches have turned unused lawn space into community gardens--Holy Trinity Lutheran Church (Somerset, New Jersey) under the leadership of Pastor Andrew Dinger has had tremendous success and worked with Rutgers University (a state school) to help design their community garden in the best way possible. Perhaps a member has unused acreage they would like their church to use in this way.
        *My ideas: _____

Technology-

If I have a technology question, I ask the youngest child at home to help me. He or she almost always finds the solution. If you look at social media (smart phones, web sites, lap tops, You Tube, blogs, Twitter, etc,), you will have to agree that technology is a cultural domain. Immigrants hunger for technology; the research says that they are much more likely to embrace new technology, more quickly than long term citizens of comparable socioeconomic status. Christian Friends of New Americans in St. Louis, Missouri, has had tremendous success connecting with refugees and immigrants with its free computer labs, after school tutoring, delivery of home furnishings, health and wellness clinics and ESL and citizenship classes. My parents, the Rev. Dr. Al and Carol Buckman, each volunteer about 30 hours a week with this ministry. By God's grace, Christian Friends of New Americans will serve over 800 visitors to their ministry center each month. Several urban Lutheran congregations are making new relationships through this non-traditional ministry center, served fulltime by Pastor Eddie Mekasha, himself an East African immigrant. My parents' congregation--Concordia Lutheran Church in Kirkwood, Missouri--led by their Pastor, the Rev. Dr. Scott Seidler, provides tremendous support to this Great Commission driven ministry.

Technology is something of interest for all the people in your community. Can your Church provide computer labs? Are there corporate partners who would invest in your vision to serve the community?

*My ideas: _____

Time / Space-

People of Western European descent have a cultural understanding of time; my experience tells me that much of the rest of the world does not share it. To interact successfully with others in your community who come from a different culture than yours, take time to learn their understanding of time and space. Some good questions include, "What does 'on time' mean in your culture?" Also, "What does 'personal space' look like when we are greeting each other? If we are fellow-shipping? If we are negotiating?

*My ideas: _____

History / Myths-

Every culture has this domain: in America we revere George Washington, who as a youth could not lie about the cherry tree he cut down. Some questions to consider asking people from other cultures in your community include, "Who are your national heroes? What was your country's liberation story? What is your oldest celebration?

As you learn about the history and myths of other cultures, perhaps the most important thing you will do is to demonstrate to your new friends that you genuinely want to know about them.

*My ideas: _____

Action Questions:

*As you think about the 12 Cultural Domains and the average unchurched person in your community, what are key words you would use to describe these people?

_____

*How would you learn from those you are trying to reach; which of these 12 Cultural Domains are most important for them?

_____

What Is a Simple and Effective Way to Track Congregational Prayer Ministry?

Truth Lutheran Church in Taipei, Taiwan, has used a Prayer Card for years that has space at the top for the person to write their name, contact information and prayer request.

The bottom half of the Prayer Card has a "Staff Follow Up" box. In this box are listed the most likely ministries within the congregation that would follow up with a prayer request. There is also space for "other" ministries to be listed, which are assigned by the Pastor to follow up with the Prayer Request.

The Pastor meets with the Congregational Prayer Ministry coordinator every week to go through the new Prayer Cards. Together, they note which ministries will be responsible for following up with each prayer request received (no, I'm not kidding).

The Prayer Card Truth Lutheran uses is a triplicate, pressure-sensitive form; each Prayer Card has a white, yellow and pink copy. The Pastor keeps one copy, the Congregational Prayer Ministry coordinator keeps another copy, and the first ministry assigned to follow up gets the other copy.

If there is more than one ministry assigned to follow up with a given prayer request, the first ministry leader initials his or her box on the card, notifies the Congregational Prayer Ministry coordinator and passes the Prayer Card on to the next ministry assigned to follow up with the Prayer Request. When the last ministry assigned to the given Prayer Card has followed up with the request, it is turned in to the Pastor.

Jesus reminded us that His Father's house would be a house of prayer. *How seriously do we take this*?

A ministry could replace the three-part form with an electronic process. Truth Lutheran also uses modern technology / social media to help with ministry. A ministry could also disseminate the information simultaneously instead of sequentially to the ministries following up.

The point here is not to lift up some particular format or technique; that could very easily become idolatrous worship. No, the point here is to say, "What are we doing to be good stewards of the ministry entrusted to us?" With spreadsheets it is very easy to track and quantify our Mercy Ministry. It is vital to communicate clearly with our stakeholders.

> When people share a prayer request on Sunday, they are hoping this matters to the church; they would like to think it means more than a passing glance and a couple of words before being tossed in a trash can.

If we believe that God truly cares for us, then it makes perfectly good sense to make prayer a priority for the Pastor and leadership.

> In Acts 6, we see the first Pastors of the New Testament Church being pruned and getting refocused on the two things that matter most--Prayer and the ministry of the Word.

How much of our Pastor's time is devoted to Prayer? How much of our ministry is devoted to Prayer? Ministry "success" is often measured by only two numbers: noses and nickels. Stop laughing, it's true. ☺ The Apostles realized they needed to devote themselves to Prayer if they were going to accomplish the Great Commission. Do we realize this?

> Mercy Ministry is vital if you want the relationships first gathered through Prayer to develop beyond ministering through Prayer and into planting new worshipping communities.
>
> Another way to say this is, "Care is the bridge between Prayer and Planting." Or, even, "The path from Ministry to Multiplication runs through Mercy."

Prayer + Mercy = Gospel Opportunity in a Disaster

When Storm Sandy first came ashore in New Jersey and then New York, the North East had not seen a storm of this magnitude in the lifetimes of any resident.

Musical artists came together and did a relief concert; neighbors helped each other and as of when this book went to press, the members of the Lutheran Church Missouri Synod had contributed almost $3,000,000 for disaster relief. In addition to their financial contributions, we are expecting hundreds of short term mission team members to come and help with the cleanup.

Village Lutheran Church in Lanoka Harbor, NJ was directly impacted by the storm- emeritus Pastor, the Rev. Roy Minnix personally suffered damage to his home. Village Lutheran Church will be one of the key rallying points for short term mission teams coming to New Jersey.

I met with Pr. Mark Stillman of Village Lutheran to discuss the need to not only train volunteers in safety issues but also spiritual ones. With Pr. Mark was Pr. Ed Brashier, Director of Shepherd's Heart Disaster Response Ministry; Pr. Ed is in New Jersey coordinating the volunteers working out of Village Lutheran; Alabama is where Pr. Ed hails from, but he is found wherever disaster strikes.

Pr. Mark Stillman and Pr. Ed Brashier

Simply, I suggested that all volunteers receive a simple training in how to ask those whose physical needs they are taking care of, "How can I pray for you?" It would be explained to the volunteers that the Prayer requests they collect would be turned into Pat Ashford, the church secretary who will add them to the Prayer Ministry database. Pr. Mark will then meet weekly with his key leaders to Pray for these needs and then the ministry leaders will go over the new Prayer requests and choose which families their respective ministries can follow up with. Next, Pr. Stillman will go over the list of Prayer requests that the ministry leaders had previously taken responsibility for and get updates on their situations.

In this way, Village Lutheran Church will develop faith focused relationships with many new families in their community. Also, the volunteers will receive practical spiritual training which they can take with them, the rest of their lives. Pr. Mark and Pr. Ed thought this was a good idea and agreed. An additional benefit of this approach is that Village Lutheran Church will be able to give a numerical accounting for their Gospel outreach to the donors that supported them.

My Prayer training for disaster volunteers will be available at: www.HouseChurchPlanter.com

Mercy Is at the Heart of "Ministry, Mercy and Multiplication"

Rev. Dr. Matt Harrison was the Executive Director for LCMS World Relief and Human Care before being elected to serve as President of the LCMS. He brings with him an intense passion for serving the needs of our neighbors. This is not "social Gospel," but rather caring for our neighbor in close proximity to Word and Sacrament ministry.

Prayer Ministry for others enables us to provide better Ministry; in some cases, this can lead to multiplication of worshipping communities. *Mercy ministry is the bridge that Congregational Prayer Ministry must cross in order to get from Ministry to Multiplication.*

In our training of House Church Planters, one of the textbooks we use is *Christ Have Mercy,* by Matt Harrison. The following quotes and reflections come from this book.

"Nearly 15% of the adult population of western Kenya is infected with HIV…" (pg. 27)
   * What issues do <u>we</u> have to help our people wrestle through so they can attempt to do the good works that God has prepared in advance for them? _____

"Mercy (ministry) is the key to:
      -seizing the moment
      -the future of the church
      -mission and stewardship
      -moving boldly and confidently into the future" (pg. 11)

      *How does following up with Prayer requests help guide our Mercy Ministry?
_____

"In Christ, compassion means action because of who He is. In Christ, God acted and acts for the temporal and eternal blessing of the world." (pg. 39)
      *What resources does your Church have to serve the physical needs of others?

_____

      *How will you organize the Mercy Ministry of your Church to follow up with the Prayer requests you receive?

_____

"Baptism is a hurricane of grace and mercy in Christ." (pg. 66)
      *How messy are hurricanes? _____

The Five Steps to Establishing a Lutheran Mercy Ministry (pg. 187-194):

      1. Get the right people involved and give them the space to be creative
      2. Identify critical issues
      3. Assess the potential for partnerships to increase capacity
      4. Look for best practices
      5. Go with what you can be good at

V. Prayer Improves Ministry to Members- Starting With the Household of Faith

Jesus came first to the Jews then to the Gentiles. In sending the Apostles, He directed them to begin their ministry in Jerusalem and then move progressively further and further even to the ends of the earth.

The Apostle Paul tells us, *"Therefore, as we have opportunity, let us do good to all people, especially to those who belong to the family of believers.*" (Galatians 6:10) The Good Shepherd who will bring sheep that are not of this flock into the fold; , nevertheless always has His eye and heart upon any sheep already within His flock who is wayward.

In sharing the role of Prayer in Ministry, Mercy and Mission; **we will begin first with the Household of God**--specifically, the people who are members of your congregation. From here, we will move on to discuss how Prayer can help your ministry to those who visit your ministry; and finally, we will look at how Prayer can be used to reach those in your community at large. (I am <u>not</u> saying that Church membership = personal salvation. I believe we need to really help people understand the difference between membership and discipleship; but these are the terms and church structures in use, so by the power of the Holy Spirit, let us redeem them for His purpose).

It is important in beginning any ministry to lay a good foundation. This foundation must be measured according to the blueprint of Scripture and correct doctrine; just as any building has inspectors who make sure the work is done correctly, so also <u>ministry must be done under ecclesiastical accountability</u>. Jesus, the Son of God, said that <u>He did not do anything of His own authority</u>; but only what the Father told Him. <u>Jesus' humility should be the model</u> of all who would lead a ministry.

In very practical terms, it is important in developing this aspect of your Congregational Prayer Ministry to cast a vision <u>so that everyone in your congregation sees a role and a reason for their involvement</u>. That is why we are first beginning by focusing on how to <u>serve your current members</u> better through Prayer.

Prayer is something <u>every</u> believer is supposed to do. <u>Interestingly, not a single list of Spiritual gifts mentions "Prayer"</u>; this is because Prayer is something <u>every</u> Christian will be doing.
<u>Prayer is not a program</u>; Prayer is an indelible feature of faith. <u>Prayer is not a human effort</u>; it is only by the Holy Spirit that we can cry, "Abba, Father."
In the following chapters, we will talk about ways that Prayer can be of help; but Prayer is not a program; it is the work of the Holy Spirit and the Holy Spirit blows as He desires. <u>We can attempt to describe the work of the Holy Spirit, but He is dynamic. He cannot be manipulated through ritualism or even reason.</u>

The following ideas are not "silver bullets"; you will probably not be the next mega church if you use them; this isn't "church growth." **The power is in the Word of God**; He works through the Sacraments; His eye is always upon us; His heart inclines to the voice of His children. He renews those who call on Him. May we truly love our neighbors as we love ourselves and diligently be in prayer <u>for</u> them and <u>with</u> them.

I will make you this promise: if you are a believer in Jesus (Romans 10:9-10) and you pray out of a sincere heart for God to help you better serve your neighbor through the sacrifice of Prayer, you will absolutely see God work. And once you have seen God work, you want to see Him more. To God alone be the glory, praise and honor!

Why Is Prayer Effective for Ministry?

1. You connect at a personal level with those who share Prayer requests with you
2. Almost any age can pray
3. You can pray anywhere
4. You can ask someone of any religion how you can pray for them
5. It is cost free
6. Post Moderns are very comfortable with Prayer
7. Ministry can be directed much more effectively to the actual needs of people
8. It's a good discipleship priority for our members
9. You have a Godly reason to follow up with people
10. You're not trying to get money
11. You're not trying to get them to go somewhere or even do something
12. It is the best thing that we can do for someone
13. It fulfills the 2nd table of the Law (the 4th through 10th Commandments)
14. It fulfills the 2nd Commandment (honor God)
15. God is building the ministry; not some humanly devised program
16. No government license is needed ☺
17. You are taking their needs to God in Jesus' name
18. You are praying God's Word over them
19. This is what God told us to do
20. The Holy Spirit prays for us when we pray

How Can Prayer Help Delinquent Members Reconnect?

Sixty-five percent of the members in The Lutheran Church--Missouri Synod choose not to come to Church on any given Sunday. Responding to delinquent members is viewed as a thorny issue by most fellow members and their ministers.

What are our options when it comes to communicating with delinquent members? Impersonal letters… "Inquisition" visits…. Ignoring them…. Inactivating membership…?

Prayer is a better way.

Imagine this--you have not been to church for a month; pick the reason why. Your phone rings and you answer. It is your Pastor or Elder. Now here is the amazing part; they don't ask why you have not been to church; they don't tell you about the next five things coming up on the church calendar; they don't mention church finances; in fact they don't do any of the stereotypical things you would expect.

Instead, the reason for their call is to simply ask you this question, "**How can I pray for you**?"

Imagine you tell them the truth. You tell them what is really of concern in your life. Maybe it is a sin you have slipped (or jumped) into; maybe it is embarrassment from the loss of a job, spouse or significant other. Maybe it's a new work schedule and you just can't be in Church on Sunday morning. You share your reason and now you wait for their response.

Your Pastor or Elder listens to everything you feel comfortable sharing, perhaps asking questions as appropriate in order to understand better your thoughts and feelings. And then, they say, "You are important to us and we are going to be praying for you." You may ask them if it is ok to pray right now; they may even feel led to suggest it themselves. As the Holy Spirit guides, prayers are lifted up before the throne of God.

How would you feel if your Pastor / Elder called to see how the Church could be in prayer for you?

What if the next thing the Pastor / Elder did was to get together with other leaders and prayerfully share and seek God's leading for how the Church can minister to your needs. Maybe it is the Social Concerns Group; the Youth Group; perhaps it is the Women's Mission group (LWML); or maybe it is something that the Church can't offer but they can make available to you through another avenue.

> If you were going to go to Church, would you want it to be with people who really cared about you, just for you? Would you want to go because you were responding to the Holy Spirit's work in your heart?

How Can Prayer Help Raise Attendance?

For members who have not felt the loving touch of Christ for an extended period of time, the Church leadership will probably need to discuss the steps involved with updating the membership list to reflect more accurately those who are under their Spiritual care. As always in the Christian life, this is a time to confess that we have not loved others as we have loved ourselves. More importantly, it is important to hear Absolution and know we are forgiven, that the Holy Spirit will bring forth new fruit.

> *It is very simple to set up a Prayer Care Plan for Delinquent Members*:
>   1. Define what delinquency is.
>   2. Prayerfully select someone to be the Prayer Care Coordinator, someone who will work directly with the Pastor. If possible, develop someone not already responsible for an area of ministry..
>   3. Carefully recruit Prayer Callers (Prayers) who will call the members. Care must be given to choosing those with a humble spirit, a cheerful attitude. and a desire for the members to be fed and cared for again. The Prayers must agree to follow the training they are given. A good ratio to consider is recruiting one Prayer Caller for every 20 delinquent households.
>   4. Hold regular meetings of Ministry Leaders in the Congregation to track specifically the care the Church gives in her follow up to these delinquent members.
>   5. Have the Prayers report their activity and insights; their primary concern is that people are touched with God's love through Prayer. The "bottom line" for the Prayers is a robust prayer ministry for the members they are directed to focus on.
>   6. In Church, celebrate this ministry and the work of the Holy Spirit through it.
>
> Jesus is our model, "*I have not lost one of those You gave Me.*" (John 18:9) Jesus never forced any to follow Him; many turned away. May our prayer be that we are not responsible for the loss of any; may this be so for His glory.

How Can Prayer Help With the Discipleship of Members?

When doctors examine you, they poke a little, push a little, shine some light, take your temperature and ask questions. Through their training and observation, they are able to give you an honest assessment of your condition and provide recommendations for your routine.

A wise patient seeks honest counsel and strives to honor the guidance received. Asking members how you can pray for them is a very powerful way to learn their Spiritual circumstances. As the Pastor / Elders / Congregational Prayer Ministry members listen to the answers given, they will learn not only individual perspectives, but also what areas of Spiritual growth are most commonly voiced by the flock.

As Lutherans, we believe that the 6th function of the Priesthood of the Baptized (LW vol. 40; pgs. 29-30)--all Christians--is to pray. If our hope is to have healthy members, we must help them grow in their Prayer life. In school, when you help a classmate prepare for a test, you learn the subject better yourself; the same thing is true of our Prayer life.

> Prayer helps with the Discipleship of both the person being prayed for and the Prayer.

How Many Members Can Participate in Our Congregational Prayer Ministry?

Children can begin praying at a very young age; Jesus reminded us that His Father ordained the praise of infants. Adults can continue praying until they take their last breath. Congregational Prayer Ministry is probably your best chance to get 100% participation from your membership in a particular ministry.

Redeemer Lutheran Church in Westfield, New Jersey, is blessed to be led by Pastor Paul Kritsch; this man is running the race of ministry at full steam like a race horse. The fastest horses get faster as the race closes; they burst through the finish line at the fastest pace of their entire race. Pastor Kritsch is one of those who presses; he leans forward in the saddle (he is also my Pastor.).

When Pastor Kritsch gathers his elders for their monthly time together, they all bring their cell phone. There is half an hour set aside in the Elders meeting for each Elder to take their list of families and scatter to different parts of the Sanctuary / Church.

Each Elder then calls their families and says, "Hi, this is _____. The Elders and Pastor are gathered at Church to pray for the families of Redeemer. How can we pray for you?" If no one is home, the Elder leaves the message and the invitation to call back with requests.

The elders will typically get about 30 prayer requests from the families. Every member is touched with the ministry of Prayer. The Elders believe they have been fulfilling their Spiritual responsibility--not just reading the list of upcoming events from the Church newsletter.

Not only are the members prayed for, but Pastor Kritsch knows how best to organize the care of the congregation for the members of the congregation. This follow up is something everyone can participate in.

Prayer Lists can be updated and sent to the members to include in their personal family prayers throughout the week. Social media can be used for such Godly purposes.

In the military it takes about 14 people to support each person on the front lines. In Congregational Prayer Ministry, most people will serve **in support of** those who ask the question, "How can I pray for you?" The biggest priority is organizing the care for those in need. In Acts 6, we learn the names of those who brought the food to the widows; but many more were involved--gathering and preparing the food.

In Congregational Prayer Ministry, many will need to be recruited, trained and organized to facilitate the support for those asking, "How can I pray for you?" The ratio may be 14 to 1 or even higher.

How Much Focus Should Our Pastor / Staff / Elders / Leaders Have on Prayer?

How much of a priority was prayer for Jesus?

In Acts 6, the disciples identified two priorities for their time--Prayer and the ministry of the Word. Should prayer come first? Is it perhaps "more important"?

Luther supposedly said that when he was too busy, he had to stop everything and pray for a couple of hours, that in this way, God accomplished everything.

If we say that every good thing is from above and that any good work is done only by the power of the Holy Spirit, then maybe we should spend more time with God.

What would the leaders in a local church say if their Pastor agreed with the statement of the Apostles in Acts 6 and said that Prayer was going to be one of the most important things he was going to devote his life to?

Pastors with an Apostolic focus on prayer have the support of their secretary--appointments are not scheduled during the time the Pastor has set aside for Prayer. If a church like this has a staff, the staff are also expected to set aside a block of time (often an hour) for prayer.

This prayer time is done during the work day; it is not in addition to the work. We have to understand Prayer as part of the work a Pastor / others who serve in ministry do on our behalf.

Jesus often withdrew to be in prayer; it is important for the Pastor and those who help with leadership to also have times to completely get away for Prayer Retreats. It is appropriate to spend time in planning and evaluating the effectiveness of the current Congregational Prayer Ministry. Also, time should be spent in prayer for the members. But a significant and intentional amount of time must be set aside for these leaders to hear individually from God in their prayers. This does not count as vacation time.

A journal with the highlights of this Prayer Retreat should be kept and shared with accountability boards / key leaders / church members as best fits the situation.

Twenty Ways to Use Prayer in Congregational Ministry:

1. A Coordinator for Your Congregational Prayer Ministry would be a great place to start. At first, this should probably be your Pastor. As he establishes the purpose and procedures for this role, he can begin to develop someone to help him. Your ministry situation may warrant the development of more than one person to help your Pastor in this role.

The Coordinator would give an accounting for every prayer request received. He or she will work with the leaders of your church's ministries to organize and expand the follow up for prayer requests received. In most ministries the Coordinator will be accountable to the Pastor. The Prayer Ministry Coordinator will work with those who communicate to the congregation through print / electronic means so your Congregational Prayer Ministry is strong and serving as desired. The Coordinator will report on the efforts of the other church ministries regarding their support of the follow up to prayer requests received.

Action Question:
    *Who comes to mind for your Congregational Prayer Ministry Coordinator? _____

---

2. Prayer Vigils, Worship Services and Retreats are all great ways to have dedicated blocks of time for discipleship and service in Prayer. The variety of forms these can take is almost endless.

Prayer Vigils are usually for specific, short blocks of time, usually less than 24 hours. If they go longer, the overall time is usually broken up into smaller blocks. This is done to facilitate the participants' schedules. Vigils can happen virtually, with the participants praying from their homes / places of work, etc.

Prayer Services can be scheduled regularly; often they are for special ministry needs / opportunities being considered. These services can be very interactive and responsive, or they can be a simple time of gathering, where the Pastor has prepared a handout with the items to pray for and accompanying Scriptural passages.

Prayer Retreats are held somewhere other than the normal worship location, such as in the countryside, the city, or even at another church's retreat center. These special times are helpful for team building, reconciliation, renewal, vision casting, etc., as the group gathers and has extended time for prayer, hearing from God and sharing with each other.

Luther in his commentary on Genesis 3:1 said that Adam "hears from the LORD His very thoughts." Isaiah heard the still, small quiet voice of God. Prayer, like a conversation should be spent in listening as well as talking.

3. Prayer Partners are a very special form of Prayer ministry. My wife, Cathy, has very fond memories of being a Secret Prayer Sister with other ladies in the Congregation. The ladies participating would gather once a year to put their names in a jar and then draw out someone else's name. The idea was to keep your identity a secret for the rest of the year; which almost never happened.   You could arrange Prayer Partner ministries for new members who are "adopted" by long-time members. Youth could have adult mentors. Prayer Partnerships could be arranged for the sick and those confined to their homes or in nursing homes; college students away from home; and members in the military. Men could call their fellowship "Prayer Warriors."

4. Prayer Chains are common in many churches. General concerns to address include confidentiality, gossip, and length of time it takes for the last "link" in the chain to get the Prayer request. Establish that the person at the end "closes the loop" and calls the leader to check in.

5. Prayer Hotline / Prayer Website / Prayer Blog are variations of the same idea--offering Prayer support to others in a way that offers the possibility of anonymity. These uses of technology are appealing to some members and are a way for them to serve in ministry that utilizes their Spiritual gifts. There are great stories of Christians who have handicaps ministering to others in this way.

6. Private Confession and Absolution--early in my Pastoral ministry I asked an elder Pastor to be my Confessor. I found it a great blessing to have a Pastor I came to for confessing my sins and hearing forgiveness. Many things people will ask us to pray for entail sin in some way. Certainly any Christian can go directly to the Father for forgiveness (and should); a Christian can also turn to another Christian and be assured of the forgiveness of their sins (this is a blessing). But there are also great benefits in confessing your sins privately to your Pastor--there is complete confidentiality; he has been trained in theology and seasoned with experience; he will be better able to preach and teach you by knowing your needs and concerns. Your Pastor can then personally pray for you., You might encourage your Pastor in love to have a Confessor for himself. In our Congregational Prayer Ministry, we should be certain to include Private Confession and Absolution as part of the care we offer to members.

7. Prayer and Fasting is a New Testament practice and should be encouraged today. Jesus was asked one time why His disciples did not fast. His reply is instructive; He said that the guests of the Bridegroom do not fast while He is with them; but the time is coming when He will no longer be with us and that "... *in those days they will fast.*" (Luke 5:35) These are "*those days.*"

Fasting held an unpleasant smell in Luther's nose. As a monk he bought into the devil's lie of good works. Being of sincere heart, Luther strived harder than almost any other to please God by not eating, sleeping on cold floors, even whipping himself. Luther would later surmise that these activities contributed to some of his health problems. We are careful to encourage fasting as an activity of those who are saved, not as a way of entering salvation.

In the Bible, we find many examples and varieties of fasting. Daniel limited his diet in a certain way, John the Baptist in another. When I was at the Seminary, I heard a Lutheran Pastor share that his practice was to set aside one day each week for fasting; I have adopted his practice. But I am not legalistic about it. If I am supposed to be at a celebration on that day and everyone is eating, I will eat with them. My salvation is secure in the grace of Christ.

8. Sending Personal Notes to the person who shared the prayer request the same day you received the request is a very touching and powerful practice. Typically, the person will receive your note (it does not need to be a store bought card) a couple of days later, bringing a pleasant reminder of God's love for them.

9. Prayer Resources should be made available to members. Luther's Personal Prayer Book was one of his most popular books; it went through 24 editions due to the demand. Prayer is still strongly practiced; a recent ABC News poll found that 90% of Americans pray daily.

What is shaping our members' conversation with God? Who is providing their Prayer resources?

10. Prayer Chapels / Prayer Closets are very nice to have in church. Many times people look for a place to get away and be with God; this is where a dedicated space for worship is a real benefit for ministry.

Prayer Chapels can be very elaborate spaces where significant effort and resources are dedicated to creating a space, which, through ecclesiastical art, icons, candles and perhaps incense, transport worshippers mentally and emotionally, so they can focus Spiritually on their Father.

Prayer Closets utilize the "less is more" approach that many understand. A simple, utilitarian space with comfortable chairs, perhaps a prayer altar / prayer kneeler, Bibles and devotional helps, Christian music playing softly, and limited artwork. It will probably be used often on Sunday morning before, during or after worship services.

11. Praying the Lord's Prayer should be encouraged. First, it should be taught just as Christ gave it to us. Next, we should train and encourage believers to expand the seven parts (petitions) of the Lord's Prayer and to apply personally each part of the Prayer our Lord taught us. In this way, the Lord's Prayer is both memorized (a good thing) and it is helping develop a believer's personal relationship with Jesus.

In "*A Personal Prayer Book*"; Luther said these things:

"Three things a person must know in order to be saved. First, he must know what to do and what to leave undone. Second, when he realizes that he cannot measure up to what he should do or leave undone, he needs to know where to go to find the strength he requires. Third, he must know how to seek and obtain that strength. It is just like a sick person who first has to determine the nature of his sickness, then find out what to do or to leave undone. After that he has to know where to get the medicine which will help him do or leave undone what is right for a healthy person. Then he has to desire to search for this medicine and to obtain it or have it brought to him."

Thus <u>the commandments teach man to recognize his sickness</u>, enabling him to perceive what he must do or refrain from doing, consent to or refuse, and so he will recognize himself to be a sinful and wicked person. <u>The Creed will teach and show him where to find the medicine—grace</u>—which will help him to become devout and keep the commandments. The Creed points him to God and his mercy, given and made plain to him in Christ. <u>Finally, the Lord's Prayer teaches all this, namely, through the fulfillment of God's commandments everything will be given him</u>. In these three are the essentials of the entire Bible."[97]

Luther provides examples of how he personally prayed the seven petitions of the Lord's Prayer in "*A Personal Prayer Book*." This book is included in Volume 43 of Luther's Writings. A simple Google search will yield many sites where you can read his book for free. I would encourage you to do <u>at least</u> this <u>and</u> to consider getting a copy for yourself.

As I read Luther's personal examples of how to pray the seven petitions of the Lord's Prayer, I was struck by the following thought of his:

"Protect us from asking you for anything temporal or eternal *which would not serve the glory and honor of your name*. Should we petition you in such a way, do not listen to our folly. Help us conduct all our life in such a way that we may be found to be true children of God, lest we call you Father falsely or in vain."[98]

This is a great prayer! If we are wondering how to properly pray; this simple request contained in Luther's prayer is something we would all do well to remember today.

You need to get a copy of Luther's "*Personal Prayer Book*" for your own use; you will also find it very helpful in a multitude of situations requiring your prayers. Get a couple copies for your friends this Christmas or on their baptismal birthdays.

12. Recognition of Your Congregational Prayer Ministry in worship services--this is very important. A wise Seminary Professor once advised, "What we speak to in worship, the members speak to in the daily witness of their lives."

As a parish Pastor, I always made a point during the announcements in worship, of saying to the congregation, "If you shared your faith with someone this past week; raise your hands…. Everyone look-- these are our Great Commission Christians. Give God a praise clap!" <u>The very next thing I would do</u> is talk about the special DVD Bible study resource we had as a gift for our members. Without even saying it explicitly, the <u>implicit message</u> was there--visitors come to church through <u>you</u> talking to people about your faith. Every Sunday we had members who raised their hands, letting everyone know they had shared their faith with someone, and almost every single Sunday (probably at least 95%), we had first time visitors. All praise be to God; this happened in a mission start with very few members at first.

It is important to recognize your Congregational Prayer Ministry in corporate worship also. There are some simple, effective ways to do this.

  -Ask members to indicate if they have prayed for others this past week
  -Recognize those who are Prayer Walkers
  -Recognize those who organize the Mercy ministry follow up to Prayers received
  -Have special prayer testimony time (this will require working with those who will be sharing
      their story; you will want to make sure the length and doctrine are correct)
  -Include information in your bulletin on how to be a part of your Congregational Prayer Ministry
  -Print statistics / stories in your bulletin that tell part of your Congregational Prayer Ministry
      story
  -Have households help with the Congregational Prayers
  -Publicize the numbers regarding your Congregational Prayer Ministry (give God the glory)

---

[97]Martin Luther, 43:14. Fortress.
[98]Ibid., 43:31.

13. Healing Prayer Ministry is something that is powerful, speaks to people's hearts, and is a way in which the Holy Spirit works through the Priesthood of the Baptized. In the fourth petition of the Lord's Prayer ("*give us this day our daily bread*"), we affirm that we should pray for good health (Small Catechism). Prayer for healing is something Lutherans are good at doing. We always pray, "according to God's will; in the name of His Son and for His glory," if we are praying for healing or anything else.

Healing Prayer Ministry can be expressed in many ways: special worship services or even regularly scheduled Prayer and Healing services; services in response to tragedy; ministry of anointing with oil. This is a great opportunity to involve the Priesthood of the Baptized in the ministry of the Church.

I found the following thought good to reflect on:

"Augustine experienced the power of faith in sickness and constantly affirmed that God hears the prayers of believers. It would be useful to recall such examples as these which talk about faith"[99]

People are looking for God in their time of trouble. If we don't help them see God when going through their medical difficulties, then shame on us! We have not been good shepherds when we yawn and turn a disinterested ear to the experiences of others.

14. Prayer Breakfasts are a great way to have fellowship, discipleship, ministry and mercy all at the same time, on a Saturday morning. Often the time will begin with the Pastor leading a simple order of service in the Sanctuary, followed with a Breakfast. While people are eating, the presenter can start the time of equipping, followed with sharing of Prayers that can then be lifted up in small Prayer huddles or together. It would be good for those who organize the Mercy Ministry of the Congregation to have a chance to share an update on their activities as well as opportunities for possible service; prayer and care go together like root beer and ice cream.

15. The National Day of Prayer is a good thing to observe in your congregation. There is a great deal of information regarding this on the internet as well as resources to encourage participation and follow up. We are told to pray for those in authority; certainly we can do this at any time. However, in our own Sanctuaries, with the freedom to lead worship according to Scripture and our conscience, we have a great opportunity to be part of something other Christians are also participating in, but in a way that does not compromise our Confession.

16. Meet Me at the Flagpole is another way to be part of the community and to give a Confessional Christian witness in the public square. Most public high schools have a Christian student association. An active group will invite local clergy to come and share devotions or offer a prayer for their gatherings. Every Fall, the tradition is to "gather at the flagpole" for a time of prayer. (The Wisconsin Synod does not allow members to be in the Boy Scouts, provide Chaplains for their military members, or pray with other Christians. This is not the position of The Lutheran Church--Missouri Synod.)

Our nation has a growing diversity of religions; the need to Confess publicly what we believe and teach has never stood in sharper contrast to the culture. If you are going to offer a prayer at an event like this, it is wise to write your prayer down and share the prayer beforehand with the Elders board of your congregation as well as brothers in the ministry. Listen carefully to their concerns and suggestions; especially those you might perceive as "negative." It is probably a good idea to discuss this beforehand with your Circuit Counselor / District President as well. We should not exercise our Christian freedom in a way that distracts from the original intent.

17. Praying Through the Membership Directory or the Church cookbook are good ways to lift up "... *especially those who belong to the Family of Faith.*" (Galatians 6:10) This is a ministry that can easily be encouraged by the Congregational Prayer Ministry coordinator / Pastor; with just a little work, a simple Prayer Guide could be composed for this emphasis.

---

[99] AC 1. IX. 36.

18. Take-home Bible Studies on Prayer should be prepared / offered by the: Pastor; Board of Elders; Board of Education; Women's Mission Group (LWML), etc.

The first Pastors of the New Testament Church realized that their ministry had two basic components: Prayer and the ministry of the Word. (Acts 6)

It is an embarrassing travesty when we honestly assess the Spiritual maturity of our members in these two most elemental aspects of our faith. More and more Confirmation Programs are adding an additional year of instruction just so the children can learn the basics of the Bible, which they were supposed to get in their Sunday school years.

> We need to get back to the basic blocking and tackling of the Christian faith- Prayer and the ministry of the Word!

In my family, we have a tradition every night. My wife Cathy and I have five Godly children; so there are seven of us altogether (plus Kisses our golden retriever and River our calico cat). Every night we focus on a different member of our family. For example, Wednesday is our son Jim's day. So, on Wednesday nights I will ask everyone to share individually one thing they love about Jim. Then I will ask Jim to share one thing he loves about his family. After that, I will ask everyone to tell Jim that he is a blessing from God. Then I will ask Jim to tell us one thing that our family should do on Thursday for John (Thursday is John's day). Finally, I will ask Jim to lead our family in prayers and we will repeat after Jim as he leads us in prayer. When our children were very young, they would lead us in "Now I lay me down to sleep"; as they got a little older they led us in The Lord's Prayer (which they still choose sometimes), and now they lead us in prayers based on petitions we share with them first. Cathy and I are very blessed to see our children have the ability, confidence and experience of leading public prayer / lifting up the prayer requests of others. This is what they have known their entire lives; by God's grace, they will know this the rest of their lives as well.

19. Sermon Series / Sunday School Classes / VBS themes that focus on Prayer should be conducted. We are blessed to have a schedule of Scripture readings for each Sunday; this helps us *preach the whole counsel of God.* We are also blessed with Christian freedom in this, something Luther exercised frequently as he preached through a book of the Bible or on a particular Discipleship topic like the 10 Commandments.

Prayer, being one of the two priorities for the New Testament Church's first Pastors (Galatians 6), would be a logical (and Biblical) priority for our pulpits today. For starters, a sermon series on The Lord's Prayer would be an easy and agreeable place for Pastor and members to focus. From there, other sermon series on Prayer could be developed, perhaps a sermon series on the prayers of the Prophets, the Priests, the Kings, the Apostles, the Priesthood of Believers from both the Old and New Testaments, etc.

20. Annual Member Prayer Life Surveys should be conducted. This would be a good opportunity to receive feedback and suggestions for future ministry that could be of benefit to the Prayer life of your members. The responses would also be a natural part of the conversation when your Pastor / Elders make home visits. Inviting members to participate in the Congregational Prayer Ministry (especially the Mercy ministry of following up with the Prayer requests received) could yield some pleasant surprises and extra hands for the Harvest.

A good rule of thumb with surveys is to keep them as short and simple as possible--"test drive" them with a small group first, before sending them out. Also, consider using resources like Survey Monkey, which can be very helpful for your communication and analysis.

How Do We Assess the Prayer Ministry of Our Congregation?

Scripture gives us God's intent for our Prayer life; it contains specific examples and attributes (both desired / not desired). Hopefully, the first section of this book with all of the Scriptural passages regarding Prayer, as well as the second section, with excerpts of our teaching regarding Prayer was helpful. I will not plow those fields all over.

In your Annual Prayer Life Surveys of Members, you will learn a great deal about the condition of your Congregational Prayer Ministry.

If you want some ideas for a general **Prayer Assessment Tool**, the following might give you some ideas of questions to include:

- How much time should the Pastor / Staff devote to Prayer Ministry?
- How strong of a Prayer life should our church leaders have?
- How much has the Church helped you grow in your Prayer life this year?
- What additional Prayer resources should the Church offer?
- Are you serving / desiring to serve in our Congregational Prayer Ministry?
- Should the Church have a dedicated Prayer Chapel for use when needed?
- How much of the budget should be devoted to Congregational Prayer Ministry?
- Should members have an occasional chance to share a personal testimony in worship regarding their prayer experiences?
- Do you understand the purpose of our Congregational Prayer Ministry? How would you explain it to someone else?
- Who should we be trying to serve through Congregational Prayer Ministry?
- How often do you pray? For others?
- How comfortable are you praying out loud, in a public place?
- How much time do you spend in prayer? Daily? Weekly?

It is not a bad idea to go on the Web and look at other Churches to see what they are / are not doing. Just remember the idea is **not** to "do what _____ church does," but simply to ask, "As we see how the Holy Spirit is working in other places, what gifts has He given us here and, considering these strengths, how might He want to use us?"

Developing Your Congregational Prayer Ministry

You will want the following:
-Coordinator of Congregational Prayer Ministry
-Mercy Ministry Leadership Team, made up of representatives from the various ministries of the Church, which will be following up with care for those identified through Prayer. This can be a separate team, or the function can be accomplished by inviting the Coordinator of Congregational Prayer Ministry to be a part of your Church Leadership meetings.
-Creation of a single Master List for Prayer requests being followed up with
-Prayer Walkers (the people who ask members, "How can I / we pray for you?")
-Prayer Partners (the people who will be doing the Praying)
-Resources committed in the church budget
-Space in all Church communications to tell the story; share needs and invite others
-Training
- A set of guidelines developed for your ministry that are appropriately approved
-A statistical summary of your Prayer and Mercy ministry prepared for the members

It is important to develop Congregational Prayer Ministry, especially the Mercy Ministry piece, before trying to do outreach into the general community. Start with the household of faith. Work out your roles and responsibilities; understand who will be providing what kind of follow up care to those who share Prayer requests with us (members, visitors or finally, the community at large).

What Is the Connection Between Prayer and Multiplication?

Put simply, people who are cared for tell others. There is no better care than prayer and prayer that informs our care.

Great Video- Pr. Garrett Knudson, Holy Cross in Bordentown, NJ and members share about Prayer Walking the visitors to the Open House hosted by their Pre School.

http://www.youtube.com/watch?v=a5wsDuLYmRo

VI. Prayer Improves Ministry to Visitors-A House of Prayer Welcomes All of the Nations

Most church members are surprised at how much ministry their church is accomplishing. A fun and informative exercise is to ask your church, "What does our church do to serve others?" Write down all the answers; the list will be longer than you think. A related question is, "What does our church do to reach out to others?" Again, write down all the answers, because the list will be longer than you think.

Yet, for all our efforts, most of our churches are stagnate in their growth. A frightening number of churches have not had a single adult Baptism for years.

Maybe it is time we started praying about this. Maybe we should return again to our first love as Pastors--Prayer and the ministry of the Word. (Acts 6:4) Maybe we should stop trusting in humanly devised programs or gimmicks. Maybe, the Priesthood of the Baptized should not measure the growth of their church if they are not willing to commit in writing to freeing up their Pastor to focus on those who are not yet members. Maybe it's time to focus first on Prayer and then the Word; what do you think?

Church "experts" come up with snazzy words to capture some idea (and our hopes). But none of this is rocket science. Then, we spend all sorts of time arguing about these phrases; meanwhile people are dying and souls are being judged. We should all be ashamed of what we have done with the Gospel. When Christ returns will He find any of us working; or will we all just be sitting around needling each other?

Most church outreach is what the "experts" classify as "attractional"- which simply means using something to draw people to you.

Here are some problems with attractional outreach:
    -It costs money
    -Your relationship with the people is over when the event ends (maybe earlier if they walk out)
    -If you do gain members in this way, these members will be consumers, looking for you to continue to entertain them; they are, generally speaking, very disinterested in serving. Why? Because you didn't gain them by asking them to serve; you gained them by "giving" them something.
    -It is basically "bait and switch" (and everyone knows it)
    -It often cheapens the Great Commission to look like selling used cars
    -The cross is not attractive to our natural way of thinking
    -The majority of self-described Christians do not want to worship in a Sanctuary; attractional outreach is not really conversion focused; but primarily a redistribution of sanctuary worshippers.

Having said all that, here is my confession--as a church planter who helped plant two churches, I have done some of the craziest types of attractional outreach. Why? I wanted a chance to tell people the Gospel. Chief of sinners--that is I--there is a place in ministry for "attractional outreach"; and that is second place; second to the Word of God; Communion, Baptism, Prayer, and the fruit of the Holy Spirit.

In fact, there are many "solid" attractional outreaches that we have used historically in the Lutheran Church. Consider our education system for example. The Lutheran Church Missouri Synod has the second largest Christian school system in the United States- impressive considering we are 1% of the population. Usually, when we talk about "attractional outreach" we do not mean Christian education, but rather social events or community invitations to attend church celebrations (e.g., Easter Egg Hunts).

Prayer Can Break the Cyclical Nature of Relationships
Formed Through Attractional Outreach

One of the biggest shortcomings with attractional outreach is that our relationship with the unchurched who come to an attraction-based outreach ends when the event is over; maybe sooner if they have to leave for another commitment.

Take, for example, an Easter egg hunt. Your church may not do this; if that is the case, consider your own attractional outreach event during this discussion.

The typical Easter egg hunt preparation begins a couple of months in advance. A team will gather, review last year's efforts; consider suggestions for this year; assign responsibilities; create a critical events calendar; there may even be numerical goals (at the very least, numbers will be discussed for the purpose of supplies and organization) and then everyone will begin to go to work.

One of the first things that will then happen is someone will search for last year's registration list (hopefully finding it) to contact the families who attended. Typically, most of these families will return.

When the Easter egg hunt is over and everyone has gone home, the team will meet and the first thing to be discussed will be, "How many people came?" The success / failure of the Easter egg hunt will, in large part, be measured in some way by this number, which can easily become a stumbling block if we aren't careful.

Sound familiar? Be honest!

The problem: the unchurched families touched by this outreach will most likely not hear from the Church until next year's Easter egg hunt. A well-organized Church will include a flier with a list of upcoming events and this is good, but unfortunately, these other events are organized by different committees within the Church and the simple truth is that <u>most committees do not share registration lists with each other</u>.

When entities within an organization view the information they have gathered as "theirs," this creates "stovepipes" and a tremendous amount of energy, effort and expense simply evaporates right up into thin air.

I have said this before, but it bears repeating--<u>your Church needs to have a single database into which every ministry feeds its information regarding new contacts</u>. Hopefully, there are no leaders in the ministry who will be threatened by this / try to impede this information sharing.

> ****Here is the basic hurdle for Attractional Outreach--the cross is not attractive***. Neither is discipleship. Thus, there is the challenge of moving people from the "Visitor" column into the "Member" and eventually, "Disciple" column.

Certainly it is true that Jesus' ministry was "attractive." Tens of thousands would come out for a free dinner of fish and chips served lakeside. But then, Jesus got into <u>heavy</u> discipleship, "*I am the Bread of Life… unless you eat My body and drink My blood…*"
What happened to the fan club? They whined and cried, got all "theological" and left in a huff.

What did Jesus do? Jesus turned to His remaining disciples and said, "Here's the door; do you want to leave also?" Peter pipes up and correctly says, "Lord, to Whom would we go, You have the words of eternal life." Good job, Pete.

Jesus was hard as a rock! To follow Him meant letting the dead bury the dead. To be a disciple of Jesus still means picking up your cross daily and following Him.

We can hand out all the free food in the world; but if we don't get on to discipleship in a forthright and honest way, clearly laying out Law and Gospel; the Sacraments; salvation which is found only in and through Jesus; the inspiration and inerrancy of Scripture; the fruit of the Spirit; modeling a powerful prayer life, then we are just "playing church." We are saying we are "successful" just because a large crowd came. **Listen to me, Jesus' success began once the posers left.**

> *Prayer can help change a relationship initially created through an attractional outreach into a discipleship relationship.*

After your attractional outreach event is over, have a couple people who have an interest in the lost call up your visitors (or maybe even stop by for a visit), and after the appropriate amount of "small talk," ask this simple question, "How can we pray for you?"

So, the phone call goes something like this:
"Hi Mrs. Smith; this is Jim. It was great to have you at Redeemer's Easter egg hunt this year again. Hope you had a great time….

"We are going to have a special time of prayer on Sunday for the families that came. We will be lifting up the prayers of the other families and would love to include you.

How can we pray for you?"

Then, you simply take down their prayer request and turn it into Pastor. The prayer request will be lifted up in worship. If you have other Prayer Ministries in your congregation, they can be asked to pray for these needs as well.

There are two things that now need to happen:
1. Whoever is in charge of your congregation's Mercy Ministry needs to organize the follow up for this home.
2. The calling team that originally asked for the Prayer Request needs to call the visitor back and get an update from the visitor regarding the status of the item prayed for. The church caller will let them know the congregation did in fact pray for them; that someone may be reaching out to them with help, and that the church will continue to walk with them through this difficulty.

In this way the nature of the relationship between the visitor and the church will change from one based on the church providing "attractive events" for the unchurched to "consume." By the Holy Spirit's work, the relationship will change into one focused on: Prayer, the body of Christ, Mercy Ministry, and discipleship of the members in service to their community.

You no longer have to wait for the annual Easter egg hunt to "reconnect" with the unchurched (until their children outgrow this activity). Prayer can break the cyclical nature of relationships formed through attractional outreach.

Twenty Attractional Outreaches
That Prayer Walking Can Increase in Effectiveness:

Here is a short list of attractional outreaches, commonly offered by churches:

- VBS (Summer or Christmas)
- ESL
- Marriage / Parenting
- Medical Screenings
- After School Care / Activities
- Fall Festivals
- Community Celebrations
- Worship Concerts
- Guest Speakers
- Invite Mailers
- Easter Egg Hunts
- Passion Plays
- Youth Camps
- Financial Workshops
- Divorce Recovery
- Parenting Courses
- Food Pantries
- Clothing Banks
- Parent's Night Out
- Day Care, Preschool, Grade School, High School

Your church most likely has these and others. With any of these outreach activities, Prayer can be used in the way previously described to build personal relationships; extend Mercy Ministry; and incorporate visitors into your ministry before they even become members.

I would encourage you to keep track of the percentage of people attending your Membership Information class who are already part of a ministry team in your church. When you are reaching out to your visitors with Prayer, you will build a personal bond between them and your ministry and they will respond by desiring to help with other ministries your church is offering. It is not uncommon to have over 80% of those considering Membership, already participating in ministry when Prayer is a priority in your ministry to them.

One of the biggest mistakes made with trying to assimilate new members is waiting until someone becomes a member before inviting them to be part of the ministry.

Most of the ministries a church does do not require membership; so why wait for them to become members first? Be proactive! Lean forward in the saddle!

It is a good idea to include the offer of Prayer in all of your promotional efforts. Two options: a link to your church website that holds the form for filling in Prayer requests, and printing the name and contact information for your Prayer Coordinator.

What About Visitors to Our Ministry that Happens Beyond the Church?

In addition to outreach that happens at your Church address, your church has the opportunity to provide regular, scheduled ministry at other locations.   *__Nursing homes__* are a good candidate for your church to extend worship and ministry. Most of the time, ministry in a nursing home consists of inviting the residents to the fellowship hall, cafeteria or possibly a Chapel. The focus of this time is usually a simplified order of service.

A congregation with a Congregational Prayer Coordinator and a Mercy Ministry Team can begin a ministry much deeper than the simple order of service. You already are taking Prayer requests in these worship services; now you can follow up with intentional Mercy Ministry to residents of the Nursing Homes and their loved ones.

When providing ministry to a Nursing Home, don't forget the staff. Make time to visit with the staff and ask them also, "How can we pray for you?" They will be pleasantly surprised to see a Church that cares about them as well as the residents. As you follow up with Mercy Ministry to the staff, you will expand the sphere of your ministry; not to mention, you will see an even greater effort on their part to help you gather the residents for the worship services.

When calling on members who are **hospitalized**, coordinate with the Hospital Chaplain and discuss the options for providing ministry to all who list "Lutheran" as their religious preference. The Hospital Chaplain (or Social Worker) will have guidance in place to share with you. Honor the trust they have been given and seek to be helpful to them in how you go about connecting with the patients.

Most people who list "Lutheran" as their religious preference are not currently active in a congregation. A visit to a fellow Lutheran not currently active can move beyond a "courtesy call" by asking the simple question, "How can I pray for you?" then having the Congregational Prayer Coordinator and Mercy Ministry Team follow up as appropriate.

This ministry can be done by the Pastor, but perhaps a Deaconess or a trained member could develop the full potential that exists. Hospitals today are discharging patients much quicker today than in years past; this provides an increased opportunity to visit with more people in a given week.

Another great opportunity exists if you will be intentional about connecting with **the pillars of your community** (your mayor, public school superintendent, local TV, radio and newspaper reporters, business owners, celebrities, notable retirees, the police or fire chief, etc.).   It is perfectly appropriate for a Pastor to set an appointment with these pillars, the purpose of this visit would be to encourage these public servants in their tasks; learn about their vision and hopes as well as the current challenges they face.

Most newspapers have a Religion / Community Events section. Take the initiative and call the appropriate persons to arrange a meeting. They will have a wealth of information about issues facing your community and will probably be able to help your network rapidly expand. You can repeat this with people who work in all aspects of the News / Social Media / Radio / Sports / Entertainment, etc.

A logical question to ask in these visits is, "How can I pray for you?" Again, as they answer, you will likely learn of opportunities for the Mercy Ministry of your congregation to share God's love in circles beyond the walls of your congregation.

It is a great idea for the Pastor to not only reach out and connect with community pillars, but then also to invite these leaders to be the special guest of the church's leadership at your next Board of Directors / Church Council / Elders meeting. Put the special guest first on the agenda- this way you can still discuss any in house business later and you are showing respect for their time.

There will be a sense of anticipation as your special guest shares from their perspective what your church can do to serve the community. It is common for this special guest to offer resources to help you in this shared work. Your special guest will tell others about your ministry. Your leadership team and church members will see their church's ministry in an expanded way. What I am sharing here is not theory; I have personally been blessed by God to see this happen. The authority that comes from influence is helpful.

How Can We Expand Prayer Ministry on Sunday Morning?

There was also a prophetess, Anna, the daughter of Phanuel, of the tribe of Asher. She was very old; she had lived with her husband seven years after her marriage, and then was a widow until she was eighty-four. <u>She never left the temple but worshiped night and day, fasting and praying.</u> Coming up to them at that very moment, she gave thanks to God and spoke about the child to all who were looking forward to the redemption of Jerusalem. (Luke 2:36-38)

Do we make room in God's house (*"a house of prayer for all nations"*) for the Annas of today?

The story of Anna is a New Testament picture of <u>intense</u> prayer in God's house. Are there ways in which our local churches could resemble this more closely? Yes!

Prayer sheets could be prepared in advance of Sunday morning with a list of the Prayer Requests received through the various aspects of your Congregational Prayer Ministry. A special room could be designated as a place for prayer before the worship service starts. Women today, like Anna, could gather with others for prayer. Usually this works best if people feel free to come when they want and stay as long as they feel led. Some might gain purpose from walking throughout the church, stopping in the classrooms that will be used later in the morning and offering a prayer for the teachers and students who will gather there.

On these sheets could be the Ministry Leaders to contact if you want to help with the Mercy Ministry follow up. Make it easy for people to get involved.

In the worship service, when people are coming forward for Communion, the church could have Elders, or others with the recognized gift of Prayer, standing in an appropriate place, available to pray with anyone who would like to receive this ministry.

At the end of the service, again, these same Prayer Workers could be available to pray with anyone going through a difficult time. They could be positioned by the altar or be available in a private room near the Sanctuary if that would be more beneficial for the burdened brother or sister.

<u>If your church does not currently have this practice, it is best to discuss this in peace and with patience.</u>

God's vision for His house is that it would be a house of prayer. Incense is the symbol of prayer in the Bible. (Psalm 141:2 Revelation 5:8) Incense is very powerful; it permeates every space. It seems that this is God's picture of what prayer should look like in His house.

How Does Prayer Connect with Post Moderns?

To understand why it does, let's take a moment to review how "Post Moderns" came to be; this is important because by some estimates they represent 80% of our population.

Wikipedia defines postmodernism in this way:
"Postmodernism is largely a reaction to the assumed certainty of scientific or objective efforts to explain reality. There is no consensus among scholars on the precise definition. <u>In essence, postmodernism is based on the position that reality is not mirrored in human understanding of it, but is rather constructed as the mind tries to understand its own personal reality.</u> Postmodernism is therefore skeptical of explanations which claim to be valid for all groups, cultures, traditions, or races, and instead focuses on the relative truths of each person. In the postmodern understanding, interpretation is everything; <u>reality only comes into being through our interpretations of what the world means to us individually.</u>"

Post Moderns will readily agree with the following statements:
    "Truth is relative."
    "There is no black and white; just shades of gray."
    "Perspective is reality."

These statements pose significant challenges to anyone who believes that Jesus is the only way to Heaven and that the Bible is the only revealed Word of God, inspired and inerrant in every aspect.

Unfortunately, many Christians either directly attack these Postmodern statements or throw their hands up in the air and "shake the dust off their feet," muttering that there is no help for these people.

To understand how to witness to Post Moderns requires understanding a little science.

Modern science can be broadly divided into two eras: Newtonian science and Einsteinian Science (which followed Newtonian science).

Newtonian Science had a G.U.T., that is, a "Grand Unification Theory." Under Newtonian Science, everything had an explanation. Newtonian scientists believe they can put all the pieces of the puzzle together. The three laws of motion and the law of gravity provided observable truths.

The Church was very comfortable with the G.U.T.; it was an easy step from science's G.U.T. to a theologian's library of doctrinal books, replete with Biblical answers to any question. The Church did, however, wrestle with Modernism's maxim of "I think, therefore I am." Modernism itself had no place for religion, because to a Modern scientist an invisible God could not be tested in a laboratory.

Modernism and Darwinism were the humanistic parents that produced spectacles like Adolf Hitler and Joseph Stalin. In the aftermath of World War Two, the survivors agreed that a new construct was needed.

Enter Einstein. With technology, new aspects of the Creation were revealed. Under the microscope, we learned that the smallest particles of the universe were in constant motion, thus leading to the realization that what something is depends on when and from what angle you look at it. With technology, the scientists of Einstein's era began to discover the effect of speed--the faster something moves, the longer it gets, thus leading to the revelation that "what something is" depends on what is happening to it. Also, speed was proven to slow down time itself.

All these scientific facts were unfortunately taken note of by Philosophers before Theologians. Modernism was replaced in the public universities with Post-Modernism. Appropriating the scientific facts for their endeavors, the Philosophers put forward their new "meaning of life"….
    -All things are relative.
    -Perspective is reality.
It is necessary to **deconstruct** these two previous powerful statements. In order to minister to Post Moderns, we must understand their roots. At their root, post-modern ideas are based on good science. The Church's argument is never with good science, just bad philosophy.

In God's Word we find many examples of perspective being reality:
    If anyone is in Christ, they are a new creation. (2 Corinthians 5:17)
    Though I am free and belong to no man, I make myself a slave to everyone, to win as many as possible. (1 Corinthians 9:19)

When Post Moderns express skepticism about anyone having all the answers, the following verses also express similar sentiments:
    For now we see in a mirror dimly. (1 Corinthians 13:12)
    We walk by faith, not by sight. (2 Corinthians 5:7)

When Post Moderns say, "There are some things we just can't make sense out of," we again can find common ground in Scripture:

> *Very rarely will anyone die for a righteous man, though for a good man someone might possibly dare to die. <u>But God demonstrates his own love for us in this</u>: While we were still <u>sinners</u>, Christ died for us.* (Romans 5:7-8)

Truth be told, God's grace makes no "sense"; that is why it is grace.

Be of good cheer, the Gospel is needed by Post Moderns also.

Prayer has characteristics that resonate with Post Moderns:
-It's very personal.
-It is beyond full explanation.
-Each prayer request and person praying is unique.
-It speaks to their understanding of a life after this one and the way to it.

A prayer-based relationship is P.I.E.: **P**ersonal, **I**ntuitive and **E**motional. <u>These are things that Post Moderns are very comfortable with</u>. Professor Francis Rossow, Concordia Seminary, St. Louis, might call Prayer a "Gospel Handle"; that is, a way to share the Gospel with others.

The best research confirms that <u>Post Moderns in fact pray as much, if not more, than previous generations</u>. As many as 90% of Americans pray every day. This is something the liberal media has a very hard time with. If you doubt the veracity of this, just mention, "Tim Tebow."

The Apostle Paul took a stroll up Mars Hill in Athens one day. He found no Bible, no Small Catechism; but he did not walk away. He saw the Greeks' interest in religion; he even added the words of a pagan poet into the inspired and inerrant Word of God. He had one thing on his mind--the salvation of souls, and he wasn't going to be deterred.

Let us also set our faces like flint and move towards the good works God has prepared for us. People are people; they are sinners in need of a Savior. Listen with loving ears.

When a Post Modern says, "All things are relative," let us respond by saying, "Einsteinian science is good science. Now, let's think about this good science, in a good and Godly way."

<u>Our argument is not with good science but bad philosophy</u>. Spend time learning about scientific discoveries; <u>reflect on how to discuss these things in light of your faith.</u>

Who Can Be a Part of a Church's Prayer Ministry?

Potentially, any believer.

Members can pray at home for those being lifted up. Evangelism is something that many do not feel they have the "personality" for. Prayer does not require any special "personality."

<u>To be successful, an evangelism effort must provide the opportunity for every member realistically to have a chance to participate in</u>. Every member can pray. A five year old can pray; so can a 95 year old. You may only know how to speak English, but when you learn the prayer need of a Spanish-speaking neighbor, you can bring them before our Father in Heaven.

Mercy Ministry is a linchpin in Prayer Ministry.

87

Having received prayer requests, one of the key aspects of following up is caring for the needs we are praying for. When we learn a family is going through a divorce, we better get real, physical ministry organized. When a prayer request is shared for a father who has lost his job, we need to **fold our hands for prayer and then join our hands for care.**

Many in our congregations have a heart for helping others with real and practical assistance; this key part of the body of Christ must be connected to the Prayer Ministry.

Any believer can be a part of a Church's Prayer Ministry.

Is Prayer Ministry the new Networking?

Prayer is not a program. Prayer is a basic characteristic, given to believers by the Holy Spirit in their new birth.

Prayer is not new. Hopefully we don't need to explain this.

Prayer Ministry can be relationship based; but it doesn't have to be. Certainly, we should seek prayer requests from the Family of God / those we already know; but we should converse with those we meet, and intentionally and forthrightly ask them simply, "How can I pray for you?"

But *Prayer is an activity of the Holy Spirit*. The truth is, we don't even know how to pray (except for the Lord's Prayer); but the Holy Spirit intercedes for us. And the Holy Spirit moves as He sees fit. This means that Prayer Ministry is not going to fit into some cellophane wrapped package from Church Growth Central.

Sometimes churches grow frustrated with the lack of "growth" in their pews. A simple step to consider would be gathering the members and asking them, "Who do you know that we as a congregation can be praying for?"

And again, having folded our hands for prayer, join our hands to provide care to those we are praying for.

> ### *Can You Really Ask ANYONE How You Can Pray for Them?*
>
> Every culture in the world has religion.
>
> Every religion in the world has prayer.
>
> Every person has heard of prayer.
>
> #### *So, the answer to the question is, "Yes."*
>
> The childish cynic smugly says, "But not everyone will share a prayer request with you."
>
> That doesn't change either the question or the answer.
>
> #### *The answer is still, "Yes."*

How Can Prayer Walking Help Lutheran Education?

Pastor Garrett Knudson serves at Holy Cross Lutheran Church in Bordentown, New Jersey. I was invited by Pastor Knudson in 2010 to make a presentation regarding Prayer Walking to some leaders in his congregation. At that time, I shared the possibility of using Prayer Walking as way for the Church to reach the unchurched families with children enrolled in their Preschool.

The concept is basically very simple--when you have an Open House, position your Prayer Walkers in the most heavily used entry ways. As families enter the church, simply identify yourself, let the parent(s) know that you will be praying for the Preschool families and then ask the million dollar question--"How can we pray for you?"

After asking, "How can we pray for you?" the Prayer Walkers then distributed the Prayer requests received (typically about 30 responses) to the Prayer Chain to pray for these families. Also, the following Sunday, Pastor Knudson lifted up these prayers in their Sunday worship.

Through this process, the families coming to their Preschool have experienced that Holy Cross truly is a "house of prayer" and that there is a concern that runs deeper than attendance.

Another benefit of this is the strengthening of the relationship between Church and School. Sometimes, the two can feel separated. By Prayer Walking the Preschool, the Director and staff saw the desire of the Church to help them succeed.

In other churches I have worked with, the Directors / Principals have taken on the role of organizing the Prayer Walking in their school. The families who come to our schools know we are Christians; they know Christians are people of prayer. Our schools already have a much deserved reputation for excellence and faith; through Prayer Walking we reach out and strengthen the personal relationship between our ministry and these families. When we reach out with Prayer, people are touched with the power of the Holy Spirit. You can see it in their faces; you will hear it in the appreciation they respond with.

The next step is to develop an intentional plan for how the Church will follow up with the needs expressed in the Prayer Requests.

This is the "ministry of waiting on tables," which we read about in the first part of Acts 6; just as those widows had real, physical needs, so also people today who are crying out in prayer have needs to be met.

Some people say we feed people so they will want to hear the Gospel. This is wrong. We feed people because we have been fed at the Lord's Table and through His Word. Because we have heard the Gospel, the power of God's Word has changed us; there is power, life-changing power in the Word of God. Mercy ministry is not some gimmick to get people to the Gospel.

This all takes time; the results are the responsibility of the Holy Spirit. Our job is to be passionate about sharing the Good News, throwing the good seed as far and wide as possible. We already know that not all seed will yield the desired result; this does not stop us from the good works that God has prepared in advance for us to do.

President Matt Harrison has brought an intentional focus on Mercy ministry to our church body. This is a very good thing. There are many great ideas on Mercy ministry for your congregation available on our web site--www.lcms.org.

Prayer Walking is done for the purpose of ministry, mercy and multiplication. Mercy is "step two"; it is what takes the ministry of Prayer and builds the relational bridges so the multiplication of disciples can happen. Churches that demonstrate they take ministering to "the least of these" seriously, are repeatedly blessed by the Holy Spirit with increase. Mercy ministry is part of the Holy Spirit's plan for us to share the Gospel to a lost and dying world.

Another simple thing to do is train the teachers to ask parents / students for Prayer requests. These can be turned in to the Congregational Prayer Ministry Coordinator; nonmember families could be a focus.

How Can Prayer Help With Visitor Follow Up?

Shortly after moving into our new worship space in the Shadow Wood strip mall in Springfield, Missouri, I came into the office one weekday to find three police cars in the parking lot with their lights on. As I drove closer, I could see that a crime scene was being investigated; there was broken glass and some blood, and two women were grieving.

The business next to our church was a Christian-owned incentive company. I had introduced myself to the owner almost immediately; he was very friendly, giving a good testimony of his Christian faith, speaking highly of his church and giving me a sleeve of golf balls with Bible passages (which I still have).

I had never met the distraught women, so I went up and introduced myself. The one lady was the owner's wife and the other was their daughter. They shared with me that their husband / father was working late and had been assaulted and abducted; no one knew where he was or if he was even alive.

I invited the two women to come into our simple sanctuary; we sat down and prayed together. This would be the beginning of an investigation that took several weeks before it came to a rather surprising conclusion. In the meantime, hundreds of volunteers combed the fields around Springfield and untold thousands of police hours were spent tracking down leads. Eventually, it would come to light that the owner had faked his death and had run off with his girlfriend; he would be charged criminally for this and was also presented with a bill from the Police department.

In the meantime, I got to know their Pastor--the Rev. John Lindell, the founding Pastor of James River Assembly of God. I came to count John as a personal friend. When we built our church and had our "grand opening service," he sent over an arrangement of flowers that was bigger than anything I had ever seen (I still have the card he included).

Pastor Lindell had previously attempted a church plant in Kansas City; after a year of hard work he had one person to show for his efforts. To hear John tell the story, this single addition to his ministry had one focus when she came--debating him on every and any theological point. In frustration, Pastor Lindell began watching the truck-driving commercials on TV and considered another calling. So, he went to his denominational leaders and told them to stop wasting their money on him. His ecclesiastical supervisors suggested that he go to Springfield, Missouri, and meet with a small group of worshippers who were interested in starting a new church; at that time they were being served by a retired Pastor. John came to Springfield and the rest, as they say, is history. Today, over 5,000 attend worship services at James River AOG. John always shares his story of failure in Kansas City so that God gets the glory.

John and I would get together for lunch from time to time. Whenever we did, I always brought a list of questions to ask him and a notepad to take down his answers. One time, John shared something with me I will now share with you; it has to do with the power of prayer and effective visitor follow up.

Every Monday, John sits down with his staff and they go through the pile of cards filled out by first time visitors. The prospects are categorized by geography, probable ministry needs, potential ministry involvement and any connections they might have to current members.

John then takes his stack of cards and personally drives to the homes of these people on Monday night of each week. He brings with him a plate of cookies made by the ladies, some "sorry I missed you" cards to stick in the door in case the family is not at home, and his Bible.

John says, "It is always something to watch the reaction on the faces of the people when they see me at the door. It's like they can't believe the Pastor of this church (the largest in Springfield) has personally come to their home."

I asked John, "What are you trying to accomplish when you make a follow up visit to these homes?" John's answer should not be surprising, "To welcome them to our church; share a little about our vision and values; let them know where we came from and where it appears that God is taking us."

But then John shared this insight--"When I am talking with them and asking about their life, I listen to what they say. At the end of our time, before I go, I ask them if I can pray with them. They always say, 'Yes.' When I pray with them, I lift up those things they have shared with me. When we are done praying, I can tell they feel as if this Pastor and congregation care about them."

It is such a simple thing--ask people about their lives, listen, and then pray for these things. Make this a point of your follow up with first time visitors.

John and I hold different positions on important aspects of doctrine and practice; but we both rejoice that He holds us in the palm of His hand. Don't be too proud to sit down with your brothers and sisters in the faith, even if they are part of another tribe; God is at work there too. I can tell you, I always tried to follow John's focus on prayer in following up with the visitors who came to our church.

How Can Prayer Help With Membership Information Class?

Everything in Level Two of Congregational Prayer Ministry development is focused on Visitors; this question regarding Membership Class might seem as if it belongs in Level One because of its focus on Members.

I have chosen to include it in this section because one of the things we track regarding our Visitors to worship on Sunday morning is how many of them are becoming members.

Prayer Ministry can be a tremendous resource for your Membership Classes. By asking the perspective members, "How can we pray for you?" you will learn their needs / concerns / desires / joys. All these pieces of information should be helpful as you consider how they can best be assimilated into the ministry of your church.

Again, as you fold your hands for prayer, follow that by joining your hands for care. Having learned the needs of your perspective members, let them learn the power of Mercy Ministry in your congregation.

As they see the connection of the outgrowth from Prayer to Care, they will personally experience God's grace communicated through His Body.

Also, perspective members may share Prayer Requests for unchurched friends. This opportunity may be a good work prepared in advance by God for your ministry to reach out in a very natural and comfortable way; based on Prayer, not polished gimmicks.

Action Questions:

  *What percentage of your new members are still active one year later? _____

  *Who is the youngest member to start a new ministry in your Church? _____

  *Who could organize an effort to learn and care for the needs of the newest members? _____

Mission team from Christ Our Savior Lutheran Church in Louisburg, KS (with Pr. Andy Keltner)
is Prayer Walking in Jersey City, NJ

Christ Our Savior helped our Kenyan congregation- Tumaini Kristo have the first VBS in their storefront
church on Martin Luther King Drive; over 85 children came during the week.

The Jersey City Municipal Council gave us a
Resolution of Commendation for the work of
our Mission Teams and Kenyan congregation
in serving the community; the Council specifically
thanked us for Prayer Walking.

Lutheran Women in Mission.

VII. Prayer Improves Community Outreach-- Loving Our Neighbors as Ourselves

What Is the Connection Between Prayer and Loving Our Neighbors as Ourselves?

When we confess our sins in worship, often we admit, "… I have not loved my neighbor as myself." What does this mean? Certainly not loving our neighbor as ourselves includes those times we are rude to our neighbor (especially if we include other drivers on the highway in the category of "neighbor"). We would agree that "not loving our neighbor as ourselves" also includes those times when we drive home in the evening, exhausted after a full day of work, and as we pass our neighbor's home, see their garage door up. The sun has set, darkness invites temptation from any desperate person; do we stop and tell our neighbor that their property is at risk or turn a blind eye and begin to wonder what is for dinner?

The 10 Commandments are divided in two parts by many Christians. The first part covers our relationship with God; the second part covers our relationship with our neighbor.

Luther said that there is no greater way to fulfill this second part than through prayer. Why? Because, there is no greater Person to seek help for our neighbor from than God. Certainly, we should help our neighbor with a plumber, electrician, lawyer or doctor if needed; but really, no one can take care of our neighbor like God can. Amen?

So, you see, when we confess, "… I have not loved my neighbor as myself," we are also confessing that we have not been in prayer for our neighbor as much as we pray for ourselves.

Discipleship Question: Will we ask the Holy Spirit to help us pray more for our neighbor? _____

This is true isn't it? I mean, it's not hard to pray for your wife when she has cancer; it's not hard to pray for yourself when your job is on the line; it's not hard to pray for your children when they go off to college or the military. It is very easy and natural to pray for us and ours. Not so much for our neighbor. Most of us never pray for our neighbor by name, let alone offer specific petitions.

Which brings us to the connection between Prayer and loving our neighbors--none of us are mind readers. If we are going to pray for our neighbors, we need to know our neighbors and we need to know their needs. There is a very simple way to do this--ask them, "How can I pray for you?"

When we learn our neighbor's need, we then bring them before our Father in prayer. Since we care for our neighbor and their Prayer concern / Praise report, we will seek them out in the near future and inquire as to their current situation regarding the Prayer request they shared.

Scripture tells us that when one part of the body hurts, the whole body hurts. You will hurt for your neighbor because of Prayer. Your heart will break as people share aspects of their lives you would never have imagined they were struggling with.

This is where the whole body of Christ comes in. This is why it is so important for your Church to develop a functional Mercy Ministry Leadership team and for your church to have a Congregational Prayer Coordinator. Most members will serve the Prayer Walking effort through Mercy Ministry; providing care and compassion to those who share Prayer requests with the Prayer Walkers.

You are not in this Spiritual battle by yourself. God has brought you into His bride, the Church. A wise old Pastor said, "The church will divide your sorrows and multiply your joys." When you share the needs of your neighbor with your Mercy Ministry Leadership Team, the other members of your church will be blessed to have the opportunity to do good works that were prepared in advance; you will bless other members with the opportunity for their Spiritual muscles to grow and develop in service to others. Your neighbor will be blessed beyond what they imagined when they responded to your question, "How can I pray for you?" Prayer opens the door for Care, which in turn helps build the relationships through which Planting new House Churches happen. This is not rocket science.

Prayer Walking in Newark, New Jersey

One of my friends and partners in mission is the Rev. Dr. Scott Seidler, Senior Pastor for Concordia Lutheran Church in Kirkwood, Missouri. Scott is an incredibly gifted speaker, with a great vision for mission; on a personal level, he is one of the most caring Pastors you will ever know. Pastor Seidler has laid an incredible challenge at the feet of his members--their goal is for 80% of the members to be personally involved in missions (local, national or international). As a good mission partner, Pastor Seidler wanted to visit and see first-hand the work that Concordia supports. So, he and Jeremy Becker, the Family Life Minister, came to New Jersey. We had begun Prayer Walking in Newark, so they were very excited to come along on a Prayer Walking event. At that time, Pastor Bill Klettke was the District President for New Jersey. When Bill heard that Scott was coming out, he said he would like to see what this Prayer Walking was all about also. No pressure.

In Newark, a city the size of St. Louis, we have one LCMS church property. There are two congregations worshipping in the same space. The original congregation--Redeemer, Newark, has about four people in worship on a typical Sunday. The newer congregation is made up of Liberian immigrants; they typically have about 50 in worship. A Liberian immigrant, Pastor Lawrence Gboeah serves as a worker Priest and is called as the Pastor for both congregations. Pastor Gboeah is a graduate of Concordia Seminary in St. Louis (Pastor Gboeah's name is pronounced "boy").

Pastor Gboeah is a good friend and dedicated co-worker in the Harvest. When I first met him, after we got to talking, I asked if his wife made fufu and soup (a staple in West African villages, like the one I grew up in). He smiled and said, "Yes. My wife will make some for you." Jesus invited Himself to dinner; so do I. When I took the first bite of his wife's fufu and soup, it transported me back in time to my youth growing up in a village in Nigeria. This was the first fufu and soup that I had eaten in over 30 years. Definitely worth the wait!

So, I got in touch with Pastor Gboeah and let him know we were going to have some guests for our next Prayer Walking outreach. Pastor Gboeah and one of his elders came with Scott, Jeremy, Bill and me. We worked our way through the neighborhood, first opening the gates in front of each postage stamp sized yard, walking up the sidewalk and knocking on doors. When the door opened, I would greet the person and say, "We are praying for the neighborhood tonight; we would love to pray for you; how can we pray for you?"

I will never forget one house we called on. Scott and I were walking together, leading the group, catching up on old times (we were classmates at the Seminary). When we got to the front door of this simple home, I knocked on the door. A small girl answered the door; I would guess she was no more than four or five years old. I asked her, "Is your mother home?" She said her mother was home, then went to get her.

This home was very simple; you could hear everything going on inside. When the girl found her mother, she said, "Mom, there are five men outside looking for you." Sounded like something my daughter Grace might say.

The mother came to the door and I introduced myself, shaking her hand. I explained that we were praying for the neighborhood, that we would love to pray for her and then simply asked, "How can we pray for you?"

I will never forget her reply--she looked me in the eyes and said, "I got served with my divorce papers today. You can pray for my two daughters and myself." I cleared my throat, looked at my watch and smiling, said to her, "We are going to be praying at the Lutheran Church in about 15 minutes and we will pray for you." I pointed at Pastor Gboeah and continued, "This man (Pastor Gboeah) is the Pastor of the congregation He and his members will make sure that you don't go through this alone."

The mother looked at me and said, "This is the first time that a Church has ever come to my home." I replied, "Praise God!" Each person on the team offered words of encouragement and hope to her. We took down her information and soon afterwards were back at the church lifting up this family and others from the community in prayer to our Father in Heaven.

This is the power of Prayer.

In a matter of minutes we were able to connect with this family in a way that no slick advertising from an ad agency could have done. We had established a Christ focused relationship with this family, immediately. There were no gimmicks or galas required.

I am just kind of old fashioned; I believe that Jesus did everything required when He died on the cross to pay for our sins and was raised from the dead three days later. That is power! The Good News of His grace, expressed through the loving touch of His Church, connects souls to Him.

> Prayer Walking does not require church coffee mugs, fliers, tracks, videos, boxes of salt, light bulbs or any of the other trinkets and trash peddled in the name of outreach. It is very simple--just ask people, "How can I pray for you?"

Research companies will sell churches reams of demographic information. Churches are told, "You have to know your community." And these companies can tell you all sorts of information (it is almost scary what they know about us). From their database, you will learn that your neighbors have 1.25 dogs; 1.75 children; 4 magazine subscriptions; watch 4.8 hours of TV every night and on and on…

But none of this information equals a single relationship and if you are not careful, you will spend hours and hours studying it.

> If you want to truly know your neighborhood, go out into it! If you want to know how to minister to your neighborhood, ask them! Just ask, "How can I pray for you?"!!
>
> The people who share Prayer Requests with you are the ripe fruit; they are the ones you should fold hands in prayer over and then join hands together to provide care to (Mercy Ministry).

The Holy Spirit has already equipped you for every good work. Trust in His instruments--Prayer, the Word, the Sacraments, the assembly of believers. What is Madison Avenue going to teach you?

I know because I have tried it the other way as a Church Planter. I have done the massive mailings; I have had the big speakers; I have held concerts. It is not hard to get 1,000 people to come to your church. I've done it; trust me.

Churches try the attractional outreach method for many reasons--it takes no personal commitment to write a check and pay for TV spots; it is more comfortable welcoming someone to your games and festivities, <u>but when they are done enjoying watching their children play with the clown do they know Christ any better?</u>

My wife says, "In the end, ministry is about building relationships with people." Dear God, what a blessing she is! If 1,000 people come to your attractional outreach event and you don't build any relationships with them, <u>you have not done anything for the LORD.</u>

How did Jesus call His <u>disciples</u>? One and two at a time. Fact of the matter is, there were times when Jesus intentionally <u>avoided</u> the crowds who wanted to be with Him, so that He could spend time alone with the disciples, mentoring and growing them in their faith, preparing them for ministry.

In my time as a Mission Strategist, I have come to appreciate more and more the importance of Mercy Ministry in conjunction with Prayer Walking. <u>As great as Prayer Walking is, it is just the beginning of the Discipleship process.</u>

If your church does not have a strong Mercy Ministry Leadership team in place, following up with real, physical ministry to those in need, the potential that exists in every Prayer Request will be missed. <u>Three basic steps- Step One is Prayer Walking (first with members, then visitors, then the community); Step Two is Care Ministry; Step Three is Planting House Churches.</u>

The fact of the matter is, <u>your church most likely already has a Social Concerns committee</u>; this is a natural hub for your Mercy Ministry. Your Youth Ministry is a natural spoke; so is your LWML (Lutheran Women's Missionary League); your Seniors' ministry would be a strong partner; the list goes on. You probably already have one made up in your mind as you think about your own congregation.

There is an old saying, "People don't care how much you know until they know how much you care." <u>The Mercy Ministry Leadership Team of your church, coordinating the care to those who have shared Prayer requests, makes your care for others real in their lives.</u> There is no single organizational approach to this effort that works in every congregation. Organize according to **your** gifts and situation.

<u>Why Don't People Like Visits from Mormons / Jehovah's Witnesses?</u>

Almost everyone has had that knock at their door; you look outside and there they are--two young men with white shirts on, black name tag on their left shirt pocket. Mormons. What do you do? Answer the door and you know you are in for a half hour (or longer) debate.

You get the same dreaded feeling when the doorbell rings and looking out the peephole you see a couple of young ladies with a satchel over their shoulders; when you look closer, you see "Watchtower" on the magazines. They have a smile on their faces, but smiling is not something you can bring yourself to do.

Why don't people like it when Mormons or Jehovah's Witnesses come calling? _____

Beyond the obvious theological divide, you know there is no way you are going to convince them of the Trinity. Once you go down that road, you quickly learn that trying to explain that Jesus is God with a capital "G" is futile because they will respond, "We also believe that Jesus is god" (note the small "g").

What really makes it unpleasant, is that you <u>know</u> there is going to be an argument and this is Saturday, your day off! You didn't work all week to have to deal with this.

Prayer Walking is as different from the Mormons / Jehovah's Witnesses (JW) as night is from day.

Mormons and JWs spend hours and hours training in how to "answer" objections. And when you train this hard, you are looking for a chance to try your mettle. The truth is, they go out expecting arguments.

Besides investing time in training for "answering" objections, these groups bring materials with them that they feel duty bound to force into your hands.

Common manners teach us that when people say, "No thanks," we should respect them and leave them alone. For some reason, this almost never happens when they come calling.

Here is why Prayer Walking is different from what the Mormons / Jehovah's Witnesses do:
1. We are only going to ask you one question, "How can I pray for you?"
2. We are not going to bring any tracts to give you.
3. We do not spend any time training Prayer Walkers how to debate doctrine.

> We are not Mormons / JWs; therefore, we are not going to act like them.

Here is the thing--*when you try to force what you want on someone else, they almost never want it*. But, if you reach out in love and ask them, "How can I pray for you?" you will get an entirely different response.

Prayer Walking is about taking the trash out of people's lives; not trying to shove some more stuff into their homes. Then there is this: the next time Mormons or Jehovah's Witnesses knock on your door, ask them, before they leave, "How can I pray for you?"

What Questions Typically Come up Regarding Prayer Walking?

I have had the opportunity to train hundreds of churches in Prayer Walking and here are some of the questions that usually come up at this point.

1. "You mean we don't tell them what church we are from?"

If people want to know what church you are from, what will they do? They will ask. And they do. It is really cool when you have asked someone for a Prayer request and as the conversation develops, they say to you, "What church are you from?" Now, the energy is flowing in the right direction. They want to know about your church. A great reply is, "Since you asked, let me tell you…"

Do you see how different that is from walking up to someone's home and beginning by saying, "I am Jim and I am a member at Redeemer Lutheran Church…"?

Do you remember the commercial where the young girl has just been accepted to a prestigious college; she runs in the living room to tell her parents the good news but all that the father can think is, "How much money is this going to cost? And how am I going to pay for it?" Listen to me--when we go up to someone's home and say, "I am with xyz church…." Just know this, all they can hear you saying right now is, "We are **broke**; we need people in our pews and **what we really want is your money**."

Trust me.

2. "Shouldn't we carry a business card to give them?"

Here is the problem. If you start by bringing business cards with you, you are going to end up bringing all sorts of fliers. Before long you will look and act very similar to the Mormons / JWs.

It is best if you can simply introduce yourself to others. Ministry is very simple; it gets down to relationships with others. Extending your hand to shake theirs is much more personal than starting by holding a business card up to their face.

Having said this, you may have someone ask you for more information; you may even have someone ask you if you have a brochure regarding the basic aspects of your faith or what services your church provides.

Again, it is <u>great</u> when <u>they</u> ask for these things and since you don't have one with you, it gives you the perfectly honest opportunity to tell them, "I will bring one of those with me after we have prayed for you and I check to see how you are doing."

3. "What do I say if they say something that is completely wrong?"
☺ Smile.

Just smile and thank them for sharing their thought. Then, you might say something like this, "My Pastor really loves talking about this. Could we get together?"

It is important when you come across someone who is very antagonistic to let your Congregational Prayer Coordinator know. This will be something that everyone involved with this ministry will want to spend time in Prayer and God's Word, reflecting on how best to proceed. We have to seek the <u>ripe</u> fruit.

4. "What if they want to pray right now?"
Great.

Again, it is <u>great</u> when <u>they</u> want to do this. You should also be sensitive to the Holy Spirit's leading; you may feel it is right for you to ask them if you can pray with them right then and there. I have done this many times. The important thing is <u>not</u> having your own goal of getting everyone to pray with you. We have to seek the <u>ripe</u> fruit.

5. "What if they share something personal with us; should we have the church pray for this?"
When you introduce yourself, you say, "I'm _____; we are praying for the neighborhood and we would love to pray for you." You are there with other church members, so they are sharing this with the group. Before you leave, you will tell them again that you are getting together with other members to pray. They have shared this Prayer request with you because they <u>want</u> you to have others praying also.

6. "What if they invite us inside?"
This does happen. Use your sanctified common sense. There will be times when this makes good ministry sense and there will be times when it won't. A good rule of thumb is to check how your fellow Prayer Walkers feel about this offer; if there is one who does not feel comfortable going inside, then you should respect your co-worker and graciously decline.

7. "What if they offer to give us money?"
This will also happen, especially if you are Prayer Walking a business district (covered below). It is <u>vital</u> that you <u>decline</u> their offer. I know, a church turning down money?!! Yes. You will gain so much more in the end; but just fall into the stereotype if you accept. Listen, we know the theology, right? God's grace is a free gift to us; our gift of Prayer is free also.

8. "What if they say, 'I don't have a Prayer request'?"
Well, let's think about this for a minute; why would people say they don't have a Prayer request...
> -they truly don't have one
> -they are in a rush and just don't have the time right now to talk
> -they belong to a church and feel as if they would be betraying their Pastor if someone else prayed for them (trust me, it happens)
> -they are atheists

Let's look at that list of reasons for just a minute. How many of them are personally directed against you? None. In other words, <u>don't take offense where none was given.</u>

Actually, I think the biggest reason people will say they don't have a Prayer request for you is not even on that list. <u>The biggest reason is simply because you caught them unprepared.</u> When you go Prayer Walking, the people you speak with do not know you are coming (unless this is a repeat visit). When you ask someone, "How can I pray for you?" the first time, <u>it's not as if they knew you were going to do this.</u> It should not surprise you when they don't reply, "Well, I was expecting you to ask me this." or, "Let me see now, where did I put that prepared list of Prayer requests to give you?"

> *9. "Do we need a permit?"*

Prayer Walking is not solicitation. "No soliciting" signs are intended to protect businesses from panhandlers or individuals attempting to sell products or services to the patrons of the business with the posted sign, on that businesses property (talk about nerve!).

We are not taking money, goods or services, <u>even if it is offered</u>. We are praying <u>for</u> people. In the business district of Westfield, Pastor Paul Kritsch and Redeemer Lutheran have planted a House Church through Prayer Walking. The Chamber of Commerce has been very supportive of Pastor Kritsch's ministry of Prayer Walking the businesses; they think it is fantastic that a church is reaching out to lift up the spirits of the workforce in their community. The local newspaper has sent reporters to go along on Prayer Walking excursions; the resulting coverage has always been very positive. Even the local online newspaper has covered their Prayer Walking efforts in the business district, also in a very positive way. Who says the media can't help Jesus?   Sometimes, people will ask me, "What if a neighborhood is gated?" Seriously? <u>We have to respect the laws.</u> Now, if you have a church member who lives in the gated community, that may be a different matter.

On a related note: if you are ever Prayer Walking and giving out fliers (which you already know, I don't recommend), don't stick them in a mailbox; this is a big no-no.

What Do You Need to Start Prayer Walking Your Community?

(1) Congregational Prayer Coordinator--they track all Prayer Requests received by the Congregation and provide the Congregation with statistical updates on the Prayer Ministry.

(2) Mercy Ministry Leadership Team--coordinates the Mercy Ministry response to the Prayer Requests.

(3) The Blessing of the Congregation and Pastor.

(4) Prayer Walkers--A smaller group than those actually providing the Mercy Ministry follow up.

(5) Successfully providing Congregational Prayer and Mercy Ministry to members and visitors already.

<u>Each congregation is unique; tailor this to your circumstances.</u>

Why Is There an Order to the Development of Congregational Prayer Ministry?

The Holy Spirit is in charge of the Church. How He works in each congregation is unique, yet at the same time, we know certain things never change: there is power in the Word of God--it is through hearing the Word of God that people come to salvation (Romans 10:17); this will never change.

The same thing is true regarding the development of Congregational Prayer Ministry--on the one hand, how each church develops is unique; at the same time, we observe certain things to be true.

This book has intentionally begun by looking at Congregational Prayer Ministry <u>first for members</u>. This is something everyone in your church should support. This does not require talking with anyone not already connected with your church. The biggest growth step at this stage will be choosing a Congregational Prayer Ministry Coordinator and the formation of a Mercy Ministry Leadership team.

The development of a single list of Prayer requests from members and tracking how the church follows up with them will not happen overnight. This will require work, coordinating the efforts of the ministries already in place within your church to serve best the needs identified through the Prayer requests received. At this stage, you are laying the foundation for the rest of God's house of Prayer. The role of the Mercy Ministry Leadership team is one of coordinating, not controlling.

<u>The next Chapter focused on how to minister to those who visit</u> our Church or attend an attractional outreach event of the congregation. Again, the level of comfort should be relatively high--these are people who have chosen to come to you. We are not talking at this stage about going out to our neighbors and asking them how we can pray for them.

After you have developed a strong Congregational Prayer Ministry <u>for your members and visitors</u>, the next step of reaching out <u>to your neighbors</u> will come much more smoothly because you have taken the time to "test drive" the ministry "in house."

Your Mercy Ministry Leadership Team will mature in the first two stages of development, which will prepare it for the third level of ministry--serving our neighbor through Prayer Walking. <u>Before you begin Prayer Walking in the community, be sure to have successfully grown through the first two levels (members and visitors)</u>. Seriously.

Jim Rinaldi- chairman of Redeemer Lutheran Church and Pr. Paul Kritsch;
Redeemer was an early adopter of our Prayer and Planting strategy.

What Is Prayer Walking?

> **_Prayer walking is simply asking people, "How can I pray for you?"_**

After collecting the Prayer Requests, the Prayer Walkers get back together and pray for the needs of the neighbors. These Prayer Requests are then turned in to the Congregational Prayer Ministry Coordinator and the Mercy Ministry Leadership team for their follow up. The Prayer Walkers will also follow up and let those who have shared Prayer requests know that they have been prayed for, see how they are doing and update the Prayer request originally received. In this way, the Congregational Prayer Ministry Coordinator and your Mercy Ministry Leadership Team can be most effective.

The vast majority of people participating in Congregational Prayer Ministry are not Prayer Walkers. The truth is, a single pair of Prayer Walkers will generate enough "business" to keep a hundred other members busy with following up through Mercy Ministry.

It is important to understand that Prayer Walking is not the end; it is a means to the end.

When I was in the Army's 12th Special Forces Group, we had a saying: "Parachuting is not my job; it is how I get to my job." **Prayer Walking is like that; it is a vehicle; it is a means to get to the work of the Gospel and that work will happen primarily through the Mercy Ministry of your congregation as it follows up with the Prayer requests the Prayer Walkers collect**.

In the military, there is a ratio of how many people it takes to support every Soldier or Marine on the front line. It is helpful to use this understanding regarding the ratio of Prayer Walkers to every other person involved in this Spiritual battle.

> Every role is important. Benjamin Franklin supposedly said, "For the lack of a nail, the horse's shoe was not shod; for the lack of a horse shoe, the rider could not be sent; for the lack of a rider, the message was not delivered; for the lack of the message, the battle was lost."
> Every person and every piece of Prayer and Care Ministry matters.

Prayer Walking in East Orange, New Jersey.

Prayer Walking Report--Side A

Date: _____ House Church: _____
Date of our House Church's Next Community Fellowship: _____
House Church Target Group: _____
Numerical Goal(s) for our Prayer Team today: _____

Prayer Team Member #1: _____
   Ph# _____ Email: _____

Prayer Team Member #2: _____
   Ph# _____ Email: _____

Follow Up With My Prayer Team's PREVIOUS Contacts:
   Address: _____
   Name(s): _____
   Update: _____
   _____

   Address: _____
   Name(s): _____
   Update: _____
   _____

Hello, my name is _____ *Hola, mey yamo* _____
How are you? *Como esta usted*
Do you speak English? *Hable Engles?*
We are praying for the community *Estamos orando por la comunidad*
How can we pray for you? *Como oramos por Usted?*
What is your name? *Como se yama?*
Please write your prayer *Por favor, escriba un oración suyo*
Our Savior House Church *Nuestro Salvador Iglesia en casa*
Pastor *Pastor* _____
We hope you have a great day! *Esperamos que tenga un gran día*
God bless you! *Que Dios te bendiga* ☺

House Church Planter Training Track
Rev James D. Buckman, Missionary (417) 844.6989
www.HouseChurchPlanter.com

This is formatted so that you can get two of these out of a single page of 8.5" x 11' paper. Just set up the document in landscape view.

Side B (next pg.) goes on the backside of the paper. It is also set up to get two copies from a single 8.5" x 11" page; when that paper is cut in half. The finished document measures 8.5" x 5.5".

Side A	Side A
(Side B on back)	(Side B on back)

"Leaders and Learners" is the New Jersey District's ministry certification venue for lay leaders; check with your District. Our website (www.HouseChurchPlanter.com) is open for anyone to use.

** Look for future House Church Planters among the people you are reaching out to--*Disciples Make Disciples*

Prayer Walking Report--Side B

My Prayer Team's NEW Home / Business Contacts:

Address: _____

Name(s): _____

Prayer Request(s): _____

_____

Church Ministry That Will Follow Up: _____

_____

Address: _____

Name(s): _____

Prayer Request(s): _____

_____

Church Ministry That Will Follow Up: _____

_____

Address: _____

Name(s): _____

Prayer Request(s): _____

_____

Church Ministry That Will Follow Up: _____

_____

Address: _____

Name(s): _____

Prayer Request(s): _____

_____

Church Ministry That Will Follow Up: _____

_____

Summary of Statistics re Outreach to Homes / Businesses
My Prayer Team (PT) / Our House Church (HC)

\# Contacted: _____ (PT) _____ (HC)

\# Answered: _____ (PT) _____ (HC)

\# of Prayer Requests Received: _____ (PT) _____ (HC)

Start Time of Prayer Walk: _____ End Time: _____

It is important to track your actual ministry. Important numbers to look at: the percentage of people who shared a prayer request with you that you <u>actually</u> spoke to. If someone wasn't home, you can't think of them as "not sharing a Prayer request" because you don't know if they would or would not have.

As you follow up with Mercy Ministry to the homes that share Prayer requests, you will need to honestly evaluate each home / individual to determine if this relationship should continue. You only have so much time and there are <u>lots</u> of people who need to be reached. You will meet people who really like what you are doing and are very easy to talk with, especially if they are strong Christians belonging to a church. You probably need to spend less time with them and more time with those who have fallen away / are lost.

Twenty Ways to Use Prayer Walking in Community Ministry:

"It's kind of interesting: Jesus sees the multitudes, and they are harassed like sheep without a shepherd. He doesn't say, go, feed them. He doesn't say go, do this, or act, or make a plan or anything else. **You know what the first thing He says the Church should do? Pray**. Pray that the Lord of the harvest sends workers." (LCMS President-Elect Matt Harrison in the August 10, 2010 edition of the *Reporter*)

The first thing we should do in the enterprise of sharing the Gospel is pray. Prayer <u>itself</u> can be a highly effective way to reach out with Gospel.

This is the essence of Prayer Walking as I teach it: There are countless variations / applications, but Prayer Walking really comes down to keeping the Commandments regarding our neighbor by taking enough interest in your neighbor to simply and humbly ask them the eternally powerful question, **"How can I pray for you?"**

In this chapter I will share with you how to do the twenty Prayer Outreach approaches. <u>These approaches are not just theory; they are in actual use by real Lutherans today.</u> You will meet them and hear their story; I pray you are inspired to follow the Holy Spirit's guiding in <u>your</u> heart.

1. Residential Prayer Walking / Prayer Survey

One Saturday morning as I was making French toast for my children (one of my favorite things to do), my youngest daughter, Grace, who was six at the time, asked me, "Dad, can I go prayer walking with you?" See, on Saturdays, I work with various churches in New Jersey helping them establish new immigrant worshipping communities through the simple process of Prayer Walking their communities.

I was almost speechless to hear her words of faith. I said, "Sure." Then, my oldest daughter, Sarah, asked me if she could come also; I smiled and said, "Yes." Then my three sons, Jacob, Jim and John all asked if they could come. I said, "Yes!"

On the way to the apartment complex in Parsippany, New Jersey (400 units; 75% of which are Asian Indian), I wanted to review with my children what we would be doing. Now, they have heard me teach / preach on Prayer Walking a hundred times (at least); so they know my stuff. They know that I teach people not to bring anything with them when they go Prayer Walking, no coffee mugs (don't you have enough already?), no coupons to McDonalds (didn't Jesus do everything necessary on the cross?), no eco-friendly light bulbs and no tracts (who doesn't love seeing a Watchtower magazine in the purse of a Jehovah's Witness when you peek through the peep hole of your door? Me neither).

But I digress. So, I asked my children what we do when we go Prayer Walking. My daughter Sarah lowered her voice to imitate me and said, "Well, we don't bring any coffee mugs or coupons to McDonald's." I waited until we had all finished laughing and asked, "What else can you tell me about Prayer Walking?" My oldest son, Jacob, said, "Well it's pretty simple. <u>All we are going to do is go to people's homes and ask them how we can pray for them.</u>" I looked in the rear view mirror and thought to myself--he is exactly right; it really is that simple.

So, we got to the apartment complex and I asked my children, "Who is going to ring the doorbell?" My middle son, Jim, immediately said, "I will." Then I said, "Who is going to ask the question?" Jacob immediately said, "I will."

So, the six of us (my wife was spending a much deserved day of rest and relaxation with one of her best friends) went up to the first apartment. Jim and Jacob walked up to the door. I was standing with my three other children on the sidewalk. Jim rang the doorbell and an Asian Indian lady in her 50's answered. I wish I had a hidden camera like Jay Leno. My son looked at her and waited for her to acknowledge him so that he can ask "the question." This lady looked at my boys, shook her head and looked at me with a look of, "Why are you here?" I smiled, looked at her and then slowly turned to look at my son Jacob. Her eyes followed mine and she was once again looking at my son Jacob standing in front of her. She shook her head again and looked back at me. I again smiled and slowly turned to look at Jacob. She again followed my eyes and again found herself looking at Jacob. My son wanted to ask her "the question" and he was going to get his chance.

This time, when her eyes rested on Jacob, he said, "Hi, I'm Jacob. My family and I are praying for people. How can we pray for you?" I wish you could have seen her face. You could see her heart just melt. Here was a <u>teenager</u> asking her how he could pray for her. Teenagers don't do this! They are supposed to be self-centered and disrespectful to adults. She shared a request of prayer for a loved one's health. And then, I was so proud; Jacob remembered to ask what her name was. We took down her name, apartment number and prayer request.

In the next hour, we spoke with six families. Five of them shared prayer requests. Two asked us to come in right then and there and pray with them on the spot. My sons Jacob and Jim would reverse their roles; sometimes Jacob would ask "the question"; sometimes Jim would.

Jacob was 13 and Jim was 12. Neither of them have a Masters of Divinity. Neither was wearing a clerical collar.

Can I tell you the truth? **<u>They got a better percentage of responses than I usually do</u>**. If you have children / youth in your church, one of the best things you can do is invite them to go Prayer Walking with you.

And if your youth agree to come along with you, celebrate! Celebrate their participation, their faithfulness in the Priesthood of all Believers, their doing the good works that God prepared in advance.

Residential Prayer Walking is very simple and highly effective. As with any kind of Prayer Walking, this is designed to help you build Christ-focused relationships with people from the very beginning of your acquaintance with them. Very little time has to be wasted on trivial conversation. No effort / resources are expended by the congregation on silly gimmicks to get people to come to church (trust me, as a Pastor who helped plant two churches, I know all about resorting to gimmicks.)

Apartment complexes can be a very good use of your time, IF the doors are on the outside of the building. Some apartment complexes have interior hallways, with interior doors; these complexes sometimes have controlled access through a main lobby. In cases like this, it is best if you have members who live in this dwelling who can personally reach out to their neighbors.

Urban Prayer Walking holds perhaps the greatest potential. The population density provides a tremendous opportunity to quickly reach multitudes of people.

You can "tweak" this Prayer Walking approach and turn it into a "Prayer Survey" by simply changing your question to, "What do you think we should be praying about for this community?" When you detect interest on the part of the person sharing their answer, God may be providing you with the opportunity to develop a partner in ministry; which you might be able to determine by simply asking, "You seem pretty passionate about that; is this something you would like to help with?"

2. Prayer Walking the New Move-ins to Your Community

This is an old idea improved through Prayer. For years, businesses like "The Welcome Wagon" offered churches and businesses the opportunity to get their material in front of the new move-ins to the community--for a fee.

You can gather the names of new move-ins to your community yourself. There are businesses who will sell you these lists. They are generally fairly accurate--they collect names from real estate records, utility hook up records, etc.--in years gone by they would get the names of people with new phone numbers, but as land lines diminish, this source for names is shrinking.

In this variation of Prayer Walking, your team simply calls on the new move-ins; welcome them and then say, "We are praying for all the new move-ins; we would love to pray for you. How can we pray for you?"

Prayer Walking in East Orange; part of planting a House Church there.

One way of reaching out into our communities that has been around for a decade and shown results is- **"Planting Gospel Seeds While Serving Human Needs"**. Founder and lead trainer, Rev. Carlos Hernandez describes the approach as, "An experiential, hands-on Congregational Revitalization Process".

Some of the key components of this approach are:

1. A community outreach training process
2. Christ's compassion- the mercy and caring relationship
3. Verifying, in person, self-study demographics
4. Hands-on experience conversing with the community
5. Hands-on Agency Interview Training
6. Hands-on training going door-to-door! – Residential Interviews
7. "Lending" congregational leadership to the community – building the relationship
8. Modeling Jesus own practice of first inquiring about critical needs
9. Significant contacts and close relationships – fertile ground for planting gospel seeds

For more information or to schedule an on-site training, contact Rev. Carlos Hernandez at 314-956-2005 or carlos.hernandez@lcms.org

Carlos Hernandez, M.Div., STM, serves as the Director of Church and Community Development in the LCMS Office of National Missions.

3. Business District Prayer Walking

Jesus was often found in the market place. He was very comfortable going into a person's place of business and recruiting them away from their occupation in order for them to become His disciples. He didn't care if they worked for a family business; He took them too:

> "*Going on from there, he saw two other brothers, James son of Zebedee and his brother John. They were in a boat with their father Zebedee, preparing their nets. Jesus called them, and immediately they left the boat and their father and followed him.*" (Matthew 4:21-22)

Pastor Paul Kritsch is the First Vice President of the New Jersey District; he has served Redeemer in Westfield, New Jersey, for over 20 years. He and his members have a vision for starting a new worshipping community they have called "Anchor of Hope" (taken from Hebrews 6:19).

In the winter of 2009, Pastor Kritsch and his church plant team began implementing a strategy of Business District Prayer Walking. Ten months later, a core group of 30-40 owners and employees from the business district of Westfield gather with Pastor Kritsch and his members for worship, prayers and fellowship at the Robert Treat Deli.

Business District Prayer Walking is basically the same thing as Residential Prayer Walking except that you are taking prayer requests from owners and employees right in their place of employment. A couple of suggestions specific to Business District Prayer Walking:

-Go to the businesses when they don't have a lot of customers (4 p.m. is a good time).
-Don't bother the customers.
-Have the same Prayer Walking team members follow up with the same businesses.
-Do not accept any offers of cash from the merchants (and this will happen).

Prayer Walking is not the ultimate goal. Gathering people into worshipping communities where they experience the grace of God through His Son is the goal.

For every Christian who attends church there are three Christians who have no interest in going to a typical looking church building. Yet, where do we put the majority of our local church's budget? Into the building and staffing for events at the building we call "church."

Greg Kasich is a co-owner of the Robert Treat Deli. When we set out to plant Anchor of Hope, Jim Rinaldi, a member of Redeemer and great man of faith, suggested that we meet for our Bible study time at the Robert Treat Deli, which we did. Through this we met Greg, who became interested in our ministry of Prayer Walking and the vision to plant a House Church for the owners and employees in the Westfield business district. Greg was raised Catholic, but over the years had slipped away. Today, he is a member of Redeemer and in training to be an elder of the church. Greg and his family make the Deli available for Anchor of Hope whenever it is needed and at no cost. Greg and his family have been in the Deli business for generations. Every day a hundred people come through his place of business, and every day Greg probably shares the Anchor of Hope story with at least 20 or 30 people. Do the math. It's a no brainer.

One of the keys to achieving the numerical and Spiritual growth that God has in store for your ministry is the identification, recruitment and training of the Priesthood of all Believers. For Redeemer or any church involved with a Business District Prayer Walking ministry, the Pastors and people must be completely committed to the development of leaders who will work under the authority and direction of their called Pastor in conjunction with the board of elders.

Another key to keep in prayer from the very beginning is for God to reveal His will and for the local church to follow it regarding the long term status of this group that has been gathered through the Business District Prayer Walking. Is God's vision for this to become a free standing congregation that has its own constitution; a satellite ministry, or is God's vision something else?

Having begun this outreach through prayer, <u>be sure to continue in prayer</u>.

4. Workplace Prayer Ministry

Earlier I shared how you can begin Business District Prayer Walking; this is a potential development that can come out of a Prayer Ministry to businesses.

I have seen Prayer be a very effective way to reach into the workplace. In 2010, I had the opportunity to do a Mission Sunday with Pastor Paul Appold and the members of Trinity Lutheran in Lansing, Illinois.

After worship services and Bible study, we had a lunch with Pastor Appold and some key leaders he had gathered to learn about Prayer Walking. I shared with them that we could either go Prayer Walking in a residential neighborhood or in their business district; that it would be their choice. The group chose to go Prayer Walking in their business district.

Briefly, I shared that what we would do is look for businesses that were not busy, because we did not want to hinder the businesses. When we found one that didn't seem busy, we would enter and find an employee or owner and simply share with them, "We are praying for the employees and owners in our business district; we would love to pray for you. How can we pray for you?" I let them know that I would demonstrate this to them and that they could try their hand at it afterwards if they wanted.

So, I asked, "Where would you like to go?" The group talked amongst themselves and smiling at me said, "To the Laundromat." We piled in a van and off we went to "the Laundromat."

I would describe this Laundromat as something frozen in time from the 70's. Nothing really unusual about it, just old school.

When we got there, the place was practically empty. Entering the business, I began to look for an employee. Not seeing any, I continued to walk through the building (it is a decent sized, L-shaped space). Rounding the corner, I saw two employees standing behind a counter.

I approached the older employee, a lady, and said, "Hi, I'm Jim. I'm here with a couple friends. We are praying for the employees and owners of the businesses in Lansing. How can we pray for you?"

The lady smiled at me and expressed her surprise over our kindness. She then shared a Prayer request for a loved one. When she was done, her fellow employee, a younger man, spoke up and said, "You ought to ask them to pray for you to stop smoking." We all smiled.

So I asked this lady, "Is this true, would you like to stop smoking? Would you like us to pray for this?" She replied, "Yes, and yes I would like prayers for this. It has been very hard. I have tried several times and failed."

Then something happened I did not expect. One of the ladies in our group said, "All you have to do is succeed one more time than you quit." She went on to share, "I used to smoke. I tried to stop so many times but kept giving up. Finally, I was successful…." And she described the method that worked for her.

This began a conversation between the church member and employee that lasted quite a while. Tears and hugs were shared, names and phone numbers were exchanged, and Trinity Lutheran in Lansing, Illinois, made a connection with a long time business in its community.

On a side note--I shared this story at a church and about a month later I began getting financial support (I am a network-supported Pastor) from a church member. She explained that when she heard this story she promised God that if she was able to quit smoking, she would give the money she had been spending on cigarettes to support my work.

Through Prayer Walking a business district, by the power of the Holy Spirit, you will build connections with employees and owners. Once this happens, it is fairly simple to approach the owner and have a discussion about the benefits they have observed that your Prayer ministry provides for the employees in terms of attitude, effort, stability, values, etc.

The format your Workplace Prayer Ministry takes will vary with each employer; it will need to be tailored for their context. The reason your Workplace Prayer Ministry should always be the same: to build relationships with others, serving them through Prayer and the Ministry of the Word.

As you get to know the needs of those you are serving in this way, the Mercy Ministry of your local congregation will have doors of opportunity swing open. As your Church members see the potential for ministry beyond the walls of the church building, their witness will grow throughout the week.

From July 13-26, 2010, we hosted over 50 short-term missionaries who came to New Jersey from churches in Indiana, Kansas, Missouri and Virginia. I trained these 50 people in Prayer Walking with special attention to the realities of outreach in a heavily urban setting. We then went out on the streets of Newark and Jersey City (and one day to Westfield, a very nice suburban community).

Our Prayer Walking teams connected with over 500 individuals in those two weeks. One immediate result of this was the attendance of 87 children at the Vacation Bible School hosted by our immigrant congregations. It was truly a blessing to see the leaders of our immigrant churches looking with eyes wide open at all these children in their churches (it was the first time they had offered VBS).

One day when I was leading one of the Prayer Walking teams on streets of Newark, we came to the Garden State Adult Day Care Center. I asked the group of youth who were with me if they would like to go in and take prayer requests. With their agreement, we went inside.

When you walk inside this Adult Day Care, you are looking at a counter that separates you from the staff and residents. So, when we came inside, the receptionist looked up at me and asked what we wanted. I smiled and asked if there was a social worker on staff. She replied that there was and went to get her. When the social worker came, I explained that I was a Pastor and the youth with me had come from Indiana to do a worship service for the community and that next week another group would be here to do VBS I suggested that maybe her residents would have children, grandchildren or neighbors who would want to attend. The social worker smiled and said I really needed to talk with their Activities Director.

When the Activities Director came, I told her what we were doing and she said she would be very interested in driving her residents over to our activities (which she did). She then offered to promote everything our church in Newark was doing to her residents through their monthly newsletter. Then, she explained to me that they were looking for a Chaplain and was wondering if I could find her one.

God is so awesome. I said that I was quite confident I could find a Pastor for her who would serve as their Chaplain and she was very happy. That afternoon, I shared the good news with our immigrant Pastor in Newark, Rev. Lawrence Gboeah (from Liberia, West Africa); he was very excited about this, so I took him over to meet the director. Today, Pastor Gboeah is the Chaplain for the Garden State Adult Day Care Center and its 150+ adult residents, plus their staff. He is welcome to come anytime and utilize their facilities for his ministry.

There are many businesses that will pay a Pastor to serve as their Chaplain. Tyson, the chicken people in Arkansas, has over 17,000 employees. They also have over 120 full-time chaplains on their staff working at locations throughout the United States. A good friend of mine, Air Force Chaplain, Col. Charlie Bolin worked for many years as a Chaplain at a major casino on the strip in Las Vegas, Nevada. (only a Southern Baptist could think of something like this.).

One strategy for funding urban church work could very easily begin by Business District Prayer Walking and then, through the contacts that are made, develop a Chaplain Ministry in the Workplace. These businesses would provide salary support to the Pastor, and their workforce would be accessible for evangelization. A Pastor who is interested more in this can find a lot of practical information on the ministry of workplace Chaplains through the internet.

As we see with the Garden State Adult Day Care Center, space and other resources necessary for holding a meeting can be used by the enterprising evangelist, and at no cost to them. The local Pastor and his leadership team can seek God's will regarding the vision as to what happens with the group(s) gathered among employees from these larger businesses.

5. Prayer Hotline

This idea has been around for years and there is a reason: it ministers to people and it gives some in the Priesthood of all Believers a meaningful way to touch others with Jesus' love for healing and service.

Jesus said, *"My Father's house will be a house of prayer."* What a statement it would be if our local churches were known in their communities in the way Jesus envisioned--as *"houses of prayer."*

For any outreach to be successful, it must provide the opportunity for every member to be involved. We can't force members to participate and we should not be disappointed when not everyone jumps in and helps out with every activity we do as a church. But, careful attention must be paid by the leadership to make sure that every member has the chance to participate.

Prayer Hotline outreach is something that might appeal to those who: like talking; are physically handicapped and can't literally walk through a neighborhood or business district; have a warm, soothing voice or enjoy meeting new people.

You don't need to have 24 / 7 coverage on your Prayer Hotline. When you first start out, you may have enough support to offer ministry one or two nights a week. That is okay. Let God grow it from there. People in your community will appreciate what you <u>can</u> offer. Just be sure to state what days / hours there will be someone for people to talk to / pray with.

The basic idea with this Prayer Outreach approach is to identify members to take phone calls from people in the community who are looking for someone who will pray with them. *Research has shown over and over again that people who are dealing with a traumatic event want these three things the most*:

-A religious representative to talk with

-Prayer

-Community

This is why Prayer as an Outreach tool is so effective.

Once you identify who your Prayer Hotline workers are and to what times they can commit, all you have to do is advertise this service to your community. There are many ways to get free or no cost advertising. One of the most effective ways is by doing a press release to the local media. When I was a parish Pastor, I made it a goal to put out a press release every week. Prayer is something the media is very comfortable talking about and obviously, your Prayer Hotline would be open to the entire community, so that also has the feel of being "open" and "ecumenical" to the press--something else they like.

As with any of the Prayer Outreach approaches, it is important to look for opportunities to recruit fellow workers from those you reach. Think about it--if someone was touched by your Prayer Hotline ministry, wouldn't they be a good candidate to approach about being a part of your Prayer Hotline ministry? Yes!

6. Prayer Online

Social media is highly effective for sharing the Gospel. My wife, Cathy, finally got me to open a Facebook account. Today, I have almost 1500 friends; a good number of these people I have never met-- they are friends of friends who either asked me or whom I asked to "friend."

As I sit here in Starbucks writing this book when I Google "prayer requests online," I get 630,000 results (the stopwatch on Google records that it pulled all 630,000 results in 0.19 of a second); "LCMS website with prayer ministry" pulls up 7,490 results (in 0.19 of a second).

Online Prayer Outreach could take a multitude of approaches; for example, you could have a stand-alone, dedicated web site your church runs that is completely dedicated to prayer ministry in your community. It could have its own name and identity and serve as a "side door" or "back door" for your church's outreach.

Each church will need to think through how it responds to the different types of prayer requests; how it protects confidentiality; how it follows up with personal visits to those requesting prayer.

7. Streets of Prayer Sponsorship

This is a very simple and effective way to recruit lots of people in your church to be a part of becoming known as a House of Prayer in your community, fitting in neatly with your overall vision.

Get a map of your community and answer this very simple (but important) question: "What is our church's Jerusalem?" Jesus told the disciples that we would first be His witnesses in Jerusalem, then in Judea, then in Samaria and finally, to the ends of the earth. (Acts 1:8)

So, did Jesus mean that you and I have to move to Israel? Or maybe that part of Scripture is not relevant anymore? Ah, the answer to both of those would be.... No!

So, what is the application of Jesus' command for us today? Simple! Jesus wants us to begin right in our own community, sharing His love with other people.

So, what is your church's "Jerusalem"?

Jerusalem is a physical location. In Jesus' day, any disciple could tell you exactly where Jerusalem was. It was so many streets wide by so many streets long. It was a definite, physical location.

So, what is your church's Jerusalem?

I have friends in the military who are incredible shots; to watch their marksmanship is an amazing thing. But I want to tell you something--you are a better shot than they are. You might be saying, "How is that possible? I have never shot anything. How can you say this?"

All I have to do is blindfold them, spin them around in a circle for 5 minutes and tell them to hit the target and you will be a better shot than they are.

You say, "Well that's crazy! How can you expect <u>anyone</u> to hit a target they can't see?"

Precisely. How could we ever achieve Jesus' command of first being His witnesses in our Jerusalem if we can't even identify our "target"?

So, what is your church's Jerusalem?

Once you identify the physical location of your church's Jerusalem, you can start getting serious about taking responsibility before God for people's souls. Until then, you are shooting from the hip, with a blindfold over your eyes. And, I'm guessing, the results aren't that impressive.

So, once you have identified your church's "Jerusalem", the next step is to invite people personally to sponsor a street in your Jerusalem. The requirements we expect of believers who sponsor a street are pretty simple:

1. They will pray for the families / businesses on the street(s) they sponsor.
2. They will watch the news for anything that happens to the people who live / work on their street.
3. They will follow the Holy Spirit's guidance regarding follow-up steps to take.

Once you have a couple of people "recruited" as Sponsors for your Streets of Prayer ministry, put a map of your Jerusalem in the entry way to your church, your fellowship hall, or some other prominent place for people to see. Put a sign-up sheet inviting anyone else who is interested to join this effort. Be sure to recruit your Pastor. <u>List all the names of the people who are part of this effort on your sign-up sheet.</u> <u>People will sign up for something **when they see that others are already a part**</u>; almost no one will be the first person to "sign up." And don't count on bulletin announcements or public service announcements on Sunday mornings before / after worship; this will not work. You simply have to invite people personally to be a part of what you are doing. They will say, "Yes" to <u>you</u>.

8. Treasure Hunting

This is a great way to do Prayer Walking and is definitely something that appeals to the adventuresome type of Christian.

In Matthew 21, we read the following, "*As they approached Jerusalem and came to Bethphage on the Mount of Olives, Jesus sent two disciples, saying to them, "Go to the village ahead of you, and at once you will find a donkey tied there, with her colt by her. Untie them and bring them to me. If anyone says anything to you, tell him that the Lord needs them, and he will send them right away.*"

A fair reading of the text (see also Mark 11) has to agree that these disciples had never seen either the donkey or the colt before and most likely, they had never met the earthly owner of these creatures either. Jesus was sending His disciples on a treasure hunt. Why? Because He had need of these things.

What did the disciples do? What Jesus told them. They simply trusted what they heard from Jesus and went looking for what He wanted.

When Jesus sent His disciples out to share the Good News, the following was a key part of His instructions, "*Whatever town or village you enter, search for some worthy person there and stay at his house…*" (Matthew 10:11)

Jesus had a "simple business plan"--get going! How were these disciples going to know exactly who these "righteous people" were? Did they have a big "W" on their doors (for "worthy")? Was there some sort of heavenly light radiating out their windows?

No; the disciples were going to trust the Holy Spirit to lead them to the right people. Kind of crazy. Kind of Godly.

Treasure Hunting Prayer Walking is really something to watch--youth love it.

What you do is gather the people who are going out Treasure Hunting and pray for God to guide you to specific people and then pray for Him to give you the right words to say (crazy, huh?).

In this prayer time, it would be perfectly normal to ask God to give you clues to look for. After all, Jesus gave the disciples some clues as to what kind of donkey (I'm sure there was more than one in that town) they were supposed to grab.

So, just as Jesus gave specific hints about what to look for regarding the donkey, God can still give us hints about who to look for. After all, He has prepared the good works in advance for us to do. So why not spend some time in prayer asking God for any specific directions?

Then, after you have prayed, take the group and go to the public place you have in mind and look for the clues God has given you regarding who to look for. Sometimes, the clues God gives you may be as specific as the clues Jesus gave the disciples; sometimes the clues will come to you as you are walking along: the Holy Spirit will just give you a "nudge" to go and talk with someone.

What if Jesus told you, "Go into town and find a certain man and tell him we need his family room; we are going to celebrate the Lord's Supper there, in his house." And you had never been to his house before; in fact you had never even met him before. What would you do?

When Jesus gave us the New Covenant in His blood, it was in the home of someone who was most likely a complete stranger to the disciples. Kind of crazy. Kind of Godly.

People today are looking for a Spiritual experience that is highly personal. You have a choice. You can condemn them for this OR you can turn to Jesus and see what He did. The Holy Spirit is waiting. Ready to let God be in control?

9. Prayer Walking According to God's Agenda

This is old school Prayer Walking. When you study up on it, you will find catch phrases like, "praying on site, with insight."

Basically, the concept is very simple: start walking and start praying as you go. You can choose to walk through a neighborhood, a shopping mall, a business district, etc.

A cornerstone of this approach is that you don't have any agenda; where you go and what you do, you leave totally up to the Holy Spirit's guidance.

I am German. I like structure. But all I had to do was go Prayer Walking in this way with Pastor Gregg Ramirez (Calvary Lutheran Church in Verona, New Jersey) one time to see the validity of this approach.

We hopped in his van and he drove us to a local grocery store. One of his key leaders, a Nigerian immigrant by the name of Olugbenga Adeshakin came with us. When we parked in the parking lot, we just stayed in the van for a while, praying for everyone we saw. We prayed for God to bless them; Scripture tells us that we don't know how to pray, but that the Holy Spirit intercedes for us.

After a while, we got out of the van and approached the grocery store, praying for the customers, employees and managers. Then we went inside, quietly walking around and praying silently for everyone we saw. I believe we all bought something small and checked out.

As we were walking outside, a young mother with an overflowing grocery cart was struggling to navigate the multiple doors and keep her young children in tow. All three of us men are blessed to have several children ourselves and our hearts went out to her.

Approaching her, we asked if we could be of any assistance. She smiled and we told her we were Praying for people and would love to help her. She accepted and as we walked outside, we asked her where her car was. This young mother did not have a car; she was planning on calling a taxi to take them home. Pastor Ramirez immediately offered to give her and her children a ride home, which she accepted. We loaded everyone up with the groceries and drove them home.

The interesting thing is, she was also an African immigrant. This made for a very easy and natural conversation with Olugbenga. Of course we asked her how we could pray specifically for her and her family. She shared some prayer requests and when we got to her home, we bowed our heads and all prayed together before getting her unloaded and carrying her groceries to her front door.

My wife, Cathy, says, "Prayer Walking is really not a program. It is not something you should only do at a certain time each week with a team of people. Prayer Walking is supposed to be your life style." I couldn't agree more.

10. Restaurant Prayer Walking

This is one of my favorite ways to Prayer Walk. Really, it is very simple. The next time you go out to eat, when the wait staff has taken your order, simply say to him or her, "We are going to be praying for this food when it comes. We would love to pray for you; how can we pray for you?"

I can honestly say that every time I have asked this question of restaurant workers, they have shared a Prayer request. What is really cool is watching the pleasant surprise come over their faces when you ask them this question.

I have waited tables. If you have, you know what this job is like. It is hard work. You don't get paid very much; you have to depend on tips to make your effort worthwhile. Yet, much of your customer's experience is beyond your control--you are not cooking the food. If the customer has a problem with the food, the best you can do is hope that the cook gets it right the second time.

Waiters work hard throughout their shift trying to make others happy. I believe this is why they are always so pleased when a customer shows genuine concern for them.

Prayer Walking a restaurant is a valid way to Prayer Walk--you know how to follow up with the person sharing the Prayer request: they work at that restaurant.

I used to do a lot of flying out of Newark International Airport. Most of the time, my flight left from the same terminal. One day, I actually got to the airport early. Not being used to having extra time at the airport, I went to the restaurant by my gate to get a quick bite.

When the waitress came to my table, I could tell she had been having a bad day. After giving her my food request, I simply said, "I am going to be praying for this food when it comes; I would love to pray for you also; what can I pray for?"

I will never forget her response. She asked me, "Can you do that?" I smiled and said, "Yes, I am a Pastor," and pointed to my Bible. She then shared some Prayer requests with me and I assured her I would pray for her.

About 10 minutes after bringing my food, she came back to my table with a piece of paper. She had written out her Prayer requests, and handing them to me she said, "I wanted to make sure you had my Prayer requests." I thanked her, then put her list in my Bible.

Every time I flew out of that terminal I would look for her. The first couple times, I did not see her. The truth is, I did not have much time, I was usually cutting my flights pretty short. Then one time when I was there, I had a couple of minutes and looked around for her and there she was.

Walking up to her, I said, "I don't know if you remember me, but a while back I was eating here and asked you how I could pray for you." This smile came across her face and with no restraint she gave me the biggest bear hug. I was glad I was in a public place. We caught up on how she was doing and she updated her Prayer requests for me.

You can Prayer Walk any restaurant, even ones at the airport. But it is easier to follow up with people when they work at your local diner.

One time when I was at a restaurant with my wife, a young man working in the restaurant was emptying the trash cans in our area. I told Cathy, "I am going to ask him how we can pray for him when he walks past." Cathy smiled and when the young man came by, I simply said to him, "My wife and I are praying; we would love to pray for you; how can we pray for you?"

It was really neat watching his response. You could tell he was surprised that a customer was talking with him; his job was to take out the trash, It seemed that hundreds of people could sit and eat all around him for hours <u>but none ever talked with him</u>.

He gladly shared some Prayer requests and shook my hand. Before we left the restaurant, this young man personally stopped by our table twice to check on us and make sure that our experience in his restaurant was up to our expectations; and he was not even our waiter.

What I have learned over the years of Prayer Walking is that it is really very easy to get Prayer requests from people; but that <u>what really is important is doing this in conjunction with a strong Mercy Ministry Leadership team</u> that will take the Prayer requests gathered and follow up with them. In this way, the body of Christ, as a whole, connects with and serves those in our community who are in need.

11. Prayer Quakes with Short-Term Mission Teams

Shortly after accepting the call to be an Urban Mission Strategist for the greater Newark area, I was wakened one night in the middle of a peaceful sleep. God had given me an idea regarding Prayer and mission teams coming to New Jersey, which was based on Acts 4:31: "*After they prayed, the place where they were meeting was shaken. And they were all filled with the Holy Spirit and spoke the Word of God boldly.*"

The vision God was laying on my heart was to provide mission teams the opportunity to come to New Jersey to experience "Prayer Quakes."

The basic idea was to structure a week of mission opportunity around Prayer, each day's Bible study reflecting on a Scriptural teaching regarding Prayer; coupled with Prayer Walking; Worship; and providing an experience-based opportunity to see firsthand how to build relationships with key community leaders.

If you have ever gotten an idea from God like this, you know what I am talking about. When God speaks to you, you get out your pen and paper or laptop or tablet or whatever you use and start writing as furiously as you can to keep up with the ideas God is pouring into you. You don't want anything to distract you; you know that this is a special moment and that you need to get it down in the moment.

The following is the base schedule for a Prayer Quake that God laid on my heart. If you would like to send a mission team to New Jersey to experience this, we can talk about dates. If you would like me to help you set this up for your community, I am happy to do that as well.

Over time, we have modified the following schedule to fit particular interests / needs of Mission Teams coming to New Jersey. Mercy ministry is something we have come to see as something that needs to be integrated into the Prayer Quake experience. When we see that Prayer leads to Care, everyone is blessed.

Also, many of the Mission Teams have indicated a desire to do a Community Outreach (usually on Friday / Saturday) during their time here. The Mission Team members have been very blessed by the chance to see how many people in the community will respond to just one week of Prayer-based outreach.

Basic Schedule for a Prayer Quake in the Garden State

Saturday
-Arrive in New Jersey
-Get to Host Congregation / House Church //   -Meet the Team //   -Meet the Hosts
-Review the Schedule // -Review Safety Procedures   //   -Commit to Ministry Covenant
-Bible Study (Prayer Quake theme)
        Assorted Verses on Prayer in Scripture

Sunday
-Commissioning Service
-Sight Seeing
-Leadership Dinner

Monday – Friday
-Bible Study (Prayer Quake theme)
        Day 2. Jesus' Prayer Life
        Day 3. The Apostle's Prayer Life
        Day 4. The Prophets' Prayer Life
        Day 5. The Patriarchs' Prayer Life
        Day 6. The Prayers of Women in Scripture
-Knowing the Neighborhood
        Day 2. Small Business Owners
        Day 3. Law Enforcement
        Day 4. Hospital Staff
        Day 5. Elected Local Official
        Day 6. Public School Representative
-Prayer Time
-Lunch
-Prayer Walk
-Sight Seeing
-Dinner
-Prayer Walk
-Preparation for Ministry Celebration Event on Sunday
-Prayer Quake Journaling Time
-Go to Sleep

Saturday
-Bible Study (Prayer Quake theme)
        My Life of Prayer
                -Short Term Missionaries share what God has shown them regarding Prayer Quake theme
-Final Preparations for Ministry Celebration on Sunday

Sunday
-Ministry Celebration
-Ministry Survey
-Ministry Covenant
-Go Home

12. Hosting a City-Wide Prayer Walk

My family and I love to go camping. My wife did not grow up camping--her mom's idea of camping is a basic hotel.

So, I was pleasantly surprised when my wife told me, "Let's go camping." We got a simple pop-up tent and went out for a weekend. Cathy had a great time, and it wasn't long before she told me, "Let's get a simple camper." So I agreed and Cathy volunteered to look for a used, simple model.

Within a couple months we were the proud owners of a 12-foot long, 1970 Yellowstone camper. We didn't even give $800 for it; but it was really very nice (if you could look past the orange and brown interior color scheme.)

At the time, we just had three children and this camper was plenty big enough. We had a great time camping at State parks. One of our favorite places was the White River campground in Arkansas. For about $15 a night, we could get a campsite with water and electric hook ups. This means we could sleep in AC at night and keep as many groceries in our little fridge as we wanted. Camping is a great budget stretcher, not to mention leaving the idiot box at home and just spending lots of time together with family.

We finally outgrew that little Yellowstone camper and had to get something that could handle seven Buckmans. The great thing about buying an old camper is that when you sell it seven years later, you get back just as much as you paid. And, along the way, we were blessed with weeks and weeks of very low cost, high quality family vacations.

In 2011, our family went camping at Naval Weapons Station Earle in New Jersey. The grandparents had gotten us passes to Six Flags Not only is NWS Earle a close campground, it is a military base, which is always a great place to camp. There are amenities, usually a museum and just really cool military stuff to show your family. NWS Earle has the second longest pier in America--it goes over three miles out into the Atlantic Ocean. The pier has a railroad line on it that runs all the way to the end; this is how we load the supply ships with things that go bump in the middle of the night. The Navy built that long pier so in case something went wrong with loading / unloading of the ammunition, no civilians would be in jeopardy.

Anyhow, we were enjoying a week of going out to Six Flags and sightseeing on the base. One day, as we were driving around the base, we saw the base Chapel. If you have ever seen one of those small, classic military Chapels, you know what I am talking about. Just a beautiful house of worship: built out of bricks in the classic design with white pillars in front. When you look at one of these chapels, you can picture in your mind how many service members have gotten married here over the years.

At Ft. Bragg, North Carolina, there is a Special Operations Chapel, nicknamed the John Wayne chapel, which looks almost exactly like the one at NWS Earle. When John Wayne made the movie, "The Green Berets," he donated a life-size statue of a Green Beret in the well-known pose with his weapon in his right hand, running forward and looking over his left shoulder. He is raising his left hand and waving forward the indigenous troops he has trained to overthrow their oppressors, to follow him. Before we went into Iraq, I baptized a lot of grown men in that Chapel. The statue stands outside the little Chapel; generations of heroes have worshipped here; some have been laid to rest. Base chapels will always be near and dear to me.

Back to the story. We were at NWS Earle and spotted their Chapel. Cathy and I were saddened to see that the Chapel looked as if it was not in regular use. As I mulled this over and ministry possibilities started percolating, I remembered Muriel Smith, the civilian who worked on base and ran, among other things, the campground. Muriel and I had a good relationship- when I was making our reservations, we had some lighthearted banter about the respective qualities of the Navy and Air Force ☺ I think she probably prevailed ☺

So, I called Muriel up and asked her about the Chapel, mentioning that it didn't look as if it was getting much use. Muriel replied that they had not had a Chaplain in over six years and had been without regular worship services ever since. Then Muriel's voice changed to a hopeful tone when she asked me, "You are a

Chaplain, do you think you could help us out?" I told Muriel I thought that I could, but that she would need to talk with Base Commander. I gave her some suggested questions to ask.

About a month later I got a phone call. The voice on the other end announced himself, "Hi, this Chaplain Mike Vitcavich with the Navy. I am a Reserve Chaplain. In the civilian world, I'm a Newark Police Department Chaplain. The Navy has me on orders for six months and one of the things I am supposed to do is help start a community-based worship service. Are you still interested in doing this?"

I can't make this sort of stuff up. This is God's favor on a sinful man.

And, it is really cool when a Navy Chaplain asks an Air Force Chaplain for help!

So, I told Chaplain Vitcavich that what I do is help existing LCMS congregations plant new worshipping communities through the development of House Church Planters that work under the supervision of the regularly called and ordained Pastors serving these congregations. I went on to explain that we had a House Church Planter by the name of Bill Schmidt who was a retired Bergen County Prosecutor, and just as importantly, had served with the Navy in the Vietnam War as a Corpsman.. I shared with Chaplain Vitcavich that I was sure Bill would want to do this. I also said that we had a great Pastor with over 20 years in a military friendly congregation nearby--Pastor Paul Huneke (at Luther Memorial in Tinton Falls, New Jersey), and that Pastor Huneke would probably be interested in being the supervising Pastor for this endeavor.

Chaplain Vitcavich said, "Great, when can we get together?"

I can't make this sort of stuff up. This is God's favor on a sinful man.

So, Pastor Huneke and Bill Schmidt have begun the process of planting a House Church on NWS Earle. In 2012, the base Commander's wife, Nancy Harrison, personally invited our House Church to host the Vacation Bible School for the military children. First time in at least seven years that these children of heroes had been given their own VBS. Of course, we used Concordia Publishing House's material, and it was very well received by the base.

There are times when I am afraid that my military commitment as a Chaplain takes away from my ministry, but my wife reminds me, "Look at all the doors God is opening through the military."

Chaplain Vitcavich and I have become good friends. He has a BIG heart for the city of Newark, and I am working as a Mission Strategist for the Newark area... hmmmm, maybe God does really have a plan.

Through Chaplain Vitcavich, I have been blessed to meet Sgt. Leslie Jones who has served 40 years as a Newark Police Officer. This alone is quite an accomplishment, but on top of all this, he has also served as a Pastor in Newark for 40 years. Talk about serving God and Country.

Pastor Jones currently serves as the Police Officer assigned to the Newark Police Department Chaplain's Office. In addition, Pastor Jones has helped gather a coalition of Christian clergy--Pray for Newark. As their name describes, their goal is quite simple--to pray for Newark. The vision God laid on my heart was to use Prayer to help churches reach their communities..... hmmmm, maybe God does have a plan.

Pastor Jones is a retired New Jersey Air Guard member. He was assigned for 20 years to the base where I now serve. When he found out that I was an Air Force Chaplain, it was like old home week. When I shared with him that I serve as a Mission Strategist with my denomination, helping congregations reach their communities through Prayer, he immediately invited me to come and share with the clergy of Pray For Newark about my ministry and resources they might consider using.

Pray For Newark has a team of church members from the various congregations who have signed up to pray specifically for each block in Newark. Every street in Newark now has a Christian praying specifically for the members of that block as well as all who travel on it. What was it God said, "*My house will be a house of prayer*."

Newark, New Jersey, has a very Biblical history. Newark was founded in 1666 by Connecticut Pilgrims led by Robert Treat from the New Haven Colony (interestingly, one of our House Church plants meets at the Robert Treat Deli in Westfield, New Jersey.). Their goal being to establish a Christian community, settler Abraham Person suggested the name "New Ark" to capture the essence of their task. This name was shortened in time to "Newark." The Puritan theocracy continued until 1746 when Episcopalian missionaries were invited by Josiah Ogden to plant a church there. Josiah had been disciplined for Sabbath breaking, having harvested wheat on a Sunday (due to a series of intense rainstorms).

Hosting a city-wide Prayer Walk can happen anywhere. As Lutherans, we are free to pray with other Christians; this is not altar or pulpit fellowship and we are not talking about a worship service. Mercy ministry may find us joining hands with Roman Catholics and Baptists.

Obviously, when you are getting together with clergy from other denominations, you have to have your game face on and be fully alert so you are not lulled into agreeing to statements we cannot agree to. Not that you need to be told this, but one of the benefits of belonging to our denomination is that when you confront a question as a Pastor, you have Circuit Counselors, District Vice Presidents, the District President / Bishop as well as other Pastors to go to for counsel.

Church members are generally encouraged when they see their Pastor working with other Christian clergy in efforts to serve their community at large. There is a place for the LCMS in the public square. Dear God, if we don't get out there in it, who in the world is going to tell people that we are saved by grace, through faith and not by works; that His grace comes to us in the efficacious Sacraments of Baptism and Holy Communion? If we aren't going to do this thing that needs doing most of all, then shame on us; we will have taken the great treasure God freely gave us and <u>buried it</u> from others!

Another thing--the media loves this sort of thing (Churches working together). And for as much grief as we in the Church give the media, <u>we should always have our eyes open to the possibility of using this tool for His purpose.</u>

Pr. Haron Orutwa, Tumaini Kristo Lutheran Church in Jersey City welcomes Pr. Andy Keltner, Christ our Savior Lutheran Church in Louisburg, KS and his mission team members to worship.

13. Adding Prayer Walking to Your Existing Church Ministries

If you ever get the chance, read the book, *Good to Great* (by Jim Collins); I first read this book a couple of years back and have recommended it many times. The premise of the book is pretty simple (the best ideas usually are): figure out what you do well and do some more of that.

Every congregation is unique; yours has a special gift mix. In your church are a unique collection of saints--men and women filled with the Holy Spirit, each with good works that God has prepared in advance for them to do.

The Holy Spirit moves as He sees fit and He sees fit to move in your congregation.

Here is a simple idea--take a look around your Church (not the building; but the Church--the people); and ask, "Where is God producing fruit in the ministry of our congregation?"

Don't ask, "What does God want us to do?" It's not about you.
Simply ask, "Where is <u>God</u> producing fruit in the ministry of our congregation?"

> Jesus said, "*I am the true vine, and my Father is the gardener. He cuts off every branch in me that bears no fruit, while <u>every branch that does bear fruit</u> he prunes <u>so that it will be even more fruitful</u>.*" (John 15:1-2)

*Scripture Application is not that difficult!! <u>Look for the branch that bears fruit; this is where the Father is going to work in order that it will be even more fruitful!</u> Come on! If I can see this; anyone can!

And don't believe for a second that trash theology that says, "God doesn't care about results." That theology is delusional dribble that comes from the devil. There is a purpose to John 3:16; there is a <u>goal</u> in God's mind! Consider Luther on this: "The Holy Spirit does not bestow His gifts on procrastinators."

"Good to Great for Christians"

Adding Prayer Walking to your existing church ministries is not difficult once you have identified the areas of your ministry in which God is producing fruit; then you know this area of ministry (maybe it is your Youth ministry) is an area you want to focus on in connection with your Congregational Prayer Ministry. Let's look at Youth Ministry for example.

1. Ask the members serving as leaders in this area how you should ask, "How can we pray for you?" to those being served through their ministry. Perhaps:
   - ask it of the youth themselves
   - ask the children's parents
   - the youth should be trained to ask the question
   - the youth should be involved in the Mercy Ministry follow up to the Prayer requests received by the Prayer Walkers.

2. Ask the ministry leaders in the Congregation (the Elders, Board of Directors, Pastoral Staff, etc.); how the Youth Ministry should be utilized specifically in the Prayer outreach of the Congregation.

3. Ask leaders in the Community for their ideas on how this area of your ministry that God is blessing could be used to serve the Community at large in conjunction with your Prayer outreach. Whenever I have had this conversation with community leaders, I have always been surprised at the wealth of suggestions <u>and</u> resources they make available to see their idea come to fruition.

14. Community Events

A simple way to use Prayer to connect with your neighbor is to be involved with (if not organizing) community gatherings. Your community has gatherings; I have probably never been to your community, but I already know your community has gatherings. Communities gather; it is inherent in the word "community."

Your community may gather for sports events, cultural celebrations, historic remembrances, educational reasons or other reasons. When your community gathers, individuals, businesses and charitable organizations are invited to participate; this helps the steering committee raise funds and attendance.

Prayer fits very nicely and peacefully in this setting. A simple sign letting people know, "Prayer Requests Received Here," will let people know exactly what you are offering. A simple table and folding chairs are all that is needed to welcome people so they can sit down and share their Prayer requests with you.

When you do this, you will see many people stop and look at your sign. You will be able to tell that they are considering your ministry and reflecting on the circumstances in their life. Many will not feel comfortable sharing their Prayer request at that particular time. For this reason, it is a good idea to have a very simple handout / postcard you can give to these people. This will give them a resource to take home that gives them contact information so they know how to learn more about your Prayer ministry (maybe through your church website).

If attendance at the Community Event is decent, you will get some who stop and talk with you, sharing what is on their heart. Most of these people are not going to be from your church or even denomination. They are just going to be hurting souls, looking for God's grace. Share it with them.

In Springfield, Missouri, an annual Chili competition is held to raise money for the Boys and Girls Homes. It is wildly popular, in part due to the cause, in part due to the chili, and in equal part due to the amount of beer available at this event. I volunteered one year and was put to work in the beer tent. The instructions I was given were very simple--don't turn the tap off; just run the cups underneath the beer.

The largest church in Springfield is a Pentecostal church. (Springfield is the home of the Assemblies of God). For those of you who don't know, Pentecostals don't drink (officially).

I thought it was interesting that the largest church booth at the Chili Cook-off was rented by the largest Pentecostal church in town.

Why did a Pentecostal Church have a booth at the Chili Cook-off when there was so much beer being sold (and served nonetheless by a Lutheran Pastor.)?

Because, this is where the community was gathered and, by golly, they were going to be a witness, they were going to build relationships. And they did! Seems to me Jesus did a miracle involving a party and wine....

Baptism of Capt Rob Gearhardt; he drives A-10's.

15. E Sword and Prayer Ministry

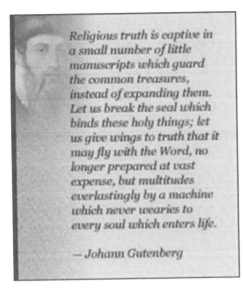

Religious truth is captive in a small number of little manuscripts which guard the common treasures, instead of expanding them. Let us break the seal which binds these holy things; let us give wings to truth that it may fly with the Word, no longer prepared at vast expense, but multitudes everlastingly by a machine which never wearies to every soul which enters life.

— Johann Gutenberg

About 10 years ago I came across an incredible resource I have utilized ever since and recommend to everyone. The name of the ministry is "e-sword"; the web site is: http://www.e-sword.net/index.html.

In January of 2000, a Christian by the name of Rick Meyers wrote the computer code for his ministry web site, which was dedicated to providing Christian resources in the public domain, in an electronic format to the public for free (donations accepted). In 2011, there were 5,000,000 downloads of his software. Altogether, a total of 20,000,000 downloads have happened.

Since Rick started, Christian Publishers like the American Bible Society have come on board and have given his ministry access to their works. Additionally, Sovereign Grace Publishers now includes a copy of the e-sword DVD with all new editions of the "Modern King James Bible" and "Literal Translation Bibles."

The resources available on an E Sword DVD are found on for sale software, which often costs about $500. This is available for a donation of any size.

Next time you have a visitor to church,; don't give them another coffee mug or eco-friendly light bulb; give them a Christian library. Here is a simple Prayer outreach idea: offer an electronic Christian library to anyone who shares a Prayer request with you. Their request could be received over your web site or with a traditional card on Sunday morning. I did this for many years. Trust me, it's a winner. The picture below is from Pr. Rick Vossler, Grace Lutheran Church in Livingston, NJ; they are utilizing this resource

House Church Planter candidates can complete their training on our web site:
www.HouseChurchPlanter.com

16. A Prayer Table in Front of Your Church

Pastor Dave Born is someone I have known for many years. As a Seminary student, I first heard him share about Jewish evangelism in 1993. I remember being inspired by his ministry; I never imagined that 20 years later, I would be a mission strategist in New Jersey and that I would have a chance to collaborate and share ideas on ministry.

At the church where he holds his membership, Pastor Born has a very simple and effective form of Prayer Outreach. He or his church members simply set up a card table in front of their church with a sign, "How Can We Pray for You?" They will sit at their table and smile as neighbors walk past the church. When someone is curious or open to sharing a Prayer request, they come forward and talk with Pastor Born or the church member.

In 2009, I helped our Kenyan congregation in Jersey City (Tumaini Kristo Lutheran Church) hold its first Vacation Bible School. One of my buddies in ministry, Pastor Andy Keltner (Christ Our Savior in Louisburg, Kansas), brought a mission team to New Jersey, and they brought their Midwestern work ethic with them. At the beginning of the week, they Prayer Walked every morning in the neighborhood around our Newark congregation; every afternoon they Prayer Walked around our Jersey City congregation. As they Prayer Walked, they let the families know there would be a VBS at the end of the week. So on Wednesday, Thursday and Friday, Pastor Keltner and his team offered VBS in the mornings for families in Newark, and in the afternoons for families in Jersey City. At night, they slept on air mattresses in the fellowship hall in Newark.

Our Jersey City congregation rents store front space on Martin Luther King Dr. So, when VBS was running, I would stand outside on the sidewalk, and every time a parent walked by with little children, I would grab the adult and tell them, "You need to come in here. We are having Vacation Bible School. It doesn't cost anything. We have food, snacks, crafts, and Jesus. Bring your children in here and sign your name. We aren't letting any kids go until their parent comes to get them; so be back here at 5 p.m."

Many parents took me up on my offer. If your church is located in an area with a lot of foot traffic, get outside the walls of your building and find a "reason" to interact with those passing by.

One of the mothers who I invited to bring her children to our Jersey City VBS was Rasheeda Wint. She told me later that she was very impressed with how seriously we took the security and safety of the children. Rasheeda was looking for a church home, and even though she isn't Kenyan, she now is a member of Tumaini Kristo Lutheran Church. The past two years, Rasheeda has been the VBS Director for her congregation. In 2012, Rasheeda graduated with her Bachelor's degree in Elementary Education. God brought the perfect person to the church.

In 2010, I called Pastor Keltner to tell him the good news about the VBS that year and how one of the mothers we had reached through the VBS was in fact going to be leading their new VBS ministry. When I shared with Pastor Keltner that it was Rasheeda who would be heading this ministry up, he interrupted me and proceeded to describe her two daughters and their mother perfectly. One year later, this Pastor could still describe the sheep of the flock with detail. This is the kind of Pastor you want for your flock.

This Prayer Table might also be set up in front of a store, from which permission has been granted, for several hours on a weekend or during the busiest store hours. Think grocery or variety stores that do a lot of business on the weekends.

17. Street Sponsorship

One of the most meaningful days of my ministry is when I was installed at my first congregation--Alive in Christ, in Columbia, Missouri. This church was so new, it was still meeting in rented space at Townsend Hall on the campus of Mizzou (University of Missouri). My call was to be the Associate Pastor, working with Pastor Feldmann as the Senior. I was very excited about this opportunity; but it would be short lived. Within months, Pastor Feldmann had a call to a Chicago area church and I was in a building program, fresh out of the Seminary. In 2012, Pastor Feldmann and I had a chance to reconnect at the 20th anniversary of the planting of Alive in Christ. It was great to see him and catch up.

My dad, Rev. Dr. Al Buckman was the preacher at my installation, and the text he used has since become one of my favorites:
> *"You will receive power when the Holy Spirit comes on you; and you will be my witnesses in Jerusalem, and in all Judea and Samaria, and to the ends of the earth."* (Acts 1:8)

Let's talk about "Jerusalem" for just a minute.

When Jesus said this, His purpose was not to share a metaphor or parable. Jesus was talking about a real, place--Jerusalem. This city had a defined boundary; the residents knew the streets by name; neighbors knew each other.

With the passing of 2,000 years we "spiritualize" many things in Scripture, turning very real stories and instructions into metaphors. We have the freedom to do this with Scripture in the interest of the Gospel proclamation. But when we make a metaphor out of something in order to help people draw meaning from it today, we need to make it "real" to them today also. A good metaphor applies theological insight to today's condition.

The inspiration for "Street Sponsorship" comes from Acts 1:8. The basic idea is for a local congregation to have "their Jerusalem": a real, defined geographical area around their church.

The church's Jerusalem will be identified as such on maps the church members have. The people living in the church's Jerusalem will be a first priority for the prayers, outreach and mercy ministry of the congregation. The church members will be Jesus' witnesses in their Jerusalem.

Jesus wanted everyone to hear the Good News, yet He took care to remind the disciples that they should be sure to witness to their fellow Jews--those right around them, those from whom they came. Sometimes, the easiest mission work to support is what happens 10,000 miles away, not in our own backyard. Sometimes we may feel more comfortable with paying someone else to be our missionary, thinking that we don't also have to be a witness. And yet we are witnesses, for it wasn't a question Jesus asked that demanded an answer; it was a statement of fact. Those who love the Lord **are** His witnesses.

In practical terms, Street Sponsorship is the opportunity for church members to sign up and commit to pray for the residents of a particular street. As the Prayer Walkers identify the residents of the homes within the congregation's Jerusalem and their Prayer requests, the sponsoring Church member will have more information with which to pray specifically.

Street Sponsors who take their job seriously will follow up with their church's Mercy Ministry Leadership team and keep updated on the care their congregation is providing to the homes on the street they are sponsoring; these updates will also help guide their Prayers. The Street Sponsor may even feel led to help with the Mercy Ministry of their congregation, perhaps for the homes on their street or perhaps for a specific need that has been raised on another street in their congregation's Jerusalem.

18. Pet Prayer Walking

One way that many find to be a fun way to do Prayer Walking outreach involves pets.

My wife, Cathy, grew up with a family dog; she has a big place in her heart for pets. Every cat or dog our family has had came to us through trying to save the animal. Over the years, in addition to our own pets, we have taken in more cats and dogs than I can remember that had gotten lost / abandoned. By God's grace, every one of these pets was placed in a good home / returned to the owner looking for it.

Currently, our family has a Golden Retriever, a calico, about 20 fish, and two bunnies are on the way. All I need is a partridge in the pear tree and I will have the whole song!

Whenever we take Kisses, our Golden Retriever, out, she gets <u>tons</u> of compliments. I should rent her out to young men looking for dates; it could pay for her dog food.

Anyhow, Pet Prayer Walking is about as simple as it sounds. You get a tee shirt for your dog that says, "How can I pray for you?"; take your dog for a walk at the park and watch the conversations start.

I know people who raise horses and they do the same thing with their horses at horse shows. If you are a pet lover, your pet can be a very natural bridge to starting a conversation about faith and receiving Prayer requests from other people with a shared love for your breed of pet.

Lutheran Church Charities of Chicago, Illinois, in addition to their many other ministries, also helps place trained dogs that congregations can use for Pet Prayer Walking.

A challenge of Pet Prayer Walking as an approach is that you are not meeting people at a fixed place where you are likely to find them again (e.g., their work or home). This is yet another example of how important Mercy Ministry is for Prayer Walking. It is very natural and logical to ask the person sharing the Prayer request with you, "After we pray for you, we will discuss ways we might help you in this situation. <u>What would be the best way to reach out to you</u>?"

19. Prayer Journals for Prayer Walking

Early in our marriage, my wife and I started a practice of journaling the things for which we were praying. We made sure to date the original Prayer request, and as significant developments happened, we would update that particular journal entry. When God had answered our Prayer request, I would draw a cross next to the Prayer request and enter the final date.

It is always interesting and uplifting to look back over the years. Many things in our Prayer Journal have long since been forgotten. There is a lesson in this--the things that seem so big today, with time and God's grace, are put in their proper place. It is also always uplifting to read again how God had answered our Prayer requests--most of the time in ways we had never imagined; always in ways that were ultimately a blessing.

I was first exposed to Prayer Journaling for members in Taiwan at a workshop hosted by the largest Lutheran cell church in the world (Truth Lutheran). Every person on staff at Truth Lutheran is required to keep a journal of the Prayer requests they receive from their church members; they update their records until each Prayer is answered.

As I reflected on this ministry discipline, it came to me that a member / staff person could also track Prayer requests received from the Prayer Walkers. Really only three things need to happen:

1. The Mercy Ministry Leadership team send out updates regarding what they are doing to follow up with the Prayer requests received.

2. The Congregational Prayer Ministry Coordinator send out updates regarding the Prayer requests not being followed up by the Ministry Mercy Leadership Team.

3. The Pastor send any additional updates he feels people need to have.

20. Prayer Walking for Public Schools

Prayer is "not allowed" in public schools, meaning that children no longer are led in prayer by their teachers, principals, or other leaders in the schools. Christians can still pray in those schools before meals, when beginning their day or a different class or before a test. No one can legislate that out of our hearts.

The adults who teach or work in public schools, the youth and children who attend there are free to ask, "How can I pray for you?" In doing so, they are not promoting "a religion," but simply showing concern about those around them. Bringing requests back to the Ministry Mercy Leadership Team and seeing how those requesting prayers can be helped can definitely make a difference in the lives of others.

In Community Prayer Walking, always make it a point to pray outside of any school, asking for God's blessings on those inside who are working or teaching or learning; asking for God to bind Satan so he has no power over those in the school; and asking for protection from harm for all who are there.

What the Holy Spirit Leads You to Do

The Holy Spirit indwells every person who confesses with their mouth that Jesus is Lord and believes in their heart that He was raised from the dead. So, if you want God to guide you, it starts with a personal relationship with Jesus, and this only happens through the Holy Spirit who enables us to cry, "Abba, Father." If you have never confessed Jesus as Lord, there is no time like the present. To help you understand more about Jesus, just go to www.lcms.org and find the Pastor who is nearest to you. On the search page, click on "Locate a Church, School, Worker" on the LCMS icon. Once there, type in your city and state (or zip code) under "Find a Church." This will take you to a list of churches located in that zip code or in your city or town. Click on the one located closest to you and you will be directed to that church's information and / or web site, including the name(s) of the Pastor(s).

Even if you have not yet acknowledged Jesus as your Savior, the Holy Spirit still cares about you and is at work with you. If you do not know Jesus as Savior, and you are reading this book, it is because the Holy Spirit worked through someone to make this happen. This is one of the things the Holy Spirit does as He calls, gathers, enlightens and sanctifies the whole Christian church on earth. The power of salvation is found in God's Word; again, I want to encourage you to find a Pastor (www.lcms.org) if you don't have one and ask him to open up God's Word to you.

Once the Holy Spirit has His way with you and by His work, you become a believer, He leads you in paths of righteousness, showing you the good works prepared by the Father in advance for you to do. In your life, you have a "circle of influence." These are people you know, including your neighbors, co-workers, relatives, friends, people your children know, your barber / hairdresser and many others. Think through the people you know; who is God laying on your heart to reach out to and ask, "How can I pray for you?"

When it comes to using Prayer to reach out to others in your community (your Jerusalem), the Holy Spirit is going to guide you, when you just pray and ask Him to do that, submitting your will to His. You may be led by the Holy Spirit to try one of the ideas you have read about here; you may be led to try a variation of something here, or you may be led to do something completely new.

If God leads you to do something new in the area of Prayer Walking, I ask that you share what you experience with others. In this way you can be blessed to be a blessing. As I was writing this book, three more people shared ways in which they use Prayer to connect with others: one Pastor shared that their church boards will, from time to time, go Prayer Walking in lieu of a regular business meeting; another Pastor shared that their church will focus on one specific institution at a time (a=such as a school or hospital. A proud Grandfather got a "How Can I Pray for You?" onesie made up for his grandson. He shared that his grandson has helped start more Spiritual conversations than he can count.

God has given you His Word so that you can test the Spirits, discerning what is approved by Him. Hopefully you have a Pastor (did I mention www.lcms.org?) who can help you in your study of His Word. Be faithful, be bold; tomorrow is promised to no person.

A Recap of Practical Suggestions for Your Prayer Walking Ministry:

-Reach out to people where you know you will find them again. For example, standing at a busy intersection and asking drivers who are stopped at a red light, "How can I pray for you?" is not a wise strategy; it will be almost impossible to follow up with them.

-Go out in groups of two or three.

-Invite children / youth not only to participate, but to ask, "How can I pray for you?" Typically, children / youth will get 50% better response rate than adults. This is why the Girl Scouts still sell cookies. It works. Some churches have incorporated Prayer Walking into their Confirmation curriculum. This makes sense when you consider what the basic point of Confirmation is--that our young adults would know true faith and confess it publicly.

-Pray immediately when you get back to where you are gathering for your group prayers
    ("sharing" your prayer requests before praying, can easily become gossip).

-CELEBRATE! You are going to see God at work when you go Prayer Walking; take time to
    celebrate what God is doing through you (Psalm 9:1-2; 89:15-18; Acts 11:18).

-Plan on your follow up (same day and time next week is best)
    (the best is if at least one person from today's Prayer Team can be there for the follow up)

-Have a system for tracking the information your Prayer Teams gather
    -If possible, train someone other than the Pastor to do this to help reduce his load
- Before going out, do spend a little time "role playing" what you will say at the door: "Hi I'm
_____. My friends and I are praying for the community; how can we pray for you?"

Ask follow up questions when appropriate.
    -For example if someone says, "Please pray for my dad's health"
        -Logical follow up questions include:
            "What is your Dad's name?"
            "Anything specific you would like us to pray for?"

    -Or if someone says, "Please pray for wisdom"
        -Logical follow up questions include:
            "For whom?"
            "What are you facing?"

-Set a time for all the Prayer Walk teams to meet afterward
    -This way you can pray together as a group and plan your follow up.

-Don't leave without getting the names of the people who share their prayer requests
-Don't go into the home (at least on the first visit)
    -After you come back and build a relationship, it may be very natural to go inside
        -But don't make it your goal to get inside the home

-Don't get into doctrinal debates
    *You are there to ask them, "How can I pray for you?"
        -By God's grace, your Church will have the chance to teach them the deeper truths of our
            Christian faith at a time and place where it is most likely to have the best results.

-Don't give handouts / brochures on the first visit
    -Your reason for being there is to:
        -Build relationships
        -Take the garbage out of their lives
    --No one is sitting around hoping Jehovah Witnesses / Mormons, etc., come knocking

-Don't feel as if you've failed if someone says they don't have any prayer requests to share
    -They still know there are Christians in their community who care for them.

Conducting a Memorial Service for an Airman.

People have a lot of things that they would appreciate you praying for.

Communion is celebrated at Anchor of Hope House Church. Anchor of Hope is a ministry of Redeemer Lutheran Church in Westfield, NJ; under the supervision of Pr. Paul Kritsch.
The House Church Planter (candidate) is Edna McClure.

Pr. Paul Huneke is working to establish a House Church at Naval Weapon Station Earle; he is working with Chaplain Mike Vitcavich.

VIII. Planting House Churches through Prayer

Once upon a time, in a land far, far away there were devout women and men of God. They had left behind family and everything familiar. Having crossed oceans, mountains and deserts, they now found themselves in a deep, dark jungle. These bearers of the Light and Truth found themselves surrounded by people whose language they did not understand, food they had never dreamt of eating, and women who were half dressed.

Their purpose was noble--to share the Good News of God's love for the fallen human race, that His grace and forgiveness was our free gift through the sacrifice of His Son. Their plan was normal--to start churches they would Pastor, utilizing worship forms that the brightest and best of their culture had developed over centuries. Their passion was noteworthy. In spite of very modest progress over several decades, these dedicated believers stubbornly clung to their vision; they were German ethnically speaking, after all.

One day, Herr Hans (not his real name) said to Herr Heinrich (not either), "Dis is nicht gut." (roughly translated, "something isn't working").

So, Hans, Heinrich and their beautiful frauleins sat down, and over some Warsteiner beer, had a theological convocation while their blond-haired, blue-eyed children played with their friends in the village. As they considered in all honesty how things were going, they were displeased. But what could they do differently? The Truth and the Light were not up for sale; so what was negotiable?

Basically, two things were identified:

-The missionaries would no longer serve as Pastors of local congregations. Up to that point, the missionaries had functioned in basically the same way that a Pastor in North America would have--they worked to gather a parish where they then served as shepherd. This would no longer be the case, from now on, the Missionary would focus on two things: Leadership Development and Planting Churches

-The second item identified as needing change was for the form of the worship to be more culturally contiguous. The pattern of the service would be true to Lutheran theology. The proclamation would be grace-based, Sacramental, and reflective of our historic Lutheran liturgy; yet at the same time, the length of the service would grow exponentially; the instruments used would be what the people were familiar with; the music played would sound like music they listened to; the words would obviously be in their language; gaiety would be evident, especially during the offerings (yes, plural).

Never would any of these changes be allowed to compromise the theological and doctrinal positions of the Lutheran Confessions or the actual statements regarding worship practice contained therein. Great care was taken not to repeat the Catholic decisions on many mission fields of folding pagan worship rituals into Christian worship (syncretism).

Today, there are almost three times as many Lutherans in Africa as there are in North America. With time, the order of service found in many Lutheran congregations in Africa has come to resemble more closely the historic Lutheran liturgy. Today, the remaining change for missionaries is still regarding their primary focus--Leadership Development and Church Planting.

Prayer coupled with Mercy Ministry will help a Church provide excellent ministry to members, visitors and their community at large. As a local church serves their community through Prayer and Mercy Ministry, by God's grace, there will be the opportunity to gather / plant new worshipping communities. For the sake of this discussion, we will collectively call these new worshipping communities, "House Churches."

America--the 3rd Largest Mission Field in the World

Why did America turn from a "Christian nation" into a mission field?

Some point to the cultural change that happened in the 1960's with the radical rejection of institutions. Others point to a lack of Mercy Ministry for the lost and least of these around us, which was replaced with slick advertising and programs designed to draw those already Christian, or nominally Christian, into our fold.

In my church body, The Lutheran Church--Missouri Synod, the early 1970's were our current high water mark (I say "current" because I have not given up hope for God to bless us once again with numerical growth). The 1970's marked a period of intense turmoil for our church body as we dealt with the issues of inerrancy and inspiration of Scripture--two positions we could not compromise. Unfortunately, since then, many future aspiring Church politicians drew our attention, not to our potential, but rather to perceived problems. And <u>the problem with always seeing problems is that the mission vision is put on hold because the Church's version of "political correctness" castrates much of leadership</u>.

Our church body has agreed what the truth is; now it is time to get on with sharing this truth. President J.A.O. Preuss once told my dad, "Some people are so closed minded, they can see through a key hole with both eyes." Think about it and consider this: if President Preuss could say this as a good Confessional Lutheran, so can we.

When I was at the Seminary, I was blessed to have Dr. J.A.O. Preuss III as my Academic Advisor. Jack was always very approachable and surprisingly, quite humorous. I always counted myself blessed to have been assigned to him; I had confidence in his perspective and position. One day, I shared this story involving our fathers; Jack smiled and said to me, "That sounds like my dad." And then he proceeded to share more stories.

The fact of the matter is, that in 2012, the best research from the Pew Center, Gallup, and George Barna says that on a typical Sunday 40% to 42% of America is in Church. This is a decline from 50 years ago, but in all honesty, this is a slight increase from five years ago.

The best research also tells us that 80% of America identifies itself as Christian. Now, there are some people who will hotly dispute the condition of these people's souls, not accepting this figure of 80%. My purpose in sharing this number is not to judge anyone's soul, but simply to share the facts with you; do with them what you want.

The average LCMS congregation has about 35% of its members in church on any given Sunday. This means that on any given Sunday, 65% of LCMS members are choosing <u>not</u> to come to church.

This is worse than the national average; the national average for worship attendance among all Christians is 50% (and this includes Christians not officially on any church's membership, which means that the national average percentage of Christians who are church members, who are in attendance on any given Sunday, is even <u>higher</u> than 50%).

> Simply put, from a statistical point of view, my church body is dying because it is not keeping up with even the <u>average</u> for worship attendance among Christians who are church members.

As of 2012, the United States has a population of 315,000,000, making it the third largest nation in the world. When it comes to population statistics, the following facts may prove helpful:

-"82% of our population live in either the cities / the suburbs (the worldwide urban rate is only 50%)."

-"The median age is 36.8 years."

-"The United States Census Bureau defines White people as those 'having origins in any of the original people of Europe, the Middle East, or North Africa. It includes people who reported 'White' or wrote in entries such as Irish, German, Italian, Lebanese, Near Easterner, Arab or Polish.' White constitutes the majority of the U.S. population, with a total of 223,553,265 or 72.4% of the population in the 2010 United States Census."

- "The American population more than tripled during the 20th century at a growth rate of about 1.3% per year."

FOUR SIMPLE TRUTHS:

#1. If you are part of a church body that is primarily rural, you need an urban plan.

#2. If you are a church body with a large older population, you need a youth plan.

#3. If you are not focused on white people, you are missing three-fourths of the population.

#4. If your church body is not growing, it is dying.

* The quotes above are taken from the United States – Age and Sex"
2009 American Community Survey 1 – year Estimates.
U.S. Census Bureau. Retrieved 2010-10-24

If you are in a church body that has had decades of declining church attendance you will be tempted to do a couple of things:

1. Attribute this decline to the purity of your position;

2. Describe the American church attendance record as <u>worse</u> than it actually is in the hope that your stakeholders take pity on you since you are apparently doing no worse than everyone else;

3. Sell out your doctrine and normative Christian practice;

4. Put your hope in some humanly contrived program;

5. Cannibalize the Church's assets to prop up ministry that is not self-sustaining (e.g., Church hierarchy, etc.). A terrible conflict of interest is created when the same people who decide to liquidate Church property also decide how much of these resources go to support themselves.

One of the challenging realities of Christianity in America is that <u>75% of the Christians who chose not to experience God under a steeple, watched at least two hours of religious broadcasting last week.</u>

Ask an "expert" why people don't go to church today and one of the reasons you will hear is, "People are just too busy. They work so many hours, spend so much time in traffic; they just don't have the time for Church."

Wrong! They just don't have the desire to be with <u>you</u> in Church.

The average worship service in America lasts roughly an hour. Even after you add it travel time, the simple truth is that people who watch their Preacher on TV are spending more time with God than the people who are going to a brick and mortar church building.

If nothing else, can we all agree that just because someone doesn't come to a brick and mortar church building on Sunday morning does not mean they don't love Jesus or don't want to hear the Gospel?

I will be the first to say that the doctrinal content found (or more accurately, missing) in most TV religion is <u>appalling</u>. By no means am I supporting or in agreement with their teaching / preaching!

If nothing else, we might draw encouragement from the fact that 75% of the Christians who did not go to Church are still exercising their faith in some way, shape or form. Some might argue that it is easier to start with a blank slate than to try and untie the Gordian's knot that comes with a lifetime of bad theology; perhaps, but with God, <u>all</u> things are possible.

Here is a strategic irony--people who attend House Church, go to Sunday worship (on average) three times as often as Christians who are <u>not</u> part of a House Church. This is why Luther would say that Christians who <u>love</u> God's Word will join together for House Church. <u>House Church is a sign of Spiritual maturity; Pastors who promote House Church encourage discipleship</u>. It is as simple as that.

If you only fed your body once a week, what would it look like? The more you eat the Bread of Life, the stronger your faith will be. If you only ate one meal a day, what would your attitude be like? <u>House Church is but one of the times and ways in which devout Christians are fed</u>. The Holy Spirit causes us to hunger for righteousness and then, by His work, we recognize the honey sweet taste of His Word.

<u>One of the misperceptions of American Christianity is that Americans used to all go to Church</u>. This has never been true and it certainly was not true in 1776.

It is interesting to study American church attendance. In the 1600's over 50% of America could be counted on to be seen in Church; but gradually, this percentage shrunk and shrunk, to the point that by the time of the American Revolution, Church attendance in America had fallen below 20% (*"Founding Faith"*, by Steven Waldman).

Why? Because the Church had largely become associated with the Government of England. We as Lutherans who understand that God works through His right hand (the Church) and His left hand (the government), should see that it is <u>not</u> God's design for the Church to be subordinated to or a puppet of, the government. When the American Revolution came, the Church had largely lost her prophetic voice. (To get a more complete picture, I recommend that you read, *"Founding Faith"*; this book is very well researched and I believe presents a fair and balanced accounting of our nation's actual religious roots.)

The fuel for American Revivals has largely been a "personal relationship" with Jesus. For those of us who know we are saved by Grace, this phrase can cause a knee jerk reaction. But, when you take time to consider the historical context of American dissatisfaction with a State-owned church, the desire to encourage a personal relationship with Jesus takes on a different light. For those of us who know that we are saved by Grace through faith, and that this faith is a gift, not of ourselves, lest any of us would boast, we should agree with the desire of our Founding Fathers that we <u>not</u> have a State-run Church.

<u>To the left hand of God (the government), the only redeeming virtue of the right hand (the Church) is any virtue that it might get the citizens to follow; and the only reason that this is desirable is for financial stability</u>. The right hand of God (the Church), knows that the redeeming virtue is His gracious gift of faith that produces all visible virtues. <u>The left hand treasures the penultimate gift; the right hand clasps the ultimate gift.</u>

The Church in America must never again be in bed with the government; regardless of party, we must hold all politicians to the light and standard of Scripture in its entirety.

So, here we are today in America, currently the 3rd largest mission field in the world.

<u>Here are some questions to consider</u>:
1. Are members supposed to be missionaries? _____

2. What will you do to share the Gospel with the unchurched? _____

Money and Missions

Praise God, my church body (The Lutheran Church--Missouri Synod) firmly believes, teaches and preaches that there is only one Name given under Heaven by which people must be saved!

I can tell you, as a network supported Mission Strategist, when I get in the pulpit on Sunday morning, I do not have to spend any time convincing our people of the need for Jesus. Thank God their faithful Pastors have already done this!!

In Garfield, New Jersey, we have a beautiful church--Holy Trinity Lutheran Church. When I first came to New Jersey, one of the Pastors I got to know was Dan Grams at Holy Trinity; his church is in a very ethnically and religiously diverse area. We looked at their community to understand better the mission context; after just one trip to the open air market with multiple Muslim businesses and grocers, it was obvious that this is in fact a "mission field." Holy Trinity is beautifully built, but its story is even more precious: they built and paid off their school and church during the height of the Great Depression. With all the social safety nets in place today, it is hard to truly understand the seriousness of those times. Christians today are still led by the Holy Spirit to give sacrificially for the Gospel.

James Cash Penney, the founder of J.C. Penney's was a devout Christian; as such, his weekly offering exceeded the tithe of 10%. His business went through good times and bad, but he always tithed.

One day, in one of those times when the business was suffering, a skeptic asked J.C. Penney, "Don't you wish you had some of that money you gave the church?" Without missing a beat, J.C. Penney replied, "The only money I ever lost was the money that I held onto. The money I gave to God has been put to the best of use."

> *Lutherans will give to support missions; the following things help*:
> -Recruitment and development of strong Prayer support for your mission
> -Good communication regarding the state of the mission
> -Potential for personal involvement in the mission
> -Resources provided by the missionary that can be used by the member
> -Accountability and transparency at all times
> -A plan is presented that at least has the appearance of working
> -Every week the goal is to be in front of a congregation, sharing the story.
> - Encourage people to give to causes other than your own.
> -All ministries planted by the missionary are designed from the beginning to be:
>   -self sustaining
>   -self replicating
>   -locally owned (in America, this means all ministry happens through a local church)

I am a network supported Mission Strategist; this simply means that by God's grace and the power of the Holy Spirit, I am responsible for raising the funds for my family and all aspects of my ministry. I have been doing this since January 1, 2009, and can report that to God's glory, we have never been without.

So, these thoughts I share with you are based on my personal experience, not some theory. I share them with you in the hope that if you are considering this type of ministry, or if you know someone who is, that you will be encouraged.

Jesus has a big vision, "Disciple all nations." His followers still get excited about this! No one in their right mind wants to jump on a sinking ship! **Pointing out problems is child's play; anyone can point out a problem. Leadership is providing a plan and by God's grace, to God's glory, getting the team from point A to point B**. Christ's death and resurrection demand nothing less than the best from us.

> God's mission does not have a money problem.

Money and the House Church

God's mission does not have a money problem and House Church is a very effective approach:

A member can be trained to be a House Church Planter through our website-www.HouseChurchPlanter.com. Every course can be taken for the cost of only a free will donation. The Pastor who is called to the congregation will have to spend time helping the House Church Planter candidate to prepare and communicate the Mission and Ministry plan. For this investment of time and a free will donation- the District gets a trained House Church Planter, with a Mission and Ministry Plan that is fully supported by a local congregation and ready to happen. The congregation is able to develop a believer from their midst whom they know and trust and that is connected in that community. The Members also "win" because for a small commitment, they receive college level training; get personally mentored by their Pastor, and have an opportunity to do things in ministry most members never get to.

Contrast this with training a traditional Pastor to go out and plant House Churches. This man will need four years of undergraduate education (at what cost); four more years of graduate theological training (in residence, total bill is over $30K a year) and then, when the Pastor graduates, he will need full time financial compensation.

Members who prove themselves competent in planting House Churches under their Pastor's supervision will receive financial support to get additional professional education as long as they continue to demonstrate the desire and ability to plant House Churches.

In this way, House Church Planters will build up a ministry as they go through their education. With this model, if it is God's desire for House Church Planters to enter full time ministry, there will be a flock already gathered to support them. And, this flock will already know their shepherd (consider how long Pastors stay at their first call and honestly ask if the shortness of their stay is not in part due to a lack of compatibility).

A basic principle in leadership development on the mission field: the church leader is selected by the community he serves; he is also supported by them (not put on the payroll of a church bureaucracy); his first line of accountability is with the worshipping community he serves. This is why we plant House Churches through existing churches, under the supervision of the called and ordained Pastor serving them.

House Churches are held in people's homes / businesses, etc. There is no cost to the local congregation for this. Likewise the utilities, refreshments and furniture are provided by the Members; so there is no cost to the local congregation for this either. All "advertising" is word of mouth; again, there is no cost to the local congregation for this. The property insurance, maintenance and upkeep are all taken care of by the Member, so again, no cost to the local congregation. The House Church Planter is a voluntary position; so there are no staffing costs for the local congregation.

There are none of the typical costs that chew up a budget and become the "god" that is worshipped in the annual planning cycle. There are none of these costs; but there will be a collection of tithes and offerings. Simple math will tell you--if you are collecting funds but not needing to spend anything, you will be in the black. Every House Church we have planted in New Jersey is in the black.

It is very important for House Church ministry to be given line items in the official Church budget:
1. The House Church ministry becomes "real" when it is in the budget.
2. Accountability
3. House Church ministry gets a "seat at the table" (you are either at the table, or on the table.)

House Church Planters can build a vibrant House Church ministry working just 10 hours per week. If they can only work five hours a week, they can still help an individual House Church develop.

There is a tremendous amount of flexibility with the House Church model; this comes in large part because the financial pressure has been taken away.

Contrast this with those who first go through eight years of post-high school education: they begin on day one with a tremendous weight around their shoulders, especially if they have been placed in a community where they have almost no long-term relationships.

But if this Pastor will dedicate his ministry to developing leaders and planting House Churches, he may make it. On the other hand, if this Pastor feels threatened by a House Church Planter, even one working under his supervision, then he has refused to allow his co-laborers in the Vineyard to contribute. My observation has been that God does not bless these endeavors.

It is a good idea to have an Elder assigned to every House Church; it may make best sense in your Church if a group of Elders rotate responsibility for each House Church. The Elder can help with financial oversight and financial discipleship. Additionally, the Elder provides a way for members of the House Church who are new to the congregation to get "plugged in" with other members and ministries.

Constantine is traditionally given credit for Christianity becoming an accepted religion. But prior to Constantine and his oft cited, "Edict of Milan," was the Emperor Galerius and his less quoted, but very powerful, "Edict of Toleration" in 311 AD.

Emperor Galerius was also well disposed towards Christians; here in part is what he had to say:

> "Among other arrangements which we are always accustomed to make for the prosperity and welfare of the republic, we had desired formerly to bring all things into harmony with the ancient laws and public order of the Romans, and to provide that even the Christians who had left the religion of their fathers should come back to reason…
>
> Finally when our law had been promulgated to the effect that they should conform to the institutes of antiquity, many were subdued by the fear of danger, many even suffered death. And yet since most of them persevered in their determination, and we saw that they neither paid the reverence and awe due to the gods… we thought that we ought to grant our most prompt indulgence also to these, **so that they may again be Christians and may *hold their conventicles*,** provided they do nothing contrary to good order.
>
> Wherefore, for this our indulgence, they ought to pray to their God for our safety, for that of the republic, and for their own, that the republic may continue uninjured on every side, and that they may be able to live securely in their homes."
>
> (From Lactantius, *De Mort. Pers.* as cited on Fordham University's web site)

A couple interesting things to note:
    -Roman history documents that the Early Christian church worshipped in "conventicles" (small groups).
    -The Emperor Galerius wanted Christians to pray for him.

Early Christianity endured many periods of intense persecution (although the truth is that more Christians are dying for their faith today than in any year previous); Christians had no public houses of worship; they often could not represent ourselves in court; the culture of the day was often blatantly anti-Christian (think lions and the Coliseum); **yet** the Church grew.

It is worth noting that during the approximately 70 years of Communist repression in the former Soviet Union, Lutherans (and all non-Eastern Orthodox Christians) abandoned their large cathedral like church structures and continued to gather for worship in numerous, non-descript homes. Here, they were able to maintain and even strengthen their faith.

This tells us that the Great Commission does not depend on the government; legal standing--even the conformity of culture to Christian prayers or Moses' Decalogue is not a prerequisite for us to share Christ boldly and confidently. House Churches were used by the first Christians when they had no money / no resources; they can work again today.

Some Notes from a Solid Research Book on House Churches

I would encourage you to get a copy of Roger Gehring's book, *House Church and Mission--The Importance of Household Structures in Early Christianity*; published by Hendrickson. The following quotes in this section are cited from his book.

Gehring's book is an excellent research resource. He is <u>very</u> thorough in looking at the New Testament passages regarding House Churches and spends <u>plenty</u> of time discussing textual criticism questions and any impact they might have. If you belong to a church body or clergy association that emphasizes this aspect of Biblical study, you will definitely appreciate this book.

Because of his focus on God's Word, I found his thoughts regarding House Churches in the New Testament and Early Church to be worthwhile. But he does more; in his book, Gehring helps us understand how the architecture of a typical Roman house would have impacted very practical aspects of Christian worship and gathering. Gehring's book is not meant to be a "practical, how to" resource (he devotes only 11 pages out of 408 to the question of "So what does this mean for us today?"); which is fine; that is why I am writing the book that I am.

You should get his book, if for no other reason, than that on pgs. 313 and 314, he has the floor plan and isometric reconstruction of St. Peter's home in Capernaum. How cool is that?! There is no other home that Jesus spent more time in during His adult ministry. St. Peter's home is arguably the first House Church Jesus planted. On those pages, you can see what it would have looked like.

"***On one point nearly all NT scholars presently agree***: early Christians met almost exclusively in the homes of individual members of the congregation. For nearly three hundred years--<u>until the fourth century, when Constantine began building the first basilicas throughout the Roman Empire--Christians gathered in private houses built initially for domestic use</u>, not in church buildings originally constructed for the sole purpose of public worship." (pg. 1)

In the transition from House Church to Basilica, there were three architectural phases: "the *house church*--a private domestic house that remained architecturally unaltered.... A *church house*--a private domestic house that was physically altered and adapted in order to meet the social and / or religious needs of the group... A *hall church* refers to a larger, more formal, rectangular hall." (pgs. 18-19)

Later in his book, Gehring points out how there were multiple house churches in many of the cities we read about in the Epistles and how the members of these house churches would gather with other house church members in the *hall church*, all being part of the same congregation. "In recent research, scholars tend to agree that the early Christian movement was characterized by <u>the coexistence of two church forms: the house church and the whole church at any given location</u>. This means that, in the various cities, alongside the local church as a whole, there existed house churches in which most of the activities and life of the church took place." (pg. 157)

To help his reader understand that in Early Christianity, there was one church that served a city, comprised of multiple House Churches, Gehring explains, "A *house church* is a group of Christians that meets in a private home. A *local church* consists of all the Christians that gather at a geographically definable location (e.g., town or city)." (pg. 27) And again, "As we have seen, house churches coexisted within the local church as a whole in Corinth. In 1 Corinthians 14:23, a gathering of the whole church is implied... In Romans 16:23, similar terminology is used." (pg. 171)

I definitely appreciate Gehring's point that **the Early House Church was not the end, but rather a means to the end** (pg. 227); the Early House Churches were a <u>springboard</u> for all sorts of ministry into the lives of the unreached in their respective city and community.

I was enlightened by Gehring to learn that Jewish people in Jesus' day had House Synagogues. (pg. 30) This helps explain the natural development of House Churches among worshippers who originally were mostly Jewish. I have since personally confirmed this with an Orthodox Rabbi who says they still do this.

In Colossians 4:15-16 we find a very nice, concise passage from the Early Church, where we see the word used for "church" describing <u>both</u> for a House Church (vs. 15) in a city AND for the city wide Church, which this House Church was a part of (vs. 16). Much thanks to Gehring for pointing this out. (pg. 257)

> *Give my greetings to the brothers at Laodicea, and to Nympha and <u>the church in her house</u>. After this letter has been read to you, see that it is also read in <u>the church of the Laodiceans</u> and that you in turn read the letter from Laodicea.* (Colossians 4:15-16)

Recently, I met with a possible House Church Planter; as I explained our model of ministry, he asked me, "So, this is what the Bible says?" On pg. 37, Gehring cites Mark 1:29; 33; 2:1; 3:20 and 9:33 as evidence that Jesus' healing and teaching ministry "took place in and around the house of Peter."

When my dad was a missionary in West Africa, his primary job was the recruiting and training of Preachers. Part of his strategy was always to win first the chief of the village; then the elders; and then the head of individual households. When Africans were brought into the Church through confession of Christ, renouncing the devil and being baptized, it was always by an entire household.

"This brings us to the very basic question of identity: In America, what we do generally provides us with our identity. In many parts of the world, especially in the family and community focused cultures of Africa and Asia, people do not see themselves as having any identity except insofar as they are part of a group, be it family, village or entire ethnic community." (Rev. Dr. Al Buckman)

Gehring points out that this is precisely what the Apostles did. *<u>The culture of their day was that decisions were made as a unit, not as individuals</u>.* This is still the culture of most of the world, and it is definitely the culture new Americans bring with them when they come here. Know the culture of the people you are trying to reach with the Gospel!

Hear Gehring--"… in calling Peter as his follower, Jesus gained the head of a household and with him the entire household for His cause, a household that was then available to Him as an operational base for His missional outreach." (pg. 41)

<u>**Action Question**</u>:
    *How are we changing our outreach in order to communicate better in the culture of the lost?

Gehring points out that Jesus' ministry was a "house to house" ministry as well as a ministry with large, public gatherings. Lutherans would resonate with the understanding that most of the time, two seemingly opposite approaches do not have to be resolved with an "either / or" paradigm, but rather through an understanding of a "both / and" approach to the alternatives presented.

For Lutherans, we say that a Christian church has nine Fruits and seven Marks. The nine fruit of the Holy Spirit: love, joy, peace, patience, kindness, goodness, faithfulness, gentleness and self control. The seven marks: Scripture, Baptism, Communion, a Pastor, the cross, confession and forgiveness, prayer and praise.

Gehring notes that the House Churches in the first three centuries were church in all essential matters-- "Prayer, fellowship, and missional and instructional proclamation are all elements of a full-fledged house church." (pg. 46) On other pages, Gehring talks about Baptism, Communion, etc., being done through the House Church. (pg. 84)

For me, an insight from Gehring's book had to do with the *Jewish regulations regarding witnesses.* (pg. 53) In Jesus' time, every matter had to be established by two or three witnesses. When Jesus sent His disciples out in pairs, it was out of this witness regulation. The witness that God so loved the world was the visible sight of these paired up Disciples; they are God's witness.

So often we describe "witnessing" as something we <u>say</u>; but the believers <u>themselves</u> are an <u>incarnational</u> witness of God. And as Jesus' representatives, sent to speak on His behalf (the definition of an Apostle is someone who speaks for the person who sent them; they do not say their own words; they are received as if the person who sent them was there instead of their representative); <u>the believer</u> is a witness regarding the response of those she or he shares the Gospel with.

Those who reject the witness of Christ are rejecting Christ Himself. I am quite sure that most Christians have never really understood the authority of their calling--or its historical roots.

A thought that came to me as I was reading Gehring's book is simply this:
Preaching for the purpose of outreach is the domain of Pastors. Prayer for the purpose of outreach is the domain of the entire Priesthood of the Baptized.

On page 91, <u>Gehring identifies three dimensions of outreach that happened in the Early House Churches</u>:
1. mission proclamation / preaching
2. mission through lifestyle (something emphasized today in "missional communities")
3. mission through personal conversation (again, emphasized in "missional communities"). Missional community is an aspect of House Church.

<u>Two Purposes of the Early House Church (pg. 94)</u>:
1. Missional outreach
2. Training / Discipleship

One of Gehring's real strengths is that he unpacks the Jewish culture during the time of the Early House Churches. I appreciated his thoughts on Acts 6, when seven are chosen--"The group of seven corresponded to the leadership structure in a local synagogue with a council of seven elders as the leaders of the congregation." (pg. 97) Interesting.

It is my observation that mission efforts usually end in frustration and failure when the missionary / supporting church do not have a clear vision for establishing self-sufficient House Churches / church plants. God's Word will not return to Him void; it will accomplish the purpose for which it was sent. (Isaiah 55:11)

People involved with planting new worshipping communities need to believe the power of God's Word down to their very core. If there is any doubt about the new ministry becoming self-sufficient, it will manifest itself in the end; and if this doubt is not dealt with, it will paralyze the new work as the doubt turns into fear, faith-killing fear.

Gehring does a good job of noting how the Apostle Paul intentionally developed House Churches that were self-sufficient. The House Church members were always sad to see Paul the Missionary leave, but Paul the Apostle knew that his part in the play was to build a foundation, that others would come behind him to Pastor and Shepherd the House Churches. And healthy House Churches, once planted by a Missionary, will <u>reproduce</u> additional House Churches under their Pastor.

The Early House Churches collected tithes and offerings. (pg. 182) This is something we teach also in our model of House Church ministry, unlike Missional Communities, which are not self-sufficient.

139

The House Church model facilitates the quick leveraging of new relationships to grow the Church dynamically. (pg. 188) An additional advantage of House Church is that there is no church sign on the believer's home; in our model, all House Churches are under the supervision of a regularly called and ordained Pastor, so you have the best of both worlds--reliable teaching and preaching being delivered in a "neutral" environment that anyone can walk into. And, because all our House Churches are planted through existing congregations, everyone who comes to a House Church can become part of an even larger body of believers.

House Church planters can be men and women; every believer should be working to gather others to be blessed by the Gospel and God's grace in a community led by a Pastor. I appreciated Gehring's listing of 12 women in the Epistles who helped the Apostle Paul with his ministry of planting House Churches. (pg. 211)

Appearing alphabetically, not by any implied order of importance:

-Euodia
-Julia
-Junia
-Lydia
-Mary
-Nympha
-Persis
-Phoebe
-Prisca
-Syntyche
-Tryphaena
-Tryphosa

Gehring cites Leonard Sweet, a known quantity in outreach, "'the best way into the postmodern home is through the family.'... three of the most significant developments in education, medicine, and religion during this period were 'mushrooming movements toward home schools, home births, and *home churches.*' This is due to 'the cultural phenomenon of *cocooning*, a postmodern desire to seek refuge in the inner circle of the home for relief from the harsh, nightmarish outside world.'" (pg. 311)

I like institutions and rules about as much as a root canal. It is much more fun to be "free" and do what "you feel like." But here is the thing, and Gehring says it so well: "Institutionalization is unavoidable for an organization that wants to continue existing and growing beyond its first generation (Roloff)." (pg. 299)

I have been blessed to know the Pastors of some very "cutting edge" churches with rapid numerical growth. One thing they all have in common is this--they have an organizational structure and clear lines of responsibility. In fact, the faster their churches add members often corresponds to the more detailed and demanding their organization chart is.

My point is simply this--in our model of House Church ministry, all our House Churches Planters are under the supervision of a regularly called and ordained Pastor; this man in turn is under the ecclesiastical supervision of his District President.

Jesus said that He did nothing on His own and spoke only what His Father told Him. (John 8:28). Jesus, an equal Person of the Trinity, asked what His <u>Father's</u> will was. Nothing less than this should be expected of anyone who claims to follow Jesus; every person with responsibility for ministry needs to be under authority. If a House Church Planter is not accountable to a higher Pastor, then those Planters have made themselves into a pseudo Bishop and their desire is to start their own ecclesiastical entity.

What Is an LCMS House Church?

In 2008, when I was praying about this call to be a Mission Strategist, my mom, Carol Buckman, asked me, "So who is in charge of these House Churches you are planting?" If you know my mom, you know how she gets to the nub of the issue very quickly. My answer to my mother has always remained the same, "All ministry in the LCMS is done through the local congregation ultimately. These House Churches will be planted through existing LCMS congregations, under the supervision of their regularly called and ordained Pastors. We are not creating competition for our existing congregations; these House Churches are extensions of their ministry. Whatever these House Churches ultimately develop into is a matter for the local congregation to decide. I don't have a dog in that fight." My mom simply replied, "You better make sure people know this." Yes, Mom. Additionally, I would say that LCMS House Churches are:

Biblical

>--*They were continually devoting themselves to the apostles' teaching and to fellowship, to the breaking of bread and to prayer.... Day by day continuing with one mind in the temple, and breaking bread from house to house, they were taking their meals together with gladness and sincerity of heart, praising God and having favor with all the people. And the Lord was adding to their number day by day those who were being saved.* (Acts 2:42-47 NASU)

Historical
--Not until the Edict of Milan and Constantine, did we have consistent, legal status, able to have buildings, bank accounts and fair treatment under the law.

Luther's Third Model of Worship
--"The third kind of service should be a truly evangelical order and should not be held in a public place for all sorts of people. But those who want to be Christians in earnest and who profess the gospel with hand and mouth should sign their names and meet alone in a house somewhere to pray, to read, to baptize, to receive the sacrament, and to do other Christian works...." (Volume #53; Luther's Works)

The Church
--We define the Church as having seven marks (The Bible; Baptism; Communion; the Keys; Called Pastors; the Cross; Prayer and Praise) and the nine Fruit of the Holy Spirit. (Volume #41; LW)
  * House Church is not just another type of small group; it is the Church.

LCMS
--All LCMS House Churches are planted through existing LCMS congregations and under the supervision of the regularly called and ordained LCMS Pastor serving that congregation.
  --Just as in Acts, the members of LCMS House Churches study the preaching / teaching of their Pastors.
  --Most of our constituted congregations began in someone's home; this is nothing new in many ways.

Uses Every Advantage Possible in Order to Share the Gospel
  --Leverages relationships between the believers and the unchurched / dechurched / unsaved.
  --Held on "neutral" space (a home, for example, does not have a church sign planted in the yard)
  --Able to call on the resources of the LCMS congregation that is planting it.

Not Held on Sunday A.M.
  --We want it to be possible for House Church members to worship with the mother church. House Church members attend worship under a steeple three times as often as members not in a House Church

Infinitely Reproducible
  --Because it has these two key characteristics: Self Supporting and Self Replicating

Some Questions to Answer / Consider Before Planting a House Church

In both my personal experience with planting House Churches and now as a Mission Strategist working with other churches, helping them to plant House Churches, I have found that spending some time up front answering the following questions to be a good thing.

I would encourage you to put your answers in writing and to share the document with the Pastor; then the Elders; then the Governance Board; then the key stakeholders; then the congregation at large.

I do not recommend that you skip over anyone on this list (unless the group does not exist or was already covered in a previous group, e. g., the key stakeholders may have already been talked to when you covered this with the Governance Board).

1. Why do you want to plant this House Church? _____

2. Who will be on your House Church plant team? _____

    Who are your partners that will help even though they are not part of the plant (think both inside and outside the church)? _____

    Who in your church's leadership team will help you connect the House Church members to the other ministries of your congregation? _____

3. What assets do you have already available to help with this House Church plant? _____

    What assets do you still require? _____

4. How will you provide Mercy Ministry to your HC, visitors and the community? _____

    How will you do outreach? _____

    How will you assimilate visitors into members and then disciples of your House Church? _____

5. Will this House Church become a satellite? _____

    Birth additional House Churches? _____

    Become a constituted LCMS congregation? _____

6. What accountability does the House Church Planter have to the Supervising Pastor, Sponsoring Congregation and House Church he / she serves? _____

    This is a *partial* list of questions to answer if you want to have a strong Mission and Ministry Plan for your House Church plant.

    In our House Church Planter training (offered on line at www.HouseChurchPlanter.com) we have an entire course devoted to preparing an effective plan. Hopefully, this short list of questions will help you see the importance of preparation and prayer.

Luther's Concept of Worship: Three Purposes, Two Places

I. Commission Focused Worship (Constantinian Church building)

"Now there are three kinds of divine service or mass. The **_first_** is the one in Latin which we published earlier under the title *Formula Missae*.[1] It is not now my intention to abrogate or to change this service. It shall not be affected in the form which we have followed so far; but we shall continue to use it when or where we are pleased or prompted to do so. For in no wise would I want to discontinue the service in the Latin language, because the young are my chief concern. And if I could bring it to pass, and Greek and Hebrew were as familiar to us as the Latin and had as many fine melodies and songs, we would hold mass, sing, and read on successive Sundays in all four languages, German, Latin, Greek, and Hebrew. I do not at all agree with those who cling to one language and despise all others. I would rather train such youth and folk who could also be of service to Christ in foreign lands and be able to converse with the natives there, lest we become like the Waldenses in Bohemia,[2] who have so ensconced their faith in their own language that they cannot speak plainly and clearly to anyone, unless he first learns their language. The Holy Spirit did not act like that in the beginning. He did not wait till all the world came to Jerusalem and studied Hebrew, but gave manifold tongues for the office of the ministry, so that the apostles could preach wherever they might go. I prefer to follow this example. It is also reasonable that the young should be trained in many languages; for who knows how God may use them in times to come? For this purpose our schools were founded."

II. Context Focused Worship (again, the Constantinian Church building)

"The **_second_** is the German Mass and Order of Service, which should be arranged for the sake of the unlearned lay folk and with which we are now concerned. These two orders of service must be used publicly, in the churches, for all the people, among whom are many who do not believe and are not yet Christians. Most of them stand around and gape, hoping to see something new, just as if we were holding a service among the Turks or the heathen in a public square or out in a field. That is not yet a well-ordered and organized congregation, in which Christians could be ruled according to the gospel; on the contrary, the gospel must be publicly preached [to such people] to move them to believe and become Christians."

III. Commitment Focused Worship—Through the Home

"The **_third_** kind of service should be a truly evangelical order and should **not** be held in a public place for all sorts of people. But those who want to be Christians in earnest and who profess the gospel with hand and mouth should sign their names and meet alone **in a house** somewhere to pray, to read, to baptize, to receive the sacrament, and to do other Christian works. According to this order, those who do not lead Christian lives could be known, reproved, corrected, cast out, or excommunicated, according to the rule of Christ, Matthew 18 [:15–17]. Here one could also solicit benevolent gifts to be willingly given and distributed to the poor, according to St. Paul's example, II Corinthians 9. Here would be no need of much and elaborate singing, Here one could set up a brief and neat order for baptism and the sacrament and center everything on the Word, prayer, and love. Here one would need a good short catechism[3] on the Creed, the Ten Commandments, and the Our Father. In short, if one had the kind of people and persons who wanted to be Christians in earnest, the rules and regulations would soon be ready. But as yet I neither can nor desire to begin such a congregation or assembly or to make rules for it. For I have not yet the people or persons for it, nor do I see many **who want it**. But if I should be requested to do it and could not refuse with a good conscience, I should gladly do my part and help as best I can. In the meanwhile the two above-mentioned orders of service must suffice. And to **train the young and to call and attract others to faith**, I shall—besides preaching—help to further such public services for the people, until Christians who earnestly love the Word find each other and join together. For if I should try to make it up out of my own need, it might turn into a sect. For we Germans are a rough, rude, and reckless people, with whom it is hard to do anything, except in cases of dire need."[100]

---

[100]Martin Luther, 53:62-64. Fortress.

Highlights from Luther's thoughts regarding House Church worship:

-It is Sacramental
-A Pastor will oversee it
-Offerings will be collected
-The worship service would not need as much singing; a brief and neat order would suffice
-There should be official guidance regarding what happens in a Lutheran House Church
-If people want House Church ministry, the Pastor should provide it
-The young should be trained to "call and attract others to faith"
-Christians who earnestly love the Word will join together for House Church

House Church Is Church

"Properly speaking, the church is the assembly of saints and true believers." Tappert, T. G. (2000, c1959). *The Augsburg Confession : Translated from the Latin* (The Confession of Faith: 2, VIII-, 1)

"The holy Christian people are recognized by:
--their possession of *the holy Word* of God…
--Second, God's people, or the Christian holy people, are recognized by the holy sacrament of Baptism, wherever it is taught, believed, and administered correctly according to Christ's ordinance….
--Third, God's people, or Christian holy people, are recognized by the holy sacrament of the altar, wherever it is rightly administered, believed, and received, according to Christ's institution….
--Fourth, God's people, or holy Christians, are recognized by the office of the keys (they belong to the people of Christ and are called "the church's keys")…
--Fifth, the church is recognized externally by the fact that it consecrates or calls ministers….
--Sixth, the holy Christian people are externally recognized by prayer, public praise, and thanksgiving to God….
--Seventh, the holy Christian people are externally recognized by the holy possession of the sacred cross….

In addition to these seven principal parts there are other outward signs that **identify the Christian church,** namely, those signs whereby the Holy Spirit sanctifies us according to the second table of Moses."
(Ibid, 41)

Small groups get together for all sorts of good things; but when they gather, they do not have the Seven Principal Parts of the Christian Church listed above. House Church ministry is not a variation of small group ministry. House Church is Church.

House Churches may be small in size, but they are the Church. Small Groups may even have a larger attendance than a House Church, but when a small group gathers, it does not have the Seven Principal Parts of the Church.

House Church is Church; it is more than "small group ministry." Luther's idea of House Church ministry accounted for all Seven Principal Parts of the Church.

On that day a great persecution broke out against the church at Jerusalem, and all except the apostles were scattered throughout Judea and Samaria. Godly men buried Stephen and mourned deeply for him. But Saul began to destroy the church. Going from house to house, he dragged off men and women and put them in prison. (Acts 8:1-3)
* The church Jesus planted was organized around homes.

144

When Did Steeple Church Start?

When we look at God's original fellowship with man in the Garden of Eden, were any buildings involved? No. **Adam and Eve's family** worshipped God (Genesis 4:3 ff), but there is no record of any dedicated building for God to dwell in.

Let's fast forward a couple of thousand years to **Abram** and examine the nature of this Patriarch's worship of God:

> *Abram traveled through the land as far as the site of <u>the great tree of Moreh at Shechem</u>... The Lord appeared to Abram and said, "To your offspring I will give this land." <u>So he built an altar there to the Lord</u>, who had appeared to him.* (Genesis 12:6-7)

*Abram's worship facility apparently consisted of an outdoor altar near a well-known tree. Not much different from what Adam's family probably used.

How did **Moses** first worship God?

> *When the Lord saw that he had gone over to look, God called to him from within the bush, "Moses! Moses!" And Moses said, "Here I am."* (Exodus 3:4)

*In the desert; barefoot, by himself.

The last act of Jewish worship in their Egyptian captivity was the Passover Meal which happened in their.... Homes.

Steeple Church Began with a Tent and the Old Covenant

> Now <u>the first covenant</u> had regulations for worship and also an earthly sanctuary. (Hebrews 9:1)

> The Lord said to Moses, "Tell the Israelites to bring me an offering. You are to receive the offering for me from each man whose heart prompts him to give. These are the offerings you are to receive from them: gold, silver and bronze; blue, purple and scarlet yarn and fine linen; goat hair; ram skins dyed red and hides of sea cows; acacia wood; olive oil for the light; spices for the anointing oil and for the fragrant incense; and onyx stones and other gems to be mounted on the ephod and breastpiece. "Then <u>have them make a sanctuary for me, and I will dwell among them</u>. Make this tabernacle and all its furnishings exactly like the pattern I will show you." (Exodus 25:1-9)

There was no "steeple church" prior to the Old Covenant.

The Old Covenant had the following primary markers / identifiers:
- A temple
- A priesthood
- Bloody sacrifices

Speaking through His prophet Jeremiah God told His chosen people that a New Covenant would be coming:

> "The time is coming," declares the LORD, "when I will make a <u>new covenant</u> with the house of Israel and with the house of Judah." (Jeremiah 31:31)

145

Jesus always chose His words wisely; don't miss His emphasis on the new covenant God offers to all humankind through Communion:

In the same way, after the supper he took the cup, saying, "This cup is the __new__ covenant in my blood, which is poured out for you." (Luke 22:20)

The three primary markers/identifiers of the Old Covenant are gone:
- The temple was razed to the ground, just as Jesus had prophesied
- The Aaronic Priesthood has disappeared without a trace
- Animal sacrifices have not been offered according to the Old Covenant for 2,000 years (a ticklish question to answer would be, "If there is no atoning for sin without the shedding of blood, how does the Old Covenant still make us right with GOD?")

Unfortunately, many Christians do not hold the LORD's Supper in proper esteem and thereby miss the greater point He is making when He says, *"This __is__ the blood of My testament which is shed for the forgiveness of many sins."* (Matthew 26:28, my translation)
  *The Old Covenant is gone!
  *When Jesus identifies the New Covenant as His, this is a declaration of His Divinity (Jeremiah 31:31)

Some Christians will say, "Jesus paid for all our sins at Calvary; Communion can't be a payment for our sins; our sins were already paid for."

The problem with this becomes apparent quickly. If all sin was paid for at Calvary, then Hitler gets to go to Heaven. Their response at this point is, "Hitler was not a believer, so he died outside of God's grace." But if Hitler did not receive the benefit of Christ's death; then how __does__ someone receive this benefit? Their answer would simply be, "You must decide to let Jesus into your heart." In their faulty answer, they still reveal the need for people __today__ to receive the benefit of Christ's death; but rather than allow God's grace in Baptism and Communion to be the means for receiving the forgiveness that His Word attributes to Baptism and the LORD's Supper, they make humanity a co-worker in their salvation and sanctification.

There is a difference between objective justification and subjective justification. Objectively speaking, Jesus died to pay for all sins; but the subjective reality is twofold:
- We are judged __individually__ before God, not collectively
- To appropriate His forgiveness today, we must be baptized if we have the opportunity; we must confess our sins; we must confess with our mouths that Jesus is Lord and believe in our hearts that God raised Him from the dead; in short, we must be born __from above__ (John 3:3-7); born of God (1 John 5:1).

This is why Communion is __more than__ just a "memorial" meal. It is Christ's body and blood; it is payment for our sins, __today__!

The three markers of the Old Covenant are gone; but they are not absent. The three original markers of the Covenant have been replaced in the New Covenant:
  - The temple is now your body. At the same time, you are also living stones joined together with other believers to be built into a Spiritual house. So there is an individual aspect to your relationship with God and there is also a corporate, collective relationship you have with other believers and together, with God.
  - The priesthood is now every believer (see 1 Peter 2:5)
  - The bloody sacrifices were replaced with Christ's atoning death and resurrection, the benefits of which He gives us through His meal. Truly, God's mercies are __new__ every morning.

The Temple Takes on a New Meaning in the New Covenant

"The first covenant had regulations for worship and also an earthly sanctuary" (Hebrews 9:1)

"I tell you that one greater than the temple is here." (Matthew 12:6)

At that moment the curtain of the temple was torn in two from top to bottom." (Matthew 27:51)

Don't you know that you yourselves are God's temple...? (1 Corinthians 3:16)

Do you not know that your body is a temple of the Holy Spirit, who is in you, whom you have received from God? You are not your own; you were bought at a price. Therefore honor God with your body. (1 Corinthians 6:19-20)

Consequently, you are no longer foreigners and aliens, but fellow citizens with God's people and members of God's household, built on the foundation of the apostles and prophets, with Christ Jesus himself as the chief cornerstone. In him the whole building is joined together and rises to become a holy temple in the Lord. And in him you too are being built together to become a dwelling in which God lives by his Spirit. (Ephesians 2:19-22)

I did not see a temple in the city, because the Lord God Almighty and the Lamb are its temple. (Revelation 21:22)

The first sanctuary was a tent; for a time, this tent was replaced with a semi-permanent building; but ultimately in Heaven, God Himself will be our temple.

Paul compares our bodies to tents (2 Corinthians 5:1), which will pass away. Just as human-made temples are replaced with God's perfection, so also our earthly bodies (these "tents") will be made new by God.

Interestingly (to me); Paul's vocation was a tent maker.

For over 250 years after Christ's resurrection and ascension, the Church counted on members' homes as places of worship. Their initial efforts to worship in the temple / synagogues received a short-lived welcome from the Jews remaining who had not accepted Yeshua as the Messiah.

The modern church with its recognizable architecture did not exist until the 4th Century AD. House Church worship is the original form of worship for the Christian Church. The current Lutheran Study Bible notes in its commentary that the church Jesus established was a House Church.

Are Our House Churches "Conventicles"?

"A **conventicle** is a small, unofficial and unofficiated meeting of laypeople, to discuss religious issues in a non-threatening, intimate manner." (*Wikipedia*)

* The House Churches in the New Testament were official and they were officiated.
* LCMS House Churches are planted through existing LCMS congregations and are under the supervision of their regularly called and ordained Pastors; they are also official and officiated.

An LCMS House Church does not fit the definition of a "conventicle"; especially in a derogatory or pejorative sense of the word.

"In England there were three acts of parliament passed to coerce people to attend Church of England services and to prohibit unofficiated meeting of laypeople:
  -The Conventicle Act of 1593
  -The Conventicle Act of 1664
  -The Conventicles Act of 1670"
      (Wikipedia)

House Churches are currently illegal in China. But the Communist Party will build your church a building for you, if you will just agree to meet only in public…. Hmmm… No thanks.

Use of the Home for Ministry in the Early Church as Found in the Book of Acts

Citation	Comments
1:14-26	All together; constant prayer. Matthias is chosen to replace Judas
2	Pentecost
2:40	3,000 are baptized
2:42	Classic four-part description of House Churches
4:23	Peter and John's report to the believers probably happened in a home (vs. 31 says that after they prayed in this place, the building shook; I am surmising this building was someone's home)
4:34	Homes are sold to fund the ministry
5:1-10	Annanias and Saphira are struck down in someone's home ("at the door" vs. 9)
5:42	Preaching and teaching ("day after day, the temple courts and house to house")
6:2	Feeding of widows ("waiting on tables"- probably a home)
8:3	In order to destroy the Church, Saul "goes from house to house"
9:11	Saul is directed to a House Church on Straight Street owned by Judas (different one)
9:36-42	Peter raises Tabitha from the dead
10:6	Peter ministers out of Simon the Tanner's home in Joppa
10:25ff	Peter comes to a large group that Cornelius has gathered in his home in Caesarea; Peter preaches and the Holy Spirit comes on them
12:12	Mary's home is a House Church
13:1	"The Church at Antioch…" is not a Gothic structure with stained glass
14:21-23	Paul and Barnabas plant House Churches and appoint Elders
14:27	"they gathered the church together" clearly "church" does not = a building
16:15	Lydia's home is a House Church
16:32-34	The jailor's home is used for a House Church gathering
17:1-9	Jason's home is a House Church
18:3	Priscilla and Aquilla's tent (apparently) is a House Church
20:6-12	Paul preaches an "all-nighter" in someone's home
20:20	Paul did his preaching and teaching, *from house to house*
28:16 and 23ff	Paul uses the home in Rome, in which he was held for House Church ministry (28:31, *"boldly and without hindrance he preached and taught…"*)

A Really Good Picture of New Testament House Church Worship to Study:

> *They were continually devoting themselves to the <u>apostles' teaching</u> and to <u>fellowship</u>, to the <u>breaking of bread</u> and to <u>prayer</u>.*
>
> *Everyone kept feeling a sense of awe; and many wonders and signs were taking place through the apostles. And all those who had believed were together and had all things in common; and they began selling their property and possessions and were sharing them with all, as anyone might have need. Day by day continuing with one mind <u>in the temple, **and** breaking bread from house to house</u>, they were taking their meals together with gladness and sincerity of heart, praising God and having favor with all the people. <u>And the Lord was adding to their number day by day those who were being saved</u>.* (Acts 2:42-46 NASU)

This passage is a favorite of any proponent of House Churches. And it is a good one to study; you will find:

1. The Four Pillars of a House Church Gathering:
   -They <u>discussed their Pastor's message</u>. This is a critical point. The group did not vote on what Oprah Winfrey or Bill O'Reilly book they were going to discuss. Their Pastors were the Apostles and when they got together for worship, they "***devoted*** *themselves to the Apostle's teaching*." This is the model for LCMS House Churches; when we gather, it is to discuss the Pastor's preaching/teaching, whatever he feels led to feed the flock with. The Pastor is the judge of sound doctrine within the congregation. He is under authority; any concern regarding his orthodoxy should be handled through proper church structures in Biblical ways.

   -They <u>ate food.</u> This is what we do when we gather. We eat food and have fun!! This is when we find out how the family is; what is going on at work; and what movies are worth seeing at the theater.

   -They <u>celebrated the LORD's Supper</u>. Of course they did; Jesus gave us the LORD's Supper in the upper room of someone's <u>house</u>. Celebrating Communion in someone's home may seem odd to us; but <u>our practices</u> would have been odd to the Early Church.

   -<u>Prayer</u>. God's house will be a house of Prayer for all nations. There are a handful of times when something Jesus said is recorded in each of the first three Gospels; His quotation of the Prophet Isaiah regarding God's house being a house of Prayer is one of those times. **The Early Church was known for Prayer**.

2. The Two Locations Where Believers Gathered:
   -The temple <u>and</u> the home. It was the desire of the Early Church to have <u>both</u> Congregational and House Church worship. Why? Because when we gather together for worship in the Sanctuary, we experience God in a completely different way (not better or worse, but different) from how we experience God when we gather in someone's living room or place of business. Good Lutheran theology teaches us that most of the time, we don't have to make "either / or" decisions, but that rather, "both / and" is the most Godly path.
   Some people propose that House Church worship is an either / or decision; that you can't worship God in both the Sanctuary and the living room. This is not the position of the LCMS house church; we have the same desire as the Early Church--to worship in <u>both</u> the Sanctuary <u>and</u> the living room.

3. There is One Result:

-Numerical Growth. God's Word is crystal clear, *"And the Lord was adding to their number, day by day those who were being saved."* (Acts 2:47) This passage is factual; the Early Church did experience numerical growth. This passage is not only factual, it is also furnished--God had it recorded in His Word for us to know this. Listen to me! The temptation is to run to some explanation that reduces the significance and power of this passage. Don't fall to that temptation; pray and ask God to have His way with our hearts and minds, to conform our wills to that of His Son, and to grow our expectation of Him to do incredible things today also.

4. How important Mercy Ministry is to the life of the House Church. Whatever the Early Church could do to help anyone in need, they did. It is important to note that when the believers sold their property to help others out, this was voluntary; they were neither driven by guilt or the government. They chose to respond in this way, as the Holy Spirit led them. We don't have a detailed diagram of how this ministry was carried out; there are no extensive job descriptions for each of the responsibilities--that is not the point. Circumstances constantly change; there is not enough paper or digital space to capture all the endless myriad of possibilities. The point is that the Early Church took care of people!

5. Being a House Church Planter requires that you and your actions are supervised. The pattern of worship here was agreed to by the Church; people were not just doing whatever they wanted to. Jesus Himself said that He had not come to do His own will, but the will of His Father. (John 6:38) *The desire to plant a House Church is wonderful, but it requires that the men or women doing this, submit to the authority and leadership of their Pastor.* If they have any reservation regarding this, then that is probably a sign that this is not the right situation for this to happen.

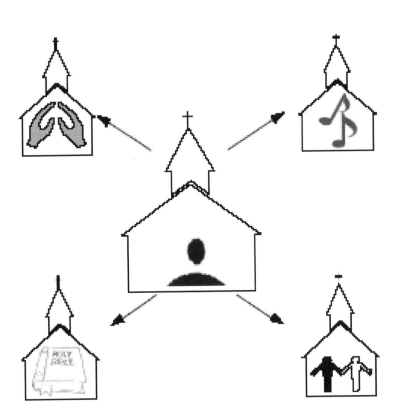

Applying a Proven LCMS Model in North America

Today, there are almost three times as many Lutherans in Africa as there are in North America. The story of how this happened includes names like Bunkowske, Rasch, Brehmer, Boettcher, Lautenschlager, Roegner, Buckman and many others. If you go to Nigeria, take the time to visit the Lutheran station in Obot Idom. There is a cemetery there, including all the missionary children who died, overcome by malaria or other maladies. The Gospel was planted at a cost.

My parents became missionaries to Nigeria in 1965; in 1977 my dad (Rev. Dr. Al Buckman) accepted the call to be the Area Secretary for Africa, Europe and the Middle East. In 1989, my dad accepted the call to be the World Areas Director for LCMS World Missions. As he was preparing to retire, my dad put down the following thoughts on how he and the other missionaries went about building the Lutheran Church in Africa, by the power of the Holy Spirit.

Their concept was basically pretty simple: develop leaders and plant churches.

As an adult, one of my favorite things to do has always been to have a Lutheran beverage with my dad and talk about ministry. Some of my best memories are the in depth conversations I have been blessed to have with him. We would take an issue and work it around from different angles, usually agreeing.

I have wondered for many years why in the world our church body did not adopt this clear focus for her work in the United States. When I became an ordained Pastor in our church body, I began this process in an intentional way. There has always been a lot of trial and error (lots of errors); but thankfully, I belong to a community of Christians who are willing to try new things and take risks for the sake of the Gospel.

The following very simple document is from my dad. It captures our strategy for missions in Africa for at least 50 years. At the end of my dad's document, I have added my thoughts for taking the principles found in this strategy and applying them to our context in the United States.

It should be noted that when our missionaries first came to Africa, we did not have Partner Church bodies with their own administration and theological education institutions; this would not come for a while. The theological practices of our partner church bodies agree with our practice regarding the office of Pastor. When the first missionaries came to these dark jungles, they were sent by our church body to establish a church where there was no church, no seminary, and no church body. Today, instead of Lay Preachers, the church bodies in Africa use the designation "Lay Evangelist" for someone who works under the oversight of a Pastor to help gather believers and potential believers for worship.

Pr. Duane Feldmann and Pr. Tim Morris at Alive in Christ, Columbia, MO.

LCMS Procedure for Opening Preaching Stations in Africa

I. Gather Approval and Assurances

Arrange a meeting with the village chief and elders, and obtain their commitment to the following:
1. Invitation to hold worship services
    Question: If a missionary comes to the village to hold services, will he be welcomed?

2. Support for the work of the missionary
    Question: If a missionary comes to the village to hold worship services, will the chief and elders encourage their people to attend?

3. Place to hold worship services
    Question: If a missionary comes to the village to preach, will the village provide a place where worship services can be held?

4. Support for those who become Christian
    Question: If the Lord blesses the missionaries' efforts and some receive Christ and are baptized, will the chief and elders support the Christians in the village? i.e., not force them to go to the fortune teller or use native medicine when someone becomes ill?

5. Land on which to build a church
    Question: If the Lord blesses the work of the missionary, and some believe and are baptized, will the village give them land on which to build a church?

Discuss the above questions with the village chief and elders. After they have given their consent to each of the above, the missionary shall set a date when he will hold the first of a series of worship services.

II. Establishing the Preaching Station

A. Worship / Commitment

The missionary will prepare and deliver a series of approximately 20 sermons. Suggested topics are:
1. Creation
2. Fall
3. God's Promise
4. Patriarchs
5. Bondage in Egypt
6. The Wilderness
7. The Promised Land
8. David's Kingdom
9. The Prophets
10. The Birth of Christ
11. The Teachings of Christ
12. The Miracles of Christ
13. The Betrayal of Christ
14. Crucifixion and Death
15. Resurrection and Ascension

At the conclusion of the worship series, the missionary will call for commitment from among those who have attended the worship services.

B. Nurture

Those who indicate that they wish to become members of the Lutheran Church shall be enrolled in an instruction class, the purpose of which shall be to:

1. Encourage entire families to become members together, as a unit (see Acts 18:8 for example)
2. Determine that each person has decided to put away all jujus, forsake traditional religion, and follow Christ.

The instruction class shall be of four to six months duration, depending on how the missionary wishes to structure it. Upon the successful completion of the class, those enrolled shall be baptized into members in the Lutheran Church.

Text: *Luther's Small Catechism*

III. Leadership Training

A. Selection of Leaders

In each preaching station, those who have been baptized are challenged to designate two men who will be trained to serve the preaching station as lay preachers. The missionary does not make the selection. From the beginning it is made clear that the preaching station is responsible for the support of the lay preacher, and the lay preacher is accountable to the preaching station. Those designated as candidates for training as lay preachers are enrolled in a leadership training class taught by the missionary. They are also responsible for leading worship services at the preaching station.

B. Leadership Training

Those designated as lay preachers are enrolled in a leadership training class consisting of two parts, each meeting once a week.

1. Sermon Study Class
The missionary meets with this class once a week to study the pericopies for the coming Sunday. The purpose of the class will be to study the Scripture readings, select one of them as the sermon text, and develop a sermon outline.

2. Lay Preacher Training
The missionary also meets with this class once a week to provide in-depth training for those who have been designated as lay preachers. The purpose of this class will be to provide instruction in Bible knowledge and the teachings of the Lutheran Church.

Texts: Koehler, <u>Summary of Christian Doctrine</u>
Reiss, <u>What Does the Bible Say?</u>

By: Dr. A. Buckman
5/3/99
jmw

"It is worth noting that, using this model, the Evangelical Lutheran Church in Liberia has grown from zero worshipping communities when work first began in 1977, to over 350 congregations and preaching stations today. Even more interesting, all this happened minus the presence of an in-country, residential Seminary program.

In the past 35 years, missionaries were only present for 13 years. Additionally, there was one Civil War and numerous military coups and yet the Church grew exponentially. Bishop Amos Bolay (of the Gbandi people) can speak even more clearly to all of this." (Rev. Dr. Al Buckman, 2013)

+   +   +

Reflection on "LCMS Procedure for Opening Preaching Stations in Africa"

Application Transition / Questions for 21st Century Urban North American Missions

1. Who are the "village chiefs / elders" in our landscape?

_____

2. In what ways could contemporary "village chiefs / elders" give their commitment to the worship and work of us as missionaries?

_____

3. What benefits come to a missionary today for taking the time to build this community team?

_____

4. What benefits could a missionary offer to a village chief? What can a missionary offer today?

_____

5. What can today's "village chiefs" do to support the rights of Christians in the public square?

_____

6. Understand how to get "free" land / buildings in America for ministry.

_____

7. How will catechesis (discipleship) happen in your House Church?

_____

8. Understand the importance of Leadership Selection and getting them into HC Planter training ASAP:

_____

Rev James Buckman
8/13/2011

Sample Covenant for Your House Churches:

This is not "covenant" of the magnitude Christ offers us in the LORD's Supper; rather the idea here is simply a group of believers making a promise to each other, their Church and their Savior. The following example is taken from one actually in use. *It is meant only as an example,* for your consideration. Please feel free to adapt as God leads you. Don't feel that you need to have this.

Our House Church Covenant-Vision

We have formed this house church by the power of the Holy Spirit who has called us to faith and equips us to bear fruit that is pleasing to our Savior and Lord, Jesus Christ.

We come together for fellowship, prayer, Bible study, confession and forgiveness, Communion, giving of our resources to support God's work, welcoming those who have visited us in worship at church and those who join us from our "Jerusalem."

We go out to practice our faith in our families, our homes, our workplace, our classrooms and our communities. We go out to live lives that draw people back with us when we return.

We promise our House Church Planter that we will recognize and respect him or her as someone who has been placed in authority by the congregation, working under the supervision of our Pastor. We will support him or her with our personal prayers and with frequent words of encouragement. We will be like the Bereans (Acts 17:11) and know our Scripture well enough and eagerly enough so we can help guide the ministry of our House Church and hold the House Church Planter accountable in an evangelical, Biblical manner.

We promise our church that we will seek in everything we do to put harmony and unity in our church ahead of our personal agendas. We will respect the Elders, Board of Directors and Pastoral Staff who have been given authority and responsibility for the ministry in our House Church. We willingly and knowingly subscribe to our church's doctrine and practice.

We promise each other that when people are hurting, we will care for them. When necessary, we will speak the truth in love, for the purpose of building each other up. We will work to have an environment that is loving, nurturing, accepting, renewing and supports our lives with meaning.

We promise our Savior that we will put His great commission to go and make disciples ahead of our personal preferences, ahead of our reluctance to birth a new group, ahead of our insecurities. We also promise our Savior that we will pay any price except denying Him and His teaching in order to maintain unity and the fellowship of love in our house church.

House Church Member(s):   x_____

                          x_____

House Church Planter: x_____

Pastor: x_____

Date: _____

Hopeful Stages of Growth in Our House Church

<u>Stage</u>   **<u>Possible Time Line</u>**

<u>Date</u>: ???

I. New Birth
   A. Focus on Growth (possible goal: add one family every month)
   B. Stay focused on mission and ministry plan
   C. Issues to look for; actions to take:
       -Excitement and expectancy-- *<u>repeatedly</u> clarify group's values and goals*
       -Anxiousness--*good ice breakers*
       -Superficial relationships--*spend <u>lots</u> of time in prayer*
       -Avoidance of acknowledging conflict--*ditto*
       -Low commitment level--*ditto*

<u>Date</u>: ???

II. Development
   A. Focus on Growth (possible goal: add one family every month)
   B. Stay focused on mission and ministry plan
   C. There are three levels that the group will go through in this stage:

I. "Storming"
       -Disappointment with one another and the group…   Apathy
       -Rebelliousness…   Spiritual warfare
* Key Actions: *Don't be surprised. Meet it with confidence that God will guide us through it. Prayer. Get help from your Pastor. Get group focused externally. Confront lovingly, yet boldly. Deal with issues, not personalities.*

II. "Norming"
       -Harmony develops…   A growing intimacy
       -A growing inclination to loving accountability…   Generally accepted group norms
* Key Actions: *Keep the group focused on the mission and ministry plan. Invite key Ministry leaders from the Church to visit for sharing the church's vision. Prayer. Begin sharing leadership responsibilities.*

III. "Performing"
       -Members work collaboratively and individually to accomplish group goals
       -Confidence and competence is increasingly demonstrated in ministry and outreach
       -Leadership responsibilities are shared with a growing number of members
       -Higher degree of support and trust
       -Group will see people led by the Holy Spirit to Christ / renewal of their walk with Christ
* Key Actions: *Plan <u>several</u> group harvest events focused on reaching lost persons. Take advantage of church-sponsored harvest events. Recognize and encourage risk takers. Begin praying in earnest about the group's multiplication. Spend time with the new future leaders that God is raising up.*

** Unless your group is guided through these three stages (storming, norming and performing), it will settle in the last stage of development and go no further; eventually the House Church will need to be reorganized.

<u>Date</u>: ???

III. Birthing
   A. Focus on preparing for birth
   B. Stay focused on mission and ministry plan
   C. Leadership team chooses the two future leaders; they begin attending training
   D. Prepare mission and ministry plans for the two new house churches
*Key Actions: *Once members realize that God's work desperately needs them to multiply, they will put that above all else. Value has been sown into the hearts of the members that declares disciple-making a primary objective of the group. Leadership development and Birthing need to have been emphasized from the beginning.*

Possible Stages in Planting a New Church Through House Churches

I. Prayer Walking
-Host a Prayer Breakfast… Have a Mission Sunday… Identify your Jerusalem…
-Key Roles: a Servant-Leader… Mercy Ministry… Hospitality… Congregational Communicator…
    "Membership" data collection … Future Pastor/Deaconess…

II. The Initial House Church (HC)
-Led by Pastor; meets weekly; HC Planter is being mentored
-Made of people committed to help the new church start (they may not go to the new church long-term)
-Focused on Prayer Walks; Personal Testimonies; Pursuing God's vision for reaching their community
-HCs will host "Community Meet and Greet" times with homes reached via Prayer Walks (quarterly)
-No Sunday worship   -No public advertising   -No big pool fishing events
-Immediately start to collect tithes and offerings; hold your first annual Capital Fund Campaign

III. Three House Churches
-Pastor leads the leaders of the House Churches; visits on a rotational basis with Communion
-Each HC has a ministry focus: Sunday School / Youth / Worship / Social Concerns / etc.
-Continue to collect tithes / offerings for the new church plant and your annual Capital Fund Campaign
-The name, values, vision and mission of the new church are agreed upon; begin process of incorporation
-Congregational worship happens once a month; not on a Sunday Morning; rented facility for one day
-Word of mouth advertising is okay   -Each house church will have approximately 5 - 25 adults and children
-House Churches praying for God to raise up a future Pastor who would probably enroll in distance learning

IV. Seven House Churches
-Same leadership model as before; but now Pastor has developed two leaders of HC leaders (could be Elders)
-Continue to collect tithes / offerings for the new church plant and your annual Capital Fund Campaign
-All Seven House Churches have a specific ministry responsibility for that first Sunday a.m. worship
-Congregational Worship happens twice a month; not on a Sunday morning; rented facility for one day
-Word of mouth advertising is okay   -HCs are praying for God to raise up a future Pastor

IV. Twelve House Churches
-Same leadership model as before; but now Pastor has developed four leaders of HC leaders
-Continue to collect tithes / offerings for the new church plant and your annual Capital Fund Campaign
-All 12 House Churches have a specific ministry responsibility for the first public Sunday a.m. worship
-Congregational Worship happens every week; not on a Sunday morning; rented facility for one day
-Word of mouth advertising for the weekly worship is okay
-Once a month have one of your public Sunday worship services be highly outreach oriented
-House Churches are praying for God to raise up a future Pastor
-Start to plan for "going public"; your first Sunday a.m. service must have excellence in everything
-40 days of prayer and fasting by the House Church members for your public launch

V. Fifteen House Churches
-Start Sunday a.m., public worship; ideally a rented place; you should already have a <u>functional</u> core of 150
-House Churches are ready to assimilate the new visitors; membership and discipleship track set
-There are five leaders of the HC leaders; hopefully, at least one future Pastor on board
-ID your 1st "signature ministry"--a bridge builder, improving lives in the community; there will be more
-Continue to collect tithes / offerings for the new church plant and your annual Capital Fund Campaign
-House Churches continue to collect tithes / offerings after public worship begins

VI. Twenty House Churches
-Plant another church out of this one   -Could be led by the new Pastor

*Everything is by the power of the Holy Spirit; this is an <u>example</u> constructed for the purpose of <u>illustration</u>

<u>SAMPLE</u> House Church Planter-- Congregational Staff Commitment

<u>1. All will follow the agreed-upon Mission and Ministry Plan for the House Church ministry. The plan will be divided into four parts, and each quarter, one part will be edited with agreed-upon updates.</u>

> *"You will receive power when the Holy Spirit comes on you; and you will be my witnesses in Jerusalem, and in all Judea and Samaria, and to the ends of the earth."... Follow my example, as I follow the example of Christ.... Join with others in following my example, brothers, and take note of those who live according to the pattern we gave you.* (Acts 1:8; 1 Corinthians 11:1; Philippians 3:17)

*Plan your work, then work your plan....   ** Hold everyone accountable to the plan....

<u>2. The House Church Planter will make congregational leadership meetings and give an update on his / her ministry.</u>

> *Finally, brothers, good-by. Aim for perfection, listen to my appeal, be of one mind, live in peace. And the God of love and peace will be with you.* (2 Corinthians 13:11)

*You are the advocate for House Church ministry in your congregation.

<u>3. The House Church Planter will make a one-year commitment, renewable annually if mutually desired.</u>

> *Jesus replied, "No one who puts his hand to the plow and looks back is fit for service in the kingdom of God."* (Luke 9:62)

*Do not try to build your own kingdom...; it takes humility to play a team sport....

<u>4. The House Church Planter is not the only conduit for ministry in their House Church.</u>

> *"The wind blows wherever it pleases. You hear its sound, but you cannot tell where it comes from or where it is going. So it is with everyone born of the Spirit."* (John 3:8)

*This isn't a cult; no one needs your "permission" to visit, talk with, or make suggestions to the HC

<u>5. Church Leaders lead by example.</u>

> *Join with others in following my example, brothers, and take note of those who live according to the pattern we gave you.... And so you became a model to all the believers in Macedonia and Achaia.... not lording it over those entrusted to you, but being examples to the flock.... Don't let anyone look down on you because you are young, but set an example for the believers in speech, in life, in love, in faith and in purity.... In everything set them an example by doing what is good. In your teaching show integrity, seriousness and soundness of speech that cannot be condemned, so that those who oppose you may be ashamed because they have nothing bad to say about us.* (Philippians 3:17; 1 Thessalonians 1:7; 1 Peter 5:3; 1 Timothy 4:12; Titus 2:7-8)

*Watch out for S.A.M. (Sex, Alcohol, Money)   *Watch out for innuendos regarding you and S.A.M.

<u>6. The House Church will submit to and support the guidance of the Congregational leadership.</u>

> *"For I myself am a man under authority, with soldiers under me. I tell this one, 'Go,' and he goes; and that one, 'Come,' and he comes. I say to my servant, 'Do this,' and he does it." When Jesus heard this, he was astonished and said to those following him, "I tell you the truth, I have not found anyone in Israel with such great faith"...And the things you have heard me say in the presence of many witnesses entrust to reliable men who will also be qualified to teach others.* (Matthew 8:9-10; 2 Timothy 2:2)

*This House Church is under the Spiritual Authority of the congregation; specifically, the Pastor.

<u>7. The House Church Planter will grow in his / her daily time commitment to Jesus.</u>

> *Then they asked him, "Where is your father?" "You do not know me or my Father," Jesus replied. "If you knew me, you would know my Father also."... To the Jews who had believed him, Jesus said, "If you hold to my teaching, you are really my disciples... Whoever serves me must follow me; and where I am, my servant also will be. My Father will honor the one who serves me... Jesus replied, "If anyone loves me, he will obey my teaching. My Father will love him, and we will come to him and make our home with him"... "I am the true vine, and my Father is the gardener. He cuts off every branch in me that bears no fruit, while every branch that does bear fruit he prunes so that it will be even more fruitful. You are already clean because of the word I have spoken to you. Remain in me, and I will remain in you. No branch can bear fruit by itself; it must remain in the vine. Neither can you bear fruit unless you remain in me."* (John 8:19,31; 12:26; 14:23; 15:1-4)

*Only when we are personally <u>in Christ</u> is ministry possible... plausible... powerful...

8. The House Church will confirm the teaching and preaching of their Pastor(s).

> *"They devoted themselves to the apostles' teaching, fellowship, breaking of bread and prayer."* (Acts 2:42)

> *The Pastor is accountable before God… the Spiritual Authorities…

9. The House Church Planter will pray daily for ministry and members of our Congregation.

> *And pray in the Spirit on all occasions with all kinds of prayers and requests. With this in mind, be alert and always keep on praying for all the saints. Pray also for me, that whenever I open my mouth, words may be given me so that I will fearlessly make known the mystery of the gospel, for which I am an ambassador in chains. Pray that I may declare it fearlessly, as I should…. And pray for us, too, that God may open a door for our message, so that we may proclaim the mystery of Christ, for which I am in chains. Pray that I may proclaim it clearly, as I should. Be wise in the way you act toward outsiders; make the most of every opportunity…. pray continually… Brothers, pray for us… Finally, brothers, pray for us that the message of the Lord may spread rapidly and be honored, just as it was with you. And pray that we may be delivered from wicked and evil men, for not everyone has faith.* (Ephesians 6:18-20; Col 4:3-5; 1 Thessalonians 5:17, 25; 2 Thessalonians 3:1-2)

> *Every aspect of your church needs to be lifted up in the prayers of your House Church.

10. The Pastoral Staff / Elders will include reports from the House Church Planter that summarize the statistics and stories of the House Churches' ministry in their official ministry updates via newsletter, bulletin, web site, annual report, etc. The congregation's financial budget will include line items for the revenues and expenses of the House Church ministry. The congregation will commit to sending a tithe (10%) of all donations received for House Church ministry to their District.

> *"The spirits of the prophets are subject to the control of the prophets."* (1 Corinthians 14:32)

X _____   date _____
      (House Church Planter)

X _____   date _____
      (Elder)

X _____   date _____
      (Pastor)

IX. Leadership Development--A Priesthood of Prayers

In our military are Privates, Sergeants, Junior Officers and Senior Officers. Privates are the "worker bees"; they mostly do the sweating and lifting; very rarely are they entrusted with thinking. At the other end of the spectrum are the Senior Officers; they haven't sweated in years; they mostly do the thinking, translating the wishes of their civilian employers into a military plan that hopefully works.

In between both ends of the spectrum, are the Sergeants and Junior Officers. The Junior Officers outrank the Sergeants, and so they often make the mistake of thinking their job is to be in charge; it isn't. The <u>wise</u> Junior Officers have one primary goal--to be trained by the Sergeants, so they will know how the military <u>really</u> works in case they are chosen to one day be a Senior Officer and have to run the military. A secondary goal for Junior Officers is to take limited responsibilities and demonstrate that they have the characteristics necessary to make something happen.

The Sergeants are where it all comes together. These men and women will take the Commander's vision and turn it into reality, even if it means turning heaven itself upside down. Good Sergeants are amazing to watch--they know what needs to be done and how to make it happen. If given the chance, they can even mold Junior Officers into leadership material.

The men and women in our churches who head up our boards, committees, task forces, small groups and House Churches are the Sergeants in the above analogy.

They are not "commissioned" (read "ordained"), but make no mistake, when it comes to actually getting the ministry (outside the altar, pulpit and baptismal font / baptistery) done, <u>the good Pastors know how this dog gets walked</u> (and they know who to let hold the leash).

One of the worst mistakes a Junior Officer (read "new Pastor") makes is not understanding that one of the first things he must learn after his formal education at the Seminary, is how the "nuts and bolts" of Parish ministry is actually accomplished and why God, in His wisdom, gave the Holy Spirit and His gifts to every believer in the body. Acts 6 is a good primer for new Pastors in any discussion regarding roles.

The basic hope of this book is that:

    1. Prayer for Others becomes Care provided by the local body of believers to those who shared Prayer Requests with us and that out of this,

    2. The Holy Spirit may provide us with the opportunity to gather new worshipping communities that are extensions of the existing congregation under the supervision of the Pastor called to serve there.

Care Is the "Bridge" Between Prayer and Planting

The lay leaders in our churches are the linchpin, ensuring that this Care gets delivered.

The Pastor is responsible for standing up in front of everyone and casting the vision developed with the lay leaders, simultaneously ensuring that everything said and done agrees with good doctrine and practice.

The members will do the lion's share of the actual Mercy Ministry; these rank and file members of our churches will be the ones who actually deliver Care to those who have shared Prayer Requests with us.

In the "middle" are the Lay Leaders: you are the ones who will <u>take this vision of following up Prayer Requests with Care Ministry, and do the on-the-scenes organization</u> without which ministry will never happen.

You will <u>collaborate with the other ministry leaders</u> in your church to ensure that those who have shared Prayer Requests with us, receive care from throughout the Body of Christ. I would argue that you are where it all happens. Most Pastors would agree that they spend far more of their time each week doing things they had absolutely no interest in doing when they went to the Seminary than they ever imagined.

Leading a small group of believers in ministry is where you have the maximum opportunity to do and lead ministry, while at the same time being dragged into the least amount of administrative headaches. Don't covet the Pastor's title. Often is the day that a Pastor wishes he could "just do ministry."

The Church is not a building or people or Pastor; we all need to get over ourselves, our insecurities and our jealousy over the calling, gifts or influence of others in the priesthood.

Ministry is not static, it is kinetic. Ministry is a <u>verb,</u> and if you are a Lay Leader, you are "the working end of the stick"; you are the "on the scene management" God uses.

Lay Leaders have a sacred trust to understand the following:

House Church Planter (candidate), Kennedy Nyangacha (third from left) brings gift cards and copies of "The Christmas Story" to families in Jersey City, NJ impacted by Storm Sandy.

Through Prayer Walking, we built a ministry with the Garden State Adult Medical Day Care Center in Newark, NJ. Here, the residents get off their buses at Christ Assembly Lutheran Church in Newark, for ministry provided by Pr. Lawrence Gboeah and the short term mission team.

The Church Is the Dynamic of God Working to Do These 10 Things:

1. Draw us

-*"No one can come to me unless the Father draws him."* (John 6:44)

-The church is made of those whom the Father has drawn to Him; without God's active intervention in history there would be no believers. Intentionally seeking Prayer requests from members, visitors and your community is a first step in His drawing others unto Him. Following up on these Prayer requests with real, physical ministry of Mercy is a next step. Most of the ministry in reaching new people is done in the follow up to the initial contact made. Your job is to seek how your area of ministry can be part of this follow up.

2. Deliver us

-*Arise, O LORD! Deliver me, O my God! Strike all my enemies on the jaw; break the teeth of the wicked.* (Psalm 3:7) *A righteous man may have many troubles, but the LORD delivers him from them all; he protects all his bones, not one of them will be broken.* (Psalm 34:19-20)

-The Church is a collection of blessed people, rescued by God's grace from their circumstances. When people share Prayer requests with us, we have the opportunity to be God's agent to deliver them from sin, death and the devil. There are all sorts of people in your community who need to be delivered from the clutches of sin and Satan. There are also all sorts of ministries happening in your community to help others. When your Church uses Prayer to serve members, visitors and the community at large, you have the opportunity to help deliver people your Church is ministering to from their difficulties. In this way, you are not just "doing good," you are building on the foundation the Holy Spirit has already laid for your Church's outreach.

3. Define us doctrinally

-*"… the Counselor, the Holy Spirit, whom the Father will send in my name, will teach you all things and will remind you of everything I have said to you."* (John 14:26) *All Scripture is God-breathed and is useful for teaching, rebuking, correcting and training in righteousness, so that the man of God may be thoroughly equipped for every good work.* (2 Timothy 3:16-17)

-As you lead the Mercy Ministry, providing care to those who have shared Prayer requests, you will minister to people who have struggled under the pain sin brings; as they wrestle through their difficulties, questions regarding God, the Bible and their faith will arise. It is very important for you to be able to give an answer for the hope that lies within you. The Prayer requests you get will touch on every aspect of human life; it is important for your Pastor to have time for expanding your understanding of the deeper truths in our Christian faith with you. As you grow in your understanding of Scripture, you will experience increasing joy over your ability to bless others from God's Word.

4. Defend us

-*My dear children, I write this to you so that you will not sin. But if anybody does sin, we have one who speaks to the Father in our defense-- Jesus Christ, the Righteous One.* (1 John 2:1)

-Jesus is our defense when we sin, and many who share Prayer requests with us will need to hear this Good News over and over.

When we gather together for public worship, we have a Pastor who is Christ's under Shepherd, chosen from among the Priesthood of the Baptized; this man stands before us and announces the forgiveness of our sins today. In between our times of public worship (which is most of the week), we who are baptized believers also have the ability and responsibility to forgive sins. (Matthew 6:15; 18:21-22; Luke 11:4; etc.)

Satan is a wicked angel; he wants to bring despair and division. Prayer requests are often the cry of the tormented. As you get to know the people better who are sharing Prayer requests with you, through the Holy Spirit you will learn the "real," deeper reasons for their Prayer requests (as opposed to the initial "presenting" reason they first gave).

As you help to lead the physical and emotional Mercy Ministry provided to those who share Prayer requests, you will have also have an opportunity to minister in Prayer and the Word. Always make sure the people to whom you minister know they are washed in the blood of the Lamb and that no accusation against them will stand.

5. Discipline us

-Endure hardship as discipline; God is treating you as sons. For what son is not disciplined by his father? If you are not disciplined (and everyone undergoes discipline), then you are illegitimate children and not true sons. (Hebrews 12:7-8)

-God prunes the branches on His Vine; His desire is for the fruitful branches to bear even more fruit. Part of your Care ministry to those who share Prayer requests is to help them have this perspective on the difficulties they are going through. As a leader, you have a responsibility to work with your Pastor and lovingly discipline believers where needed. Prayer requests can reveal areas in a person's life that need to be washed in the Word.

6. Delight us

-You have filled my heart with greater joy than when their grain and new wine abound. (Psalm 4:7)

-Joy is one of the elements of the fruit of the Holy Spirit in the lives of believers. A wife of noble character can laugh at the days to come. By God's grace, we are able to rejoice in any circumstance. As you minister to those who share Prayer requests, you will be God's instrument to help them realize this blessing of faith.

7. Distribute His grace to us

Grace and peace to you from God our Father and the Lord Jesus Christ. I always thank God for you because of his grace given you in Christ Jesus. (1 Corinthians 1:3-4)

-Through preaching and teaching, using Baptism, Communion, Prayer, Confession and Forgiveness, God distributes His grace through the Church to a lost and dying world.

8. Dress us in His righteousness

-Blessed is he whose transgressions are forgiven, whose sins are covered. (Psalm 32:1)

-In our Baptism, we are clothed in Christ's righteousness. The devil works very hard to keep this blessing from others. Never assume that those you minister to have been baptized. As the Holy Spirit leads you when you are ministering to those from the community who have shared Prayer requests, ask if they have been baptized. Share these conversations with your Pastor.

9. Direct us

-Direct my footsteps according to your word. (Psalm 119:133)

-Many who share Prayer requests are looking for direction in their lives. As your Church provides physical care to help them, you will have the chance to talk with them about their path in life. Don't be surprised when they ask, "What do you think God wants me to do?" These conversations are your opportunity to open up God's Word with them; help them to grow in their understanding of God's Word-- this is the source of true wisdom.

10. Deploy us

-Then Jesus came to them and said, "All authority in heaven and on earth has been given to me. Therefore go and make disciples of all nations, baptizing them in the name of the Father and of the Son and of the Holy Spirit, and teaching them to obey everything I have commanded you. And surely I am with you always, to the very end of the age." (Matthew 28:18-20)

-When the Samaritan woman at the well came to understand who Jesus was, she returned to her village and shared the Good News. Scripture tells us that many of the Samaritans in that town also believed in Jesus and that they were even able to talk Him into staying with them for two more days.

Often those who have been ministered to will have the desire to be a blessing to others. Jesus did not keep this new believer from sharing her faith or gathering others to hear Him, just because she had not been through some formalized training process.

As a leader in your Church, be an advocate for releasing people to do ministry; especially those who, like this Samaritan woman, are coming out of public sin. Dave and Sally were two young adults in love and living with each other when they visited our church the first time. I welcomed them and invited them to our House Church. It wasn't long before the members figured out these two were shacking. And it was even less time before a pillar of the Church came to me with their concern. I simply said, "Let the Holy Spirit work in their hearts; He will have His way with them." The next week, Dave and Sally (not their real names) shared with our House Church that they knew they were wrong for living together and that they wanted to be married. I agreed to do their pre-marital counseling and wedding. I then suggested that they should stand before the Church and share their testimony. Without batting an eye, they both agreed.

The next Sunday, I invited Dave and Sally to come forward and share their personal testimony. The congregation sat politely as they began their confession; then as Dave and Sally began to talk about the Holy Spirit and how He worked in their hearts to know they were in sin and needed to change, the members began to get visibly choked up, some started to shed tears. Dave and Sally then asked forgiveness and announced that they were going to be getting married at our Church, starting a new life dedicated to Christ and witnessing to their friends. The congregation erupted in applause and joy for the work of the Holy Spirit in this young couple's life. Today, Dave and Sally are in full time Youth Ministry on the East Coast. Releasing people for ministry while having Pastoral oversight should not be an "either / or" proposition.

People respond when they see lives that are changed. A changed life is a powerful testimony for Christ. That is what happened with the Samaritan woman in her village.

Lives don't change in a neat orderly fashion. If you look at the story of the Samaritan woman closely, you will see that she was also shacking when Jesus sought her out. In fact, she was still "in a state of shacking" when she left to tell others the Good News.

When a baby is born, it still needs its umbilical cord clipped and tied off. Rejoice over the new life in the Holy Spirit. Even if it is a little messy at times.

Having said this, we must also remember the guidance of Scripture not to be hasty in the laying on of hands. When new Pastors were installed, the Apostles, as they prayed, would lay hands on them to set them apart for their ministry and office.

"Laying on of hands" is used in conjunction specifically with the Pastoral office in the New Testament. Jesus was not placing this Samaritan woman in the Pastoral office; He was merely releasing her to share the Good News with others. These are two very different aspects of ministry.

When new believers like Dave and Sally, or this Samaritan woman, want to tell others about Jesus, let them! Encourage them! Deploy them for ministry.

The church is the dynamic of God working through His Word, Sacraments, His Son's death and resurrection, and the ministry of the Holy Spirit.

The church is the first fruit of God's work and the true believers are an evidence of God.

Jesus said that His Father's house
would be called, *"A house of prayer for all nations."* (Matthew 21:13)

164

Eight Questions for Lay Leaders to Consider:

1. What "rooms" in God's House have I agreed to help serve in?

Your area of ministry may be Youth, Worship or Education; whatever the "room" is, it is in God's house and His house is a "*house of prayer*"; which means that your area of ministry also has a role to play in providing Mercy ministry to those who are sharing Prayer requests with us--whether they are members, visitors or people in your community.

We are blessed when we are a blessing to others, because it truly is better to give than to receive. Mission gives every ministry in your Church the opportunity to exercise. Exercise is a good thing!

You can eat great food all day long; but if you never exercise you will be in poor health and bad shape. This will in turn lead to low self-worth. This is the first generation of American children to have a lower life expectancy than their adults; it's not because they don't get enough food.

Ministry needs to be muscular. Mission is the workout regimen for muscular ministry. Mission lifts spirits, expands visionary thinking, fulfills God's commissioning of the Church.

> Action Question:
> When your area of ministry, your "room" in God's house, participates in providing Mercy and Ministry to those who have shared Prayer requests with your church, you are in Mission.
>
> How is your area of ministry uniquely gifted to provide Mercy to others? _____

The irony is that Christians feel more fulfilled by serving others, than by being served. "Attractional" events will never build disciples and community the way missions can.

Mercy is what everyone expects to see the Church providing. When your community sees that your Youth Ministry (for example) exists to serve others, more than it does to serve itself, you will find there are many who will tell others what you are doing.

> When your Mercy Ministry is intentionally tied to providing care to those who have shared Prayer requests with your church, then you are being smart about how you use your resources.

2. How is prayer already evident in these "rooms"?

Hopefully, Prayer is already a part of your area of the Church's ministry. But this is not always the case. There are boards and committees in our Churches that never breathe a Prayer. This should not be.

Prayer is turning to God and trusting in Him. It is confessing and calling on Him. It is seeking His wisdom, searching His will. Unless God builds the house, the laborers will labor in vain. If we are not constant in Prayer, we are seeking to do "good" things with sinful hands and minds; this will never produce God's purpose.

A basic principle of ministry is this: look for where God is at work and go there. Look for the doors God has opened and walk through them; put your energy into these rooms. (See Ephesians 2:10.)

Don't worry so much about "what God wants me to do"; worry more about what God is doing; see where He is bearing fruit and ask to be grafted into that part of His vine.

To use a recent development from the field of counseling: Success-focused counseling is a very simple (and successful) concept. This goes by a lot of different names, but the basic principle remains:

1. Identify what success looks like for your particular endeavor (marriage, business, etc.)
2. State the next step you will take towards success
3. Take the step
4. Repeat #1

Traditional counselors have an inherent conflict of interest. If they help their client solve their problem, they need a new client. But their problem is deeper; it lies in where they are focused; most traditional counseling is not success focused; it is problem focused:

1. Identify your problem
2. Identify the cause of your problem and discuss this until tired (or broke)
3. Repeat #1

The point is to look for what God IS doing and where He IS creating passion regarding Prayer; not to spend a lot of time complaining and criticizing what is not happening or comparing your church to others.

---

*Action Questions:

How is Prayer already evident in your area of ministry? _____

What are the strengths of the Prayer ministry in your "room"? _____

How will you have your team identify the next step in the development of their Prayer ministry?

_____

---

3. How can more people be encouraged to be part of the prayer ministry in these rooms?

God's house is to be "*a house of Prayer*." Jesus said He was going to Heaven to prepare rooms in His Father's house for us. We, like living stones, are being built into a Spiritual house. If we are part of the house of God, we are to be people of Prayer.

Here are some ways you can encourage people to be part of the Prayer ministry in your area of service in the Church, understanding that each Christian is at his or her own level of Spiritual maturity:

-Invite them to submit suggestions for Prayer when you gather
-Offer them a chance to lift up the Prayers
-Ask them to develop a plan for providing Mercy Ministry to those who have shared Prayer requests
-Giving them a chance to develop a devotion on Prayer that could be used by others
-Let them share their personal story of how Prayer is a part of their life

4. What are your Prayer Priorities?

Scripture stresses over and over again the importance of Christians coming together in agreement and then going in Prayer to God, but that a house divided against itself will fall. As your area of ministry considers how it will provide Mercy Ministry to those who have shared Prayer requests, it is vital for you to come together in agreement regarding what you will Pray for.

Leaders cannot pray by themselves for victory. When Moses held his hands up, so that Joshua could defeat the Amalekites (Exodus 17), he would have failed if it had not been for Aaron and Hur who gave him a rock to sit down on and then held up his arms, one on each side, so in this way Moses could keep his hands uplifted and the battle could be won.

Listen to me. God desires holy hands everywhere to be lifted up in Prayer. When Jesus taught us the Lord's Prayer, it is in the plural, not the singular. The incense of Prayer, the lifting up of hands is something we do <u>with</u> other believers.

---

*Action Question:

What are some ways to establish agreement? _____

How will the needs of others guide the development of your ministry? _____

Give Prayer more time on your meeting agenda than just a minute or two. Take time to come together in agreement with your team over the who, what, where, when, why and how of your ministry. Then, you know it will be <u>God</u> who is building your house.

5. How will I track the prayer requests of others and follow through with them?

Your congregation needs to have a Prayer Ministry Coordinator. This person will work with you and the other Lay Leaders in your congregation to establish the exact details of how you and the other leaders will track the Prayer requests and follow through.

Part of this tracking will include recording how the various ministries of your congregation provided Mercy Ministry to those who share Prayer requests with you.

6. What organizations in the community can your room(s) of service partner up with in prayer?

Providing Mercy ministry in the community has always been an important part of the Christian faith. The Roman emperor who followed Constantine was "Julian the Apostate"; he is remembered this way in history because of his rejection of the Christian faith and his attempt to return the Roman Empire to pagan worship (which he called "the Hellenic faith").

The thoughts of Emperor Julian are preserved in the works of Cyril of Alexander, who rebutted Julian the Apostate's writings. It is insightful to read these words again:

"… <u>the impious Galileans (Christians) support not only their own poor but ours as well</u>, all men see that our people lack aid from us! Teach those of the Hellenic faith to contribute public service of this sort."

Mercy ministry "works." That is why, "*Care is the bridge between Prayer and Planting.*" This is one of the ways in which the Holy Spirit calls, gathers, enlightens and sanctifies the whole Christian church on earth.

Here is the neat thing--you don't have to reinvent the wheel. In your community are all sorts of good people and good organizations, doing really good things to serve others. You would be wise to consider which of these make sense for your area of ministry in the Church to partner with. Obviously, when considering partnering with other organizations in the community, this is something that should be discussed and agreed upon by the leadership of your church or perhaps even your entire membership (depending on how your church makes these sorts of decisions).

On a sidebar, the media love it when they see churches working together with other organizations. If you want to get free press for your ministry, this is an easy way to do it.

You can even write your own press releases and share them with the media; often reporters will take a church press release and republish large parts or even the entire article. You may be surprised at the support you can cultivate within your local media for your ministry. Be sure to invite members of the local media to your ministry celebrations for these events. Their job is all about being visible to the community; when they are invited to these events it validates their performance with their superiors.

7. What community events are popular, and how can your "room" minister through prayer?

In 2010, I attended training to become a Wing Chaplain in the U.S. Air Force. One section of training I found particularly interesting. It was not classified and contained material that is in the public domain, so I am free to talk about it.

The RAND Corporation did a study for the U.S. Government and determined two things I thought were very interesting:

First, if a foreigner learned how to properly greet someone from another culture, on average, over 80% of the host nation would have a favorable impression of this particular foreigner, even if they still had a very poor opinion of the country this foreigner came from. Obviously, this has practical implications for a U.S. soldier in a country whose culture instinctively distrusts ours.

If you feel the culture of our country is not a "churched culture," what are you going to do? Run around like Chicken Little, squawking about the sky falling? I hope not.

The Apostle Paul went to Mars Hill, and because he took the time to walk in their market place and communicate in their culture, he was able to be used by the Holy Spirit. The inspired, inerrant Word of God encourages us to become all things to all people--that you might win some to the LORD. You can't go walking around with a third eye on your forehead and not expect people to have a hard time listening to you. Don't be the distraction from the Gospel.

Second, the RAND Corporation determined that there are 12 universal cultural indicators:

-Language
-Religion
-Gender
-Politics
-Economics
-Kinship (blood)
-Knowledge / Learning
-Recreation / Sports
-Health / Sustenance
-Technology
-Time / Space
-History / Myths

Pay attention. If you want to segment an apparently monolithic society, learn what their specific 12 universal cultural indicators are and what the fault lines are that lie within them.

Take for example--language. In America, English is our official language; but you won't have to get more than two people in a room and ask them for their opinion regarding other languages being used in our country and you will get plenty of diversity on this issue.

Just go down the list. Each one of these cultural indicators is a way in which a society can be segmented. If you have a force of soldiers in a foreign country that is no more than one percent of the total population, part of your strategy will be to leverage the differences of opinions that have existed long before you ever got there. Work hard to be sure; but also be sure to work smart.

Listen to me. The community events happening around you fall into one of these 12 cultural indicators (some of the events may fall into more than one category).

Take a good look at your congregation. What are the strengths of your ministry? What gifts has the Holy Spirit blessed you with (above and beyond, Scripture and the Sacraments)? What natural connections are there between the gifts of your congregation and the gatherings of your community?

It may seem as if you are outnumbered and "outgunned," but you have the Holy Spirit! You have God's Word! You have His Sacraments! You have the fruit of the Holy Spirit! You have the Spiritual gifts with which He has blessed the members of your congregation!

This is definitely a Spiritual battle and it is one that has already been won for us by Christ. As Luther said, "The Holy Spirit does not bestow His gifts upon procrastinators." Let us not hesitate when asked, "Who will go? Whom shall I send?"

As you look at your community; both its celebrations and its challenges, these 12 Cultural Indicators are a good way to organize your priorities and help you with your plan. I pray God's richest blessings on your effort.

Taking Prayer requests from others will help you learn their needs.
Sharing Care with these individuals will demonstrate your sincerity.
Planting new worshipping communities will be possible through these relationships.

Mrs. Viola Richardson, Councilperson for Jersey City in her office- she is not ashamed of the cross. Viola is a friend to our ministry and a fellow Lutheran. Viola loves to be prayed for.

Developing the Vision of the Church Staff for Prayer, Care and Planting Ministry

Most churches have a very basic "staff"; besides the Pastor, there is often only a part-time Secretary on the payroll. Many churches have developed staff positions for devout members with demonstrated gifts who are happy to serve for no compensation; these staff members often get more done than their paid counterparts in other ministries.

Regardless of how many people are on your church's staff, it is very important to take the time and make sure the Church staff have had a chance to help craft a passionate mission vision for Prayer that helps with Ministry, Mercy and possibly even Multiplication of worshipping communities.

As we said earlier, Mercy Ministry is the bridge between Prayer and Planting.

Mercy Ministry is something every Christian in your Church should be encouraged to participate in. Your Church staff see the "big picture"; they are the ones who will "connect the dots" and are best able to insure that the Prayer requests you receive are followed up with coordinated care from the respective parts of your ministry and that your Prayer-based Care makes the agenda and is a priority.

Jesus often tried to help us understand the big picture with simple metaphors. The Early Church saw first-hand that the physical temple was gone. Perhaps better than we with our beautiful sanctuaries, they understood that God's dwelling among us was Spiritual more than spatial. There are only a handful of times when something that Jesus said is recorded in the three Gospels of Matthew, Mark and Luke. One of these is when Jesus says, "*My house will be called a house of prayer.*"

It is important to understand the theological importance of "house" in the New Testament. Every believer is a living stone, which is being built up into a Spiritual house. Jesus Himself is the cornerstone of this house. When Saul tried to destroy the New Testament Church, his plan was very simple--and it is recorded in Scripture: "*Saul began to destroy the Church; going from house to house, he dragged off men and women....*" (Acts 8:3) Believers are living stones collectively building up a Spiritual house, and we are also individually the temple of the Living God.

And so it is important to understand that when Jesus says His Father's house will be a house of prayer, He is not only describing our collective gatherings, He is also describing Christians individually. Alone or gathered together, true believers are people of Prayer.

Note that Jesus did not say Prayer happened in only one part of the house; the house is a house of Prayer. Jesus did not say that Prayer only happens at certain times in this house; rather, Prayer is one of the ongoing activities found in this house. Jesus did not make Prayer an "option" for this house; this is not a matter of personal choice or preference; Prayer is a piece of the Spiritual blueprint of this house.

Prayer is not a program. Prayer is not a legal obligation to fulfill by Christians through which they earn salvation. Prayer is not a gimmick to get material goodies from God. Prayer is not something to be motivated in believers through the use of coercion or even compliments. Prayer is the work of the Holy Spirit in the heart of a Christian, crying out, "Abba, Father." Salvation comes through hearing the Word of God and those who are saved Pray to God. When the only person who is comfortable praying with others is the Pastor, something has gone terribly wrong.

Sadly, too often believers do not turn to Prayer until their boat is about to be capsized in the storms of life. My wife has observed more than once that it is easiest to forget about God when life is going well. We both agree that a little difficulty does the soul good. There is an old saying in the military: there are no atheists in the foxhole; faith is a quick friend when the foe is near. As a Chaplain I have observed plenty of soldiers and airmen who never had any interest in a serious discussion about faith, Scripture or God, but come quickly to see me when it was time to deploy into a combat zone.

One of the greatest challenges we face in ministry is <u>the temptation to be inward focused</u>. Pick any board or committee that comes to mind. Inevitably, when it gathers, one of the big concerns will be, "How do we get people to come to what we are doing?" You might say, "Well, we want people to come to what we are doing so that we can tell them about <u>Jesus</u>."

That sounds so noble--bring people to you; but is that what Jesus told us to do? Hmmm… Seems like He said, "As you are <u>going</u>, disciple all nations…." The focus is to disciple others; in the original Greek there are three words that explain what He wants to see us doing, in our effort to "disciple all nations." The first of these is "go" or more accurately, "going." Jesus' point here was simple--get up off your backside and get <u>out</u> into the harvest. In fact, Jesus taught us to pray that the Lord of the Harvest would throw workers into the harvest (the Greek word "ekbalay" at its root means to "eject" (cf. Louw and Nida).

When the Holy Spirit descended on the disciples after Jesus' ascension to Heaven, they were supposed to become Jesus' witness, moving outward from Jerusalem to the very ends of the earth. What did the disciples do instead? They stayed in Jerusalem. What did God do? Allow persecution to come upon the Church. **If you want to be the "salt of the world" you are going to have to be shaken out of the salt shaker**. This happens in ways beyond your control. The salt does not tell the salt shaker to scatter it, let alone command the hand shaking the salt shaker. No, the hand picks up the salt shaker, tips it upside down and vigorously shakes it until the hand gets the results <u>the hand</u> wants.

It sounds so noble, "How do we get more youth into our youth group?" But really, the question we should be asking is, "How can the Youth Group serve others, <u>out there,</u> who are not part of the Youth Group?"

By beginning with Prayer and asking others how we can pray for them (members, visitors or those in the community), we learn the needs of others. This provides the perfect opportunity for your Youth Ministry (or any other ministry) to step up and ask, "How can we <u>go</u> to this person, to this family and minister to them?"

Out of this Prayer-based Mercy ministry, your church can serve others more effectively and build ongoing relationships with people in need. In this way, the people you serve in the community will not just taste the fruit of the Vine, they will have the best opportunity to be <u>grafted into</u> the Vine.

The purpose of reaching out with Prayer and Mercy is <u>not to</u> build bigger budgets or justify ourselves with spreadsheets. The purpose is <u>not to</u> build bigger buildings or even additional "campuses."

As we bring our neighbor before our Father through Prayer, we also seek to provide the Mercy Ministry they desire and build relationships so we can Multiply worshipping communities.

Among other things, <u>Pastors have the responsibility to prepare God's people for works of service</u>. When looking at the "health" of a ministry, a good place to start is by looking at who is serving in the ministry and who is not. Pastors and church leaders should have a laser focus on those who are <u>not yet</u> doing "works of service." If you want a "growing Church," take time to look closely at each member's involvement in the ministry; God did not design His Church to grow on the backs of just the Pastor and a few other servants. <u>Acts 6:3-4 is a touchstone passage in the discussion of developing the Priesthood of the Baptized.</u>

If someone asks you, '*What is that book about that you are reading?*"
A good answer would be, "**_Prayer_**. Learning how we can Pray for others so that we can provide <u>M</u>inistry, <u>M</u>ercy and by God's grace to <u>M</u>ultiply those who follow Jesus."

Prayer Walking is a very powerful tool to reach out into our communities. A pair of Prayer Walkers can easily connect with half a dozen households in an hour. It is an exhilarating experience when you see God work.

But, *this book and this ministry approach are about so much more than just Prayer Walking*. Experience has taught me that churches that do not have a vision and a plan for providing Mercy Ministry to those who are reached through the taking of Prayer requests will never achieve the full potential God had in mind for them. **The goal is not simply to get more and more people taking Prayer requests**. Getting a Prayer request is just the beginning of the ministry to those in need of Prayer.

One temptation you will have to deal with will be faced by those who receive the Prayer requests: they will want to also be the ones to provide the Mercy ministry. In Acts 6, the Church's first Pastors faced this temptation also. They wanted to do the Ministry of Prayer and the ministry of feeding the widows. These first Pastors had to learn that they needed to <u>devote</u> themselves to the ministry of Prayer and the Word and let the appropriate believers provide / organize the Ministry of Mercy. God has prepared good works in advance for <u>every</u> believer; <u>taking Prayer requests provides an almost endless supply of opportunities for believers to do good works</u>.

When Jesus called the fishermen they <u>left</u> their nets…
   -Too often we want to take ideas / resources we are familiar with (our "nets") to do <u>God's</u> work.

We are engaged in a <u>Spiritual</u> enterprise.
   -New believers are born again through w<u>ater</u> and the W<u>ord</u>
          (this water is the washing and regeneration of the Holy Spirit (see Titus 3:5-8)
   Don't confuse <u>activity</u> in c<u>hurch</u>… with <u>accomplishment</u> of the <u>commission</u>…

When we understand that it truly is <u>God</u> who builds His house:
   -We want prayer <u>everywhere</u> in His house
          -The master bedroom… the children's bedroom… the garage… the family room….
          -And at church: we want prayer not just on Sunday a.m. but also:
                 -In pre-marital counseling… membership class… evangelism meetings… etc…

Proverbs 29:18 says, *Where there is no vision; the people perish.* (KJV)

There are entire books written on the topic of "Vision." You can find books that say vision is passé; and books that say vision is paramount. You can find books that say vision is developed by the team and you can find books that say vision is found on the mountain.

Action Question:

   Here is my thought on vision- You need to answer this simple question, "How did God equip <u>me</u> regarding leadership?"

_____

One of my favorite Bible stories is when David comes to kill Goliath. The king wants David to have the best weapons and body armor to fight the giant; so the king gives David the armor he used as King. I can promise you that no one among the Jews had better gear than the King. You go to Afghanistan and I can promise you that no soldier has better protection than the top General. This is just the way it works.

So, what does David do? He is a good citizen, he respectfully tries on the King's gear but it doesn't work for him; it's the wrong size; it is too cumbersome; he has never worn anything like this before. I can just picture David staggering under the weight of this gear, looking like a Sailor on port call at 2 a.m.

So, what does David do next? He says, "Thanks, but no thanks. **I am gonna go kill this guy, the way I know how**. Keep the dinner warm." What happens? David walks out on that battlefield, mocks the giant, kills him and whacks off his head. Then he holds the giant's head up in the air for all to see; the good guys take the field and God's people are saved from their enemies. Golden!

David was a young leader, but he knew one thing--he had to fight the way God had prepared him to fight. My advice regarding vision is simple--be true to how God gifted you to fight the giants you face. **Don't try to be someone you aren't; trust God's provision.**

Having said all this, here are four steps that hopefully are helpful for you in Vision Casting to your Church, especially as it regards Prayer Ministry.

---

1. Get a Vision…

The vision for your ministry can't come from this book, some workshop, or anywhere other than the one, true, living God. Jesus gave you the Holy Spirit to guide you in all things. How do you hear from the Holy Spirit?

-Follow Christ's example of getting away from all distractions and have plenty of time devoted to this. I have found it best to bring a notepad / laptop and just start freely recording the thoughts God lays on my heart--not necessarily trying to completely "organize" them immediately; sometimes you won't see the overall structure to these thoughts until close to the end of your time.

-Spend time in Prayer. Get a vision for Prayer ministry by first spending time in Prayer. Your prayers should cover specifics like:

    -the leaders who will help make this happen (we know Jesus spent at least one entire night in Prayer regarding who His top 12 leaders should be)

    -the priorities for the Prayer ministry to focus on

    -the proclamation explaining the Prayer ministry to the church and the community

    -your openness to His guidance and shaking things up

    -the clear revelation of His will to leaders and members

    -unity as the Church goes forward with this

-Spend time in God's Word. I have always enjoyed spending some time in Psalms and Proverbs for personal worship, then reading through a book of the Bible and just letting the Holy Spirit lead my time of study and reflection. When I take notes on this Bible study time, it has always proved a blessing to share them with the leadership team back at the Church.

-Seek Godly examples. Paul exhorted Timothy to remember the faith of his mother and grandmother. Before getting away, take the time to collect resources from reliable sources on Prayer, Mercy Ministry and Planting new worshipping communities.

-Analyze the Strengths, Weaknesses, Opportunities and Threats to this Prayer ministry in your Church. This idea of S.W.O.T. analyses has been around for some time. I have found it to be a reliable way to organize my thoughts.

-Discuss with community leaders what things in your community your church should be praying about. Take the time to pray over these items and to reflect from Scripture how God has equipped your Church to address these needs. The Jersey City Municipal Council officially recognized our work; this would never have happened without taking the time to hear from and be held accountable by community leaders.

I was blessed to know Pastor E. M. Clark, a retired minister in Springfield, Missouri. Pastor Clark's oldest son, Vern, retired as the Chief of Naval Operations in 2005. I never met Admiral Clark, but his dad, Pastor Clark, was a very fine Christian man.

Pastor Clark was what we in the LCMS would call a "District President" with the Assemblies of God. Over the years, Pastor Clark helped churches and ministries raise a lot of money, and he shared with me how he did it. Pastor Clark used 1 Chronicles 29 as his model:

King David wanted to build a temple, but that was not God's plan; so David raised the funds for one of the very first Church building programs recorded in Scripture. (JIM: check out Exodus 35:4-29 and 36:2-6—although it wasn't a "building" people gave for the furnishings and "building" of the tabernacle.) King David's fundraising process was pretty simple:

Step 1: Make a personal financial commitment

Step 2: Gather the leadership and share what his personal commitment was

Step 3: Let the leaders respond with what their individual commitments would be

Step 4: Share the total raised with the people and let them respond

If you are ever looking for a simple way to raise money, I can tell you from personal experience that this can work just fine today also.

There are principles from this fundraising approach that I want to share with you regarding "Giving a Vision" in general:

1. If you are going to give a vision as a leader, you have to communicate clearly your personal commitment to seeing the vision through. You and your spouse need to be in agreement over this new shared sacrifice before you ever go before your key leaders. God does not honor a minister who doesn't honor his vows. (1 Timothy 3:2)

2. Once you and your spouse are of one accord regarding this vision, then go to the "leaders of tens and fifties" in your congregation. Start with Prayer and Scripture; then share with them what God has laid on your heart regarding Prayer Ministry, how it will help the Church minister to its members, visitors and people in the community. Talk about the strengths God has already blessed your Church with and how these Spiritual gifts can provide Mercy ministry as the Church follows up with those who have shared Prayer requests. Dream with them about the new relationships the Holy Spirit could bring and the possibilities that exist for starting House Churches or Bible studies with the 60% of your community not attending Sunday morning worship currently.

3. Allow your key leaders to make their contribution to this effort; this is what King David did. Their input will change what the Prayer ministry looks like. If Solomon's temple was built only with David's resources, it probably would not have looked the same. Apparently, it was God's plan for the key leaders to make a contribution as well.

Remember that by this time, King David had decades of relationship with these key leaders; he did not propose something this big at the beginning of his reign. This is another reminder that it is a good idea to start this Prayer ministry by focusing first on taking care of your members, then reaching out to your visitors, and finally reaching out to the community around your church. Positive momentum is easier with humble beginnings.

4. Develop an agreed-upon vision and summary of what has happened so far, which you will present to the membership at large. There is simply no way for this Prayer ministry to do what God wants it to do for your congregation without their full understanding and support. If we are not careful, we will start

thinking that <u>we</u> do the ministry for / to the members, when the vision God has is that we prepare <u>them</u> for good works.

When you share the vision for the Prayer ministry with the members, they will also want to make their contributions. Let them; King David did. And just like the contributions of the leaders changed the ministry, so also, the contributions of the members will also change the ministry. Listen to me. King David took their contributions and blessed it before God. A wise Pastor also tries first to take the contributions of the members and bless them before God as well. However, if you are looking at a golden calf, then that is a different matter.

I look forward to seeing Pastor Clark in Heaven, and I thank God for blessing me with his friendship, even if we didn't agree on all doctrinal matters.

3. Gr<u>ow</u> a Vision…

In 2007, the Air Force unit that I served as a Wing Chaplain, the 442nd Fighter Wing, had approximately 350 Airmen returning from Afghanistan. As the Wing Chaplain, I was part of the planning process for their reintegration. Most civilians are fully supportive of our military even if they don't fully understand the demands placed upon them. Our Guard and Reserve service members have the double challenge of being taken off the government payroll when their deployment is over. On top of this, Guard and Reserve units have very limited resources available for "hands on" care, not to mention that usually the service member does not live next to the military base.

When Active Duty service members come back from deployment, they have a full time job with benefits waiting for them; they live in a community that totally understands the nature of what they do <u>and</u> is set up to care for them. When we get a Guard or Reserve member back to the base, we have 48 hours to take care of them and then they are free to go.

As the Wing Chaplain, my concern was for the Airmen and how they had processed their deployment. My concern came out of my experience in 2002. In the spring of that year, the first rotation of Special Operations soldiers came back from Afghanistan. While these soldiers were gone, some of their wives were unfaithful. If you remember the news accounts, four of these returning soldiers who learned that their wives had been cheating responded by killing their wives, and then, three of these soldiers in turn, took their own lives. In a matter of days, the Army had seven homicides to deal with at Ft. Bragg.

In 2002, I was an Army Chaplain in Army Special Operations. I was directed to meet personally with every soldier in our unit who came back from combat. I told my superiors that I would do this, but that they would have to trust me, because I could not break confidentiality. They agreed. By God's grace, we never had this level of problem in our unit.

In 2006, as we prepared for these 350 Airmen to return home, I raised the concern over how the Airmen were processing their deployment. A senior officer suggested that all we needed to do was give the Airmen a survey to take on their computers and that this would be enough. I counted to 10 and took a deep breath. I responded by saying that this was not enough; what was needed was for a Chaplain to sit knee to knee with each person and look them in the eyes; to listen and probe; to do this with confidentiality; to follow up and take care of them. The Wing Commander went with my recommendation. But we had a problem--how were we going to personally interview 350 Airmen in 48 hours with a staff of three Chaplains? It was numerically impossible. I had never faced this problem. In the Army, the size of the units coming and going was much smaller, and the Army Reserves held returning soldiers much longer, giving me enough time to do it personally. This was not going to work with the Air Force constraints.

So, by God's grace, I got the idea to invite the Airmen in the Wing to nominate Clergy they knew who they thought would be interested in helping take care of Airmen in need. By utilizing other Clergy, our Airmen would still have their confidentiality protected (in fact, they might feel it was more secure since it was a civilian Clergy). It was amazing! I got over 80 nominations.

Among those nominated were fellow Lutheran Pastors like Rev. Lee Hagan and Rev. Andrew Keltner who both had members in the 442nd Fighter Wing. So, with my Wing Commander's blessing, I got in touch with these clergy and explained the situation and how they were nominated. I asked all of them if they would be interested in coming in for training; there would be no pay; they would only get a certificate and an "atta boy" or "atta girl" from the Wing Commander. Do you know, that with one exception, every single Pastor who was nominated said "Yes."

I brought the Pastors on base and gave them a tour; they were welcomed by Wing Commander Col. Steve Arthur (since promoted to General.). After that, I gave them training in how to counsel returning Airmen; how to be true to their faith and also serve every Airmen; how to document and handle any case needing follow up (we utilized a tool that I developed and had blessed by the Chaplains at Air Force Reserve Command).

When our Airmen came back, they were welcomed by their spouses, children, parents and friends. Many of these returning Airmen had also nominated their Clergy, and for them, they also saw their Pastors waiting for them. Our Security Forces, led by MSgt. James Dorl did an outstanding job of providing our team of 25 clergy with their own individual counseling rooms and made sure that every Airmen saw either a military Chaplain or civilian Clergyperson. We had 48 hours in which to do this; we were done with our screenings in about 12 hours. For the record, I made every effort to recruit a Priest (we had no other world religions represented in this deployment), but unfortunately, this did not happen.

"Growing a Vision" Is Simple

Here is my basic 12 step process:
1. Identify your goal.
2. Acknowledge your obstacles.
3. Gather a team.
4. Leverage your resources.
5. Think outside the box.
6. Learn from others' mistakes / successes.
7. Get your plan blessed by the powers that be.
8. Resource your plan.
9. Simplify your plan.
10. Pray (throughout).
11. Pull the trigger.
12. Repeat this cycle as needed.

Pr. Lee Hagan receives certificate of appreciation on behalf of the 442nd FW

By God's grace, we were able to take care of 350 Reserve Airmen. Through this process, our Wing gained over 80 key advocates in the community surrounding the base. This was all done at no additional tax payer expense. The Airmen were invited to be part of the process that provided their care. We had fun. I was awarded the Meritorious Service Medal for developing this unconventional ministry solution.

These steps / pieces in "Growing a Vision" that I list above can be used by you to develop your Prayer Ministry or other ministries.

I have come to believe that there are three values that should guide your efforts (these are in addition to your faith, Scripture, the Holy Spirit, Prayer, fellowship with other believers, etc.)
1. Put together the very best resource you can for the need being met
2. Have complete integrity throughout the process
3. Create the very best awareness possible for your effort

Return to your Savior and give thanks! Regardless of the outcome, give Him thanks.

It is a disheartening thing when you see a family in fear over a medical issue call you and ask you to come and pray with them; when after fervent and heartfelt prayers with them, God answers their prayers even beyond their honest expectations; and what do they say when a neighbor asks them how their medical situation is? Nothing!

It breaks the heart of a Pastor to see this happen for several reasons. First of all, you thought they were the type of Christian who would glorify God given the slightest opportunity and so you are truly surprised when you see them turn away from this good work that has been prepared in advance for them to do. Second, you are saddened because you know that this was truly an opportunity to proclaim the goodness of God. Here was a chance to proclaim Christ's victory over the devil and it is wasted; the opportunity slips between the fingers of time and disappears. Third, you are disappointed because the heart of the person asking the question could have been strengthened. There is a reason they were asking; probably part of the reason is because they were looking for hope also. Maybe they had even heard a good report already and just wanted to hear it themselves from the mouth of the person blessed by God.

Jesus was disappointed with the men with leprosy who did not return and give thanks. Jesus was fairly angry with the residents of the towns who did not follow Him in spite of all His miracles for them. We should remember that God has feelings too. Jealousy is certainly an emotion and we should never forget that we worship a jealous God.

God's Word will not return void; it will accomplish the purpose for which it was sent. (Isaiah 55:11) This was true for Isaiah; it was made manifest in Christ, the Word made flesh; it is true for us also today. Sometimes we see the results of His Word; it has its effect and works faith and the confession of Christ as Savior. Other times, we only learn later through others how God's Word worked in the life of someone.

God's Word tells us that if the Bible contained every account and aspect of Jesus' ministry that there might not even be enough space in all the earth to hold it. God's Word then goes on to tell us that what is recorded was preserved so that we might have faith.

The truth is that Jesus did amazing miracles we don't even know about. Odds are He raised people from the dead that we don't know about. He healed the blind, the deaf, the mute, the lame; fed the hungry; suspended the laws of nature. We know about all these incredible things; there are more miracles, just like them, that He did, which we know nothing about. That is amazing (to me).

God's Word will not return void. For all the things we know now or learn later, the fact is that there are so many more things His Word accomplishes that we have absolutely no idea about. And truthfully, we don't know if we learn about these things in Heaven after the old order of things has disappeared. It won't matter then anyway. We will have the prize.

So; make sure to take time each day to thank God for all the blessings He has showered upon your ministry of Prayer, both those you know about and those you don't.

+   +   +

My dad grew up in North Dakota. He recently told me a story about an old farmer who, when asked to pray, would always lift up the following request, "Lord, prop us up on our leanin' side." When asked why he prayed in this way, the old timer replied, "I have an old barn and one day I noticed that it leans to one side. It got this way after all the storms it has been through. As I was bracing up the leaning side of my barn, I began to think about my life and all the storms I have been through. Sometimes, I lean towards anger; sometimes I lean towards hatred; sometimes I lean towards cussin'; I lean towards lots of things I shouldn't. This is why I pray, "Lord, prop us up on the leanin' side so we will stand tall and straight again to glorify You." Pray for the leanin' side of things in your ministry and marriage.

New Numbers

Let's be honest, one of the areas that causes tension in ministry is "measuring its effectiveness." Sometimes members come across like their church's ministry is not really any different from any other business with the Treasurer's report taking up the greatest attention in leadership meetings. Sadly, some Pastors, in responding to this misunderstanding of ministry, give the impression that they are trying to avoid any sort of assessment of their ministry.

A friend and fellow Air Force Chaplain, Terry Wright, once said, "When it comes to ministry there are only two numbers people care about--noses and nickels." There is sadly a lot of truth in this.
The idea that we can "measure ministry" stands on weak theology. Ministry itself is the clear proclamation of the Gospel and a confessional administration of the Sacraments. Ministry is the discipleship of believers. Ministry is evidenced by time in Prayer, God's Word, works of Charity, fellowship, etc. To say that counting noses and nickels captures all of this is a stretch, to say the least.
At the same time; it is important for a ministry to clearly communicate its efforts to those who support the work. The Apostle Paul put a fair amount of work into keeping his donor base appraised of his work. Included in his reports were often statistical reports on the ministry's progress (Acts 11:26; 16:5, etc.).

It is difficult to quantify how much someone has grown in their understanding of Scripture or their appreciation for the Sacraments. But the evidence, the fruit of their faith can be seen in ways that can be measured. Numbers themselves don't matter at all, but the ministry they attempt to describe matters eternally. It is better to have numbers prepared to discuss than to be asked for numbers for which we have no objective answer.

Five New Numbers

In light of our focus on Prayer for the purpose of Ministry, Mercy and Multiplication; here are some numbers we could share with our members; hopefully these will move our understanding of "measuring Ministry" beyond "noses and nickels":
    1. number of Prayer Requests received from members, visitors and the community. This could be broken down to detail the ways in which these Prayer Requests were received: the Elders calling their Shepherding Groups for Prayer requests; the Prayer Walkers in the community; Sunday morning worship; Sunday School; House Church; boards and committees, etc.
    2. number of members serving in the Mercy Ministry following up with the Prayer Requests received.
    3. number of households served through the Mercy Ministry follow up to the Prayer Requests.
    4. A comparative analysis quantifying the ministry support and participation level of households served through Prayer and Mercy ministry (vs. those not). It should be fairly easy to capture their worship and contribution levels; then, you could objectively show the progress in their worship, church fellowship, ministry participation and stewardship as it relates to the level of care they received from the Prayer and Mercy ministry of the church.
    5. number of mentions in the local press regarding the Church's Prayer and Mercy Ministry. Local media outlets will have their viewership numbers available; all you have to do is ask for someone in the sales department. To understand too, the value of a news story over the perceived value of a paid advertisement is also important for members to consider as they evaluate the impact of Prayer in lifting up their ministry to the community.

There are other numbers you could use to measure ministry. There is no reason to fear numbers; we are saved by God's grace, not our works. The job we have been given is to share the Good News; the "results" are between the Holy Spirit and the person we have shared the Gospel with. My dad always ends his sermons with, "May this be so for His glory. Amen." May all of this be for His glory. Amen?

X. Additional Documents / Resources

The following resources are taken from actual ministry. These examples are being shared in the hope they will help you, not as a human endeavor but rather, simply as examples from ministry where <u>the Holy Spirit</u> is working to bring the Good News to a lost and dying world.

Prayerfully look at these resources and, as God leads through His Word, His Spirit, your Pastor and the other leaders in your church, discern how you might use the following, if at all. The purpose here is not to share some "program," but rather <u>examples</u> of how <u>the Holy Spirit</u> has worked to call, gather and enlighten the church. Do not trust in humanly devised programs; trust in the Holy Spirit and His means of Grace.

> When asked to summarize my ministry, I have shared the following:
> *"As a Network Supported Mission Strategist, I help LCMS congregations serve their members, guests and community through <u>developing a robust Prayer and Mercy ministry</u> that intentionally <u>plants House Churches and trains House Church Planters</u>, all under the supervision of the regularly called and ordained Pastors of our churches."*

This book has intentionally focused on helping churches develop *"... a robust Prayer and Mercy ministry..."*; there is only one chapter in this book devoted to Planting House Churches.

By God's grace, in New Jersey, we are now blessed to have planted seven House Churches. Initially, I began by meeting with individual Pastors, speaking with their Churches, and offering training in Prayer and Planting. By God's grace, I have been invited to provide this training for the leaders of hundreds of our churches in these first four years of being a network supported mission strategist.

My experience as a Mission Strategist has been a beautiful learning process. When I accepted the call, no one gave me a box of tricks, complete with three-ring binders ready to hand out. What I knew as a parish Pastor was that Prayer and planting House Churches were ways in which the Holy Spirit worked to build worshipping communities.

I was 100% confident in the formation the Holy Spirit had given me; what I have come to learn is that it is one thing to be a Pastor for an individual congregation, where you are on site and have Spiritual oversight. Working as a Mission Strategist means being a <u>resource</u>, providing the best principles and practices that you can, but ultimately, leaving it up to the Holy Spirit, the local Pastor, and the congregation as to how the details shake themselves out. This has been a growing experience for me; by nature, I am the kind of person who wants the ball in my hand when the clock is ticking down.

The other thing these first four years has taught me is that there is so much more to Prayer and Planting than I had ever imagined <u>and</u> the only way I would learn about this was by getting <u>out of the way of the Holy Spirit</u> and letting <u>Him</u> work through the gifts He has bestowed on the believers. <u>In this way</u> His ministry of Prayer and Planting could blossom and bear fruit. I have been truly blessed to see faithful servants in the Church follow the leading of <u>the Holy Spirit</u> and do the good works He had prepared in advance. Much of what is in this book reflects what I have learned <u>from others</u> as a Mission Strategist, and seeing them be willing tools of the Holy Spirit. Before I came to New Jersey, God told me I would reap where I had not sown, and I can heartily say, "Amen. This is most certainly true!"

After about a year of working with individual congregations, I realized that I would need to offer this training in a setting so that more than one church could be trained at a time. In the New Jersey District we are blessed to have Leaders and Learners, a lay ministry certification process that has blessed our churches for over 20 years. I approached Shirley Carpenter, the Administrator of Leaders and Learners, and discussed with her the idea of training House Church Planters under the auspices of Leaders and Learners. Shirley was excited about the possibilities, and at her invitation, I made a presentation to the Board of Directors for Leaders and Learners. By God's grace, the Board unanimously approved my proposal.

To become a certified House Church Planter in the New Jersey District requires a couple of things:
1. The candidate must have the endorsement of his / her Pastor
2. The candidate must successfully complete the following courses (I teach the first six):
    - *House Churches, House Church Planters and Mercy Ministry*
    - *Contextual-Confessional Worship*
    - *Congregational Prayer Ministry*
    - *Stewardship and Non-Profit Management*
    - *Planting a Worshipping Community and Leadership Development*
    - *Mission and Ministry Planning and Community Based Oversight Committees*
    - *Old Testament Survey*
    - *New Testament Survey*
    - *Doctrine I*
    - *Doctrine II*
    - *Lutheran Homiletics and Teaching*
    - *World Religions--Gospel Proclamation*

If you live in the New Jersey area and would like attend training in person, know that everyone is welcome. Other Districts combine my House Church Planter training with their Lay Minister Certification process.

The courses I teach can be accessed through video at www.HouseChurchPlanter.com.

Being able to offer centralized training was very helpful, but this did not provide solutions for everyone's challenges. New Americans are some of the hardest working people you will ever meet. My experience is that it is not uncommon for a recent immigrant to work two or three jobs at a time. New immigrants have tremendous expectations placed on them by their loved ones back home who perceive America as "the land of milk and honey." Early on, I asked an immigrant from Kenya when the last time was that he had been home. He smiled and said it had been several years. I asked how much airplane tickets were, to which he smiled and said it wasn't the cost of the plane ticket; it was the cost of the visit. When a Kenyan immigrant comes home, he is expected to bring money to solve everyone's needs and settle any problems.

This began the process to develop a web site where people could go to receive House Church Planter training virtually. If you go to www.HouseChurchPlanter.com you can access our training on line.

SAMPLE House Church Planter's Mission and Ministry Worksheet

Leader: (cell) _____ (Home) _____ (email) _____

Meeting Day and Time: _____ Name of House Church: _____

I. Reaching the Lost
    1. Our Jerusalem (primary focus) is: _____

    2. The needs in the community we will try to meet are: _____

    3. My commitment to inviting new people personally is: _____

II. Equipping the Saints
    1. I will meet the needs of our members by: _____

    2. We will help people increase time in prayer and Bible study by: _____

III. Praising the Lord
    1. Prepare a timetable for when your House Church gathers; attach it to your Mission and Ministry Plan.
        Worship must be part of your schedule; it should include time for:
           -Prayer (sharing prayer requests; following up on previous prayers; actual prayer time)
           -Bible study (you will receive a copy of the weekly Sermon study via email from Pastor)
           -Praise and Worship (according to the format agreed on)

IV. Leadership Development
    1. I will encourage others to enter House Church Planter training by: _____

    2. I will develop leaders in my House Church by: _____

V. Planting Ministries
    1. Our projected date of birth is: _____

    2. The Jerusalem for our present House Church will be: _____

    3. The Jerusalem for our future HC will be: _____

VI. House Church Model
We will help people grow in their understanding of House Churches by: _____

VII. Stewardship
We will encourage people to give proportionately by: _____

Final Checklist:
    --Make sure all resources needed are available.
    --Prospect list is compiled; goal of six solid prospects; Communicate to prospects first meeting info
    --Entire process is covered in prayer and concludes with one day for fasting and prayer (Luke 5:35, etc.)

Disaster Response Prayer Walking Report--Side A

Super Storm Sandy Prayer Requests

Date: _____

My Name: _____

English – Spanish

Hello, my name is _____ _Hola, mey yamo_ _____

Do you speak English? _Hable Engles?_

We are praying for the community _Estamos orando por la comunidad_

How can we pray for you? _Como oramos por Usted?_

Please write your prayer _Por favor, escriba un oración suyo_

What is your name? _Como se yama?_

We hope you have a great day! _Esperamos que tenga un gran día_

How are you? _Como esta usted_

God bless you _Que Dios te bendiga_ ☺

#1 Name(s): _____

Address: _____

Prayer Request(s): _____

_____

Church Ministry(s) That Will Follow Up: _____

_____

Phone #: _____

This is formatted so you can get two of these from a single sheet of 8.5" x 11" paper. Just set up the document in landscape view.

Side B (next page) goes on the backside of the paper. It is also set up to get two copies from a single 8.5" x 11" page when that paper is cut in half. The finished document measures 8.5" x 5.5".

Side A	Side A
(Side B on back)	(Side B on back)

As you can see, the format for the Disaster Response card is similar to the general purpose Prayer Response card (see chapter seven). This card is designed for teams that will be working specifically with homes that have requested their disaster response assistance; these teams will often work most of the day with one household.

Disaster Response Prayer Walking Report--Side B

#2 Name(s): _____

  Address: _____

  Prayer Request(s): _____

        _____

  Church Ministry(s) That Will Follow Up: _____

        _____

  Phone #: _____

+   +   +

#3 Name(s): _____

  Address: _____

  Prayer Request(s): _____

        _____

  Church Ministry(s) That Will Follow Up: _____

        _____

  Phone #: _____

☺ Be sure to turn in your Prayer requests to the Pastor, the same day

iPray

www.HouseChurchPlanter.com

As you follow up with Mercy Ministry to the homes that share Prayer requests, you will need to honestly evaluate each home / individual to determine if this relationship should continue. You only have so much time and there are <u>lots</u> of people who need to be reached. You will meet people who really like what you are doing and are very easy to talk with. If they are strong Christians who belong to a church, you probably need to spend less time with them and more time with those who have fallen away / are lost.

SAMPLE DEVELOPMENT PLAN FOR HOUSE CHURCH PLANTERS

Stage One

	HC Planter	Future HC Planter
Reaching		
-Make four Home visits to prospects each month	X	
-Make sure your House Churches assimilate one family per month	X	
-Review "Project Planning and Promotion" for HC community impact event		X
Equipping		
-Check with members who are sick or needy to insure proper care	X	
-Encourage daily devotional life in homes of members	X	
-Make sure the children in your cluster's HC are well ministered to	X	
Praising		
-Call HC members who miss public worship three weeks in a row	X	
-Coordinate quarterly fellowship gathering for HC	X	
Developing		
-Call the future HC ministers once a month and follow up with them	X	
-Help the current HC leadership recruit their future-future leaders	X	
Planting		
-Update Mission and Ministry Plan(s) for your House Church(es)	X	
House Church Model		
-Visit one HC per month; make suggestions to HC leader as appropriate		X
Stewardship		
-Keep your HC leaders updated regarding the church's finances	X	
-Approve the next year's budget as presented by the senior Pastor	X	
Administration		
-Get "Cluster Monthly Ministry Update" to Pastor		X
Staff		
-Make monthly congregational leadership meetings	X	X

Stage Two

	HC Planter	Future HC Planter
Reaching		
-Make four Home visits to prospects each month	X	
-Make sure your House Churches assimilate one family per month	X	
-Review "Project Planning and Promotion" for HC community impact event		X
Equipping		
-Check with members who are sick or needy to insure proper care	X	X
-Encourage daily devotional life in homes of members		X
-Make sure the children in your cluster's HC are well ministered to	X	
Praising		
-Call HC members who miss public worship three weeks in a row	X	
-Coordinate quarterly fellowship gathering for HC	X	
Developing		
-Call the future HC ministers once a month and follow up with them	X	
-Help the current HC leadership recruit the future-future leaders		X
Planting		
-Update Mission and Ministry Plan(s) for your House Church(es.	X	X
House Church Model		
-Visit one HC per month; make suggestions to HC leader as appropriate		X
Stewardship		
-Keep your HC leaders updated regarding the church's finances		X
-Approve the next year's budget as presented by the senior Pastor	X	
Administration		
-Get "House Church Planter Ministry Update" to Pastor		X
Staff		
-Make monthly congregational leadership meetings	X	X

	HC Planter	Future HC Planter
Reaching		
-Make four Home visits to prospects each month		X
-Make sure your House Churches assimilate one family per month	X	
-Review "Project Planning and Promotion" for HC community impact event		X
Equipping		
-Check with HC that have members who are sick or needy to insure proper care		X
-Encourage daily devotional life in homes of members		X
-Make sure the children in your cluster's HC are well ministered to		X
Praising		
-Call HC members in your cluster who miss public worship three weeks in a row		X
-Coordinate quarterly fellowship gathering for HC in your cluster		X
Developing		
-Call the future HC ministers once a month and follow up with them		X
-Help the current HC leadership recruit the future-future leaders		X
Planting		
-Update Mission and Ministry Plan(s) for your House Church(es)		X
House Church Model		
-Visit one HC per month; make suggestions to HC leader as appropriate		X
Stewardship		
-Keep your HC leaders updated regarding the church's finances		X
-Approve the next year's budget as presented by the senior Pastor	X	
Administration		
-Get "House Church Planter Ministry Update" to Pastor		X
Staff		
-Make monthly congregational leadership meetings	X	X

*** BIRTH NEW HOUSE CHURCH ***

Notes:

_____

_____

_____

_____

> ** THIS IS A SAMPLE **   May the Holy Spirit guide you in His ways
>
>   *Adjust the time line as needed
>
>   *Add / Drop items according to the vision God has given you
>
>   *Recruiting Leadership and getting them into House Church Planter training is your key

NT House Churches

Antioch	Acts 11 / Galatians 2
Caesarea (Philip)	Acts 8
Cenchrea (implied)	Romans 16
Colossae (Philemon?)	Philemon
Corinth (Prisca / Aquila, Titius Justis, Gaius, Erastus,)	Acts 18 / Romans 16
Damascus (Judas)	Acts 9
Ephesus (Prisca/Aquila)	Acts 18 / 1 Corinthians 16
Jerusalem (James?, John Mark's mother)	Acts 1, 12
Joppa (Simon the Tanner)	Acts 9
Laodicia (Nympha)	Colossians 4
Philippi (Lydia)	Acts 16
Rome (Prisca / Aquila, Asyncritus, Philologus)	Romans 16
Thessalonica (Jason)	Acts 17
Troas (remember Eutychus?!)	Acts 20

NT Households

Aristobulus'	Romans 16
Caesar's	Philippians 4
Cornelius'	Acts 10
Crispus'	Acts 18
Narcissus' (slave?)	Romans 16
Philippian Jailer's	Acts 16
Stephanus'	I Corinthians 16

Jesus' Use of Houses

Bethany	Mary, Martha, Lazarus
Capernaum	Peter
Sending of 12	Matthew 10
Sending of 72	Luke 10
Institution of the Lord's Supper	Matthew 26:17ff

*Much thanks to Dr. Claire Partlow and her research of these items as part of her doctoral paper on Immigrant House Church worship in America today, which she did with the House Churches we planted in New Jersey.

A Worthwhile Reading List

My hope in writing this book is that it would be a practical, "how to" resource that shares actual ministry practices being used in LCMS congregations; all with the understanding that ministry is not something we plan, but rather something that Christ directs through the Holy Spirit. Prayer is not a program, it is not even in any of the Spiritual gift lists of the New Testament; Prayer is something every believer does by the power of the Holy Spirit.

Even though this book is designed to be a practical "manual," I did take the time to read some well done research books. I thought it was important to hear from respected writers and share highlights from their writings, without turning this into another research book.

There are well-known authors today with books providing the current buzz words. They are easy to find; just look on the top shelf at the Christian book store--if they have a good agent, you can find them on the end cap.

I am sharing with you the books I referred to for this effort, as well as other books I have picked up over the years that I have found to be challenging / helpful in the effort to reach out with Prayer for Ministry, Mercy and Multiplication.

You will want to filter their thoughts through Scripture and solid doctrine; you won't have to look hard to find principles that are wise and nuggets that can be put to work. In the interest of space, the list is short

The Holy Bible by God ☺

21st Century Disciples with a 1st Century Faith by Waldo Werning (practical pointers for the Christian)
Christ Have Mercy by Matthew Harrison (powerful resource to help put your faith in action)
Diaspora Missiology by Enoch Wan (how to reach the massive number of people moved from place of birth)
Founding Faith by Steven Waldman (the good, the bad &and the ugly of Christian faith in colonial America)
Good to Great- Why Some Companies Make the Leap… and Others Don't by Jim Collins
House Church and Mission by Roger Gehring (invaluable research &and Scriptural study resource)
John Wesley's Class Meeting by D. Michael Henderson (20,000,000 American Christian descendants)
Life Together by Dietrich Bonhoeffer (must must-read story of a Lutheran Pastor killed by Hitler)
A Simple Way to Pray by Martin Luther (Luther's personal prayers)
Lutheran Book of Prayer by Martin Luther (great discipleship resource with/ Prayers for all situations)
Lutheran Service Book (the current hymnal for the Lutheran Church--Missouri Synod)
Never Wrestle with a Pig by Mark McCormack (buy it just for the title; read it for the ideas)
Reading the Psalms with Luther by Martin Luther (great Prayers with every Psalm; great devotional)
Secrets of Special Ops Leadership by William Cohen (beating overwhelming odds on every mission)
Solution Focused Pastoral Counseling by Charles Kollar (aid for good stewardship of a Pastor's time)
Successful Home Cell Groups by Paul Yonggi Cho (refocused the Church on ministry in the home)
The Book of Concord (contains the official Lutheran position on the important Christian questions)
Luther's Works by Martin Luther (highly recommend you get the software version &and install it ☺)
The Church that Never Sleeps by Matthew Barnett (amazing vision &and development of urban ministry)
The Shape of the Liturgy by Dom Dix (great research tool for understanding roots of Christian worship)
Urban Ministry by Harvie Conn and Manuel Ortiz (understand the city and God's work in it)

Resolution 2-02: To commend and support the ministry of the Rev. James Buckman and the Urban and Immigrant Ministry

This resolution is Overture 12-10, with the clause "Operation Barnabas" removed, as that ministry is properly covered in resolution 2-03.

WHEREAS the New Jersey District has called the Reverend James Buckman as Urban Mission Strategist in New Jersey, and

WHEREAS the goal of the Urban and Immigrant Ministry is to "help existing LCMS congregations reach more effectively into their communities by providing the very best training for men and women who will work under their Pastor and Elders to plant new worshipping communities," and

WHEREAS many congregations and individuals, both in New Jersey and other states, have been blessed and energized for ministry to their communities and the people of New Jersey, and

WHEREAS the fruit of this ministry has produced nine stand alone Prayer Walking Ministries, seven house churches, nine students enrolled in our Leaders and Learners House Church Planter Training, one SMP Vicar, two Congregational Urban Ministry Center Development Teams, and the hosting of 200+ short term missionaries, and

WHEREAS the municipal Council of Jersey City issued a resolution of commendation to the Reverend James Buckman for his work done there, and

WHEREAS Prayer Walking ministry and training (we also anticipate a book authored by Pastor Buckman on this subject) has helped revitalize outreach ministry in many congregations, and

WHEREAS the annual Mission Summit and The NJ Jam under his direction have been a blessing to many, therefore be it

RESOLVED that the congregations and people of the NJ District seek to enthusiastically embrace the ministry of the Reverend James Buckman and the Urban and Immigrant Ministry, and be it further

RESOLVED that both congregations and individuals be encouraged to give generous financial support to this ministry so that its good work may continue in our midst, and be it finally

RESOLVED that the Reverend James Buckman and the Urban and Immigrant ministry be regularly upheld in our prayers and the beneficiary of our time and efforts with a praise clap.

(By God's grace, it was adopted unanimously)

When it's all about ministry, you need a partner who understands why.

Your ministry is unique—so are the resources available to you. Thousands have invested in ministry through Lutheran Church Extension Fund (LCEF), offering your ministry a place to borrow money at interest rates you can afford and a professional staff that understands your mission. LCEF also offers Ministry Support services to put ministry in motion including VisionPath, Pastor Coaching, Capital Funding Services, Architectural Advisory Committee and Laborers For Christ.

Where is your ministry headed? Learn more about how LCEF can help at **lcef.org.**

Lutheran Church Extension Fund
> where investments build ministry

10733 Sunset Office Drive
Suite 300
St. Louis, MO 63127-1020
800-843-5233

OFFICE OF THE CITY CLERK
CITY OF JERSEY CITY
NEW JERSEY

Resolution

COMMENDING
REV. JIM BUCKMAN AND
REV. HARON ORUTWA

Council as a whole, offered and moved adoption of the following resolution:

WHEREAS, through the vision of Rev. Haron Orutwa, pastor of the Tumaini Kristo Lutheran Church in Jersey City along with Rev. James D. Buckman, Missionary with the Lutheran Church Missouri Synod, the needs of many Jersey City youth were met; and

WHEREAS, Reverend Jim Buckman brought a group of 40 youth and chaperones to Jersey City in spiritual partnership with Pastor Haron Orutwa from July 12-26, 2010

WHEREAS, a total of 46 short term missionaries from Indiana, Missouri, Kansas and Virginia worked to serve the children and community of Jersey City; and

WHEREAS, the group walked the community, offered prayer, water and fed over 100 youth and adults and provided bottled water for another 200 residents; and

WHEREAS, both pastors and a group of missionaries and parishioners provided a Vacation Bible School to the children of Jersey City, offering a much needed break for the parents; and

WHEREAS, the youth of Jersey City and the delegation of missionaries were equally touched and enriched through this experience.

NOW THEREFORE, BE IT RESOLVED, that the Municipal Council of the City of Jersey City does hereby commend Pastor Haron Orutwa and his parishioners, Rev. James D. Buckman and all missionaries involved in this endeavor for their commitment and love shown to the residents of Jersey City.

ATTEST:

Radames Velazquez, Jr., Councilperson at Large
Willie L. Flood, Councilperson at Large
Michael J. Sottolano, Councilperson - Ward A
David P. Donnelly, Councilperson - Ward B
Nidia R. Lopez, Councilperson - Ward C
William A. Gaughan, Councilperson - Ward D
Steven Fulop, Councilperson - Ward E

Peter M. Brennan, President of the Municipal Council

Viola S. Richardson, Councilperson -Ward F

Tolonda Griffin-Ross, Deputy City Clerk

Made in the USA
Lexington, KY
10 June 2014